Information Security Risk Analysis

Information Security Risk Analysis

Second Edition

Thomas R. Peltier

Auerbach Publications
Taylor & Francis Group

Boca Raton   London   New York   Singapore

Published in 2005 by
CRC Press
Taylor & Francis Group
6000 Broken Sound Parkway NW, Suite 300
Boca Raton, FL 33487-2742

International Standard Book Number-10: 0-8493-3346-6 (Hardcover)
International Standard Book Number-13: 978-0-8493-3346-0 (Hardcover)
Library of Congress Card Number 2004062725

This book contains information obtained from authentic and highly regarded sources. Reprinted material is quoted with permission, and sources are indicated. A wide variety of references are listed. Reasonable efforts have been made to publish reliable data and information, but the author and the publisher cannot assume responsibility for the validity of all materials or for the consequences of their use.

Library of Congress Cataloging-in-Publication Data

Peltier, Thomas R.
Information security risk analysis / Thomas R. Peltier -- 2nd ed.
p. cm.
Includes bibliographical references and index.
ISBN 0-8493-3346-6
1. Computer security. 2. Computer networks--Security meausres. 3. Risk assessment. I. Title.

QA76.9.A25P429 2005
005.8--dc22   2004062725

Taylor & Francis Group
is the Academic Division of T&F Informa plc.

Visit the Taylor & Francis Web site at
http://www.taylorandfrancis.com

and the CRC Press Web site at
http://www.crcpress.com

Dedication

To Jill and Tom, Justin and Julie, and David,
the best children anyone could ever want or have.

Contents

1 Introduction 1
  1.1 Frequently Asked Questions...2
      1.1.1 Why Should a Risk Assessment Be Conducted?...........2
      1.1.2 When Should a Risk Analysis Be Conducted?..............3
      1.1.3 Who Should Conduct the Risk Analysis and Risk Assessment? 3
      1.1.4 Who within the Organization Should Conduct the Risk
           Analysis and Risk Assessment? 4
      1.1.5 How Long Should a Risk Analysis or Assessment Take?...............4
      1.1.6 What Can a Risk Analysis or Risk Assessment Analyze?...............4
      1.1.7 What Can the Results of a Risk Management Tell
           an Organization? 5
      1.1.8 Who Should Review the Results of a Risk Analysis? 5
      1.1.9 How Is the Success of the Risk Analysis Measured?....................5
  1.2 Conclusion...6

2 Risk Management 7
  2.1 Overview 7
  2.2 Risk Management as Part of the Business Process 8
  2.3 Employee Roles and Responsibilities......................................10
  2.4 Information Security Life Cycle 11
  2.5 Risk Analysis Process...15
  2.6 Risk Assessment..16
      2.6.1 Step 1: Asset Definition..16
      2.6.2 Step 2: Threat Identification 18
      2.6.3 Step 3: Determine Probability of Occurrence 19
      2.6.4 Step 4: Determine the Impact of the Threat...................24
      2.6.5 Step 5: Controls Recommended.....................................25
      2.6.6 Step 6: Documentation 27
  2.7 Cost–Benefit Analysis...27
  2.8 Risk Mitigation..38
  2.9 Final Thoughts 39

3 Risk Assessment Process 41
3.1   Introduction 41
3.2   Risk Assessment Process 41
3.3   Information Is an Asset 42
3.4   Risk Assessment Methodology 44
    3.4.1   Threat Identification...45
        3.4.1.1   Elements of Threats 46
        3.4.1.2   Threat Occurrence Rates.......................48
        3.4.1.3   Risk Level Determination 50
        3.4.1.4   Controls and Safeguards 52
        3.4.1.5   Cost–Benefit Analysis 74
        3.4.1.6   Documentation 74
3.5   Final Thoughts 74

4 Quantitative versus Qualitative Risk Assessment 77
4.1   Introduction 77
4.2   Quantitative and Qualitative Pros and Cons....................79
4.3   Qualitative Risk Assessment Basics 79
    4.3.1   Step 1: Develop a Scope Statement 81
    4.3.2   Step 2: Assemble a Quality Team 81
    4.3.3   Step 3: Identify Threats...84
    4.3.4   Step 4: Prioritize Threats 84
    4.3.5   Step 5: Threat Impact 90
    4.3.6   Step 6: Risk Factor Determination 92
    4.3.7   Step 7: Identify Safeguards and Controls 93
    4.3.8   Step 8: Cost–Benefit Analysis 96
    4.3.9   Step 9: Rank Safeguards in Recommended Order 96
    4.3.10   Step 10: Risk Assessment Report...........................97
    4.3.11   Summary 99
4.4   Qualitative Risk Assessment Using Tables 99
    4.4.1   Stage 1: Asset Valuation (BIA) 101
    4.4.2   Stage 2: Risk Evaluation 102
    4.4.3   Stage 3: Risk Management 107
    4.4.4   Summary 108
4.5   The 30-Minute Risk Assessment.....................................108
    4.5.1   Overview 108
    4.5.2   Objectives...108
    4.5.3   ISRA Matrix...109
    4.5.4   The ISRA Process..109
    4.5.5   Threat-Based Controls 111
    4.5.6   Documentation..112
    4.5.7   Out-of-Control Process 113
    4.5.8   Final Notes..113
4.6   Conclusion...114

5 Other Forms of Qualitative Risk Assessment 115
   5.1   Introduction 115
   5.2   Hazard Impact Analysis 116
         5.2.1   Hazard Impact Analysis Process 116
         5.2.2   Paralysis by Analysis..119
   5.3   Questionnaires...120
         5.3.1   Risk Assessment Questionnaire Process....................121
         5.3.2   Summary..124
   5.4   Single Time Loss Algorithm 124
   5.5   Conclusion...125

6 Facilitated Risk Analysis and Assessment Process
   (FRAAP) 129
   6.1   Introduction 129
   6.2   FRAAP Overview...129
   6.3   Why the FRAAP Was Created..131
   6.4   Introducing the FRAAP to Your Organization 132
         6.4.1   Awareness Program Overview 133
         6.4.2   Introducing the FRAAP 134
         6.4.3   Facilitation Skills..136
                 6.4.3.1   Listen..136
                 6.4.3.2   Lead...137
                 6.4.3.3   Reflect 137
                 6.4.3.4   Summarize 137
                 6.4.3.5   Confront..137
                 6.4.3.6   Support 138
                 6.4.3.7   Crisis Intervention 138
                 6.4.3.8   Center 138
                 6.4.3.9   Solve Problems...139
                 6.4.3.10 Change Behavior...139
                 6.4.3.11 Recognize All Input and Encourage Participation......139
                 6.4.3.12 Be Observant for Nonverbal Responses....................139
                 6.4.3.13 Do Not Lecture; Listen and Get the Team Involved... 140
                 6.4.3.14 Never Lose Sight of the Objective 140
                 6.4.3.15 Stay Neutral
                             (or Always Appear to Remain Neutral)......................140
                 6.4.3.16 Learn to Expect Hostility, but Do Not Become
                             Hostile..140
                 6.4.3.17 Avoid Being the Expert Authority 140
                 6.4.3.18 Adhere to Time Frames and Be Punctual...................141
                 6.4.3.19 Use Breaks to Free a Discussion 141
                 6.4.3.20 The Facilitator Is There to Serve the FRAAP Team 141
                 6.4.3.21 Stop the FRAAP if the Group Is Sluggish and
                             Difficult to Control.......................................141
         6.4.4   Session Agreements 143

6.4.5   The FRAAP Team 144
6.4.6   Prescreening 147
            6.4.6.1   Prescreening Example 1 147
            6.4.6.2   Prescreening Example 2 153
            6.4.6.3   Prescreening Example 3 155
6.4.7   The Pre-FRAAP Meeting 159
            6.4.7.1   Pre-FRAAP Meeting Process 159
            6.4.7.2   Pre-FRAAP Summary 165
6.4.8   The FRAAP Session 166
            6.4.8.1   The FRAAP Session Stage 1 166
            6.4.8.2   The FRAAP Session Stage 2 182
            6.4.8.3   FRAAP Session Summary 183
6.4.9   The Post-FRAAP 186
            6.4.9.1   Complete Action Plan 186
            6.4.9.2   FRAAP Management Summary Report 190
            6.4.9.3   Cross-Reference Report 194
            6.4.9.4   Summary 203
6.5   Conclusion 204

7   **Variations on the FRAAP 205**
7.1   Overview 205
7.2   Infrastructure FRAAP 205
            7.2.1   The Infrastructure FRAAP 206
                        7.2.1.1   Infrastructure FRAAP Summary 207
            7.2.2   Application FRAAP 212
                        7.2.2.1   Overview 212
                        7.2.2.2   Summary 212
            7.2.3   Other Variations 213
                        7.2.3.1   Variation Example 1 213
                        7.2.3.2   Variation Example 2 213
                        7.2.3.3   Variation Example 3 218
7.3   Conclusion 221

8   **Mapping Controls 223**
8.1   Controls Overview 223
8.2   Creating Your Controls List 224
            8.2.1   Information Security Baseline Controls 224
            8.2.2   Control Requirements Considerations 226
            8.2.3   A Final Cautionary Note 226
8.3   Controls List Examples 227
            8.3.1   Controls by Security Categories 227
            8.3.2   Controls List by Information Security Layer 228
            8.3.3   Controls List by Information Technology Organization 229
            8.3.4   Controls List Using ISO 17799 229
            8.3.5   Mapping ISO 17799 and HIPAA 236
            8.3.6   Controls List Mapping ISO 17799 and GLBA 236

8.3.7   Controls List Mapping ISO 17799, GLBA, and
Sarbanes–Oxley 245

8.3.8   Controls List Mapping ISO 17799 and Federal
Sentencing Guidelines... 245

8.3.9   Controls List Mapping ISO 17799, HIPAA, GLBA, SOX,
and FSGCA.. 249

8.3.10 National Institute of Standards and Technology
Controls List 249

8.3.11 Controls List Mapping ISO 17799 and CobiT........................ 250

8.3.12 Other Sources 261

9 Business Impact Analysis (BIA) 289

9.1   Overview 289

9.2   Creating a BIA Process.. 290

10 Conclusion 297

**Appendix A: Sample Risk Assessment Management
Summary Report...299**

Appendix B: Terms and Definitions...............................325

Appendix C: Bibliography 331

Index...335

The Author

Thomas R. Peltier (CISM, CISSP) is in his fifth decade of computer technology. During this time he has shared his experiences with fellow professionals and, because of this work, has been awarded the 1993 Computer Security Institute's (CSI) Lifetime Achievement Award. In 1999 the Information Systems Security Association (ISSA) bestowed on Tom its Individual Contribution to the Profession Award, and in 2001 Tom was inducted into the ISSA Hall of Fame. Tom was also awarded the CSI Lifetime Emeritus Membership Award. Currently, he is the president of Peltier and Associates, an information security training and consulting firm. Prior to this, he was director of policies and administration for the Netigy Corporation's Global Security Practice. Tom was the national director for consulting services for CyberSafe Corporation, and the corporate information protection coordinator for Detroit Edison. The security program at Detroit Edison was recognized for excellence in the field of computer and information security by winning the Computer Security Institute's Information Security Program of the Year Award for 1996. Tom previously was the information security specialist for General Motors Corporation and was responsible for implementing an information security program for GM's worldwide activities.

Over the past decade, Tom has averaged four published articles a year on various computer and information security issues, including developing policies and procedures, disaster recovery planning, copyright compliance, virus management, and security controls. He has had four books published: *Policies, Standards, Guidelines and Procedures: Information Security Risk Analysis*; *Information System Security Policies and Procedures: A Practitioner's Reference*; *The Complete Manual of Policies and Procedures for Data Security*; and *How to Manage a Network Vulnerability Assessment*. He is the co-editor and contributing author for the CISSP *Prep for Success Handbook* and a contributing author for the *Computer Security Handbook*, third and fifth editions, and *Data Security Management*. Tom, along with his son Justin and partner, John Blackley, is currently coauthoring the book *Information Security Fundamentals*.

Tom has been the technical advisor on a number of security films from Commonwealth Films. He is the past chairman of the CSI Advisory Council, the chairman of the 18th Annual CSI Conference, founder and past president of the Southeast Michigan Computer Security Special Interest Group, and a former member of the board of directors for (ISC)2, the security professional certification organization. Tom conducts numerous seminars and workshops on various security topics and has led seminars for CSI, Crisis Management, the American Institute of Banking, the American Institute of Certified Public Accountants, the Institute of Internal Auditors, ISACA, and Sungard Planning Solutions. Tom was also an instructor at the graduate level for Eastern Michigan University.

Acknowledgments

Anyone who takes sole credit for any task completed or process developed has forgotten where he came from and who helped him get to where he is now. When discussing risk assessment, many people do not want to have their names associated in any way with the process. This is one of those tasks that has to be done, and the best way to do it is to make the task as simple as possible. Over the years I have been able to learn the process of risk assessment from the best teachers around, my peers.

The first group to be acknowledged is the British contingent: John Blackley, a Scotsman who has worked with me on a number of ideas and concepts for almost 20 years; Gareth Davies, a Welshman who introduced me to the subject of qualitative risk analysis; and David Lynas, an Irishman who showed me how risk assessment fits into a proper security architecture. The big Canadian, Dan Erwin, introduced the concept of facilitation to risk assessment.

My second number one is my wife, Lisa Bryson. We are both information security professionals, and it is her ability to take my big-picture ideas and help me flesh out the concepts. We have worked as a team for the past nine years and have developed some truly remarkable concepts.

Next on my list of acknowledgments is my mentor and friend, John O'Leary, the director of the Computer Security Institute's Education Resource Center. John and his wonderful wife, Jane, have sat with me through many dinners and listened to my problems and then offered the wisdom that comes from people who care.

My working buddies also need to be acknowledged. My best buddy, my son Justin, is the greatest asset any father and, more importantly, information security team could ever hope for. Over the past three years we have logged nearly 250,000 air miles together, and each day we learn something new from each other.

The other buddies are the group that sends out ideas, questions, and concepts to one another for feedback and comment. This group is always willing to offer opinions on almost any subject; they are a resource that I take great pride in knowing and working with. They include Mike Corby, Terri Curran, Cheryl Jackson, Beck Herold, Fred Trickey, Dr. Peter Stephenson, and Pat Howard.

There is a group of security professionals that have helped me in the past year to improve the risk assessment process, and they include Wayne Sumida, Robert Docken, Tom Lamog, Paula Moore, George Mathanool, Sigurjón Þór Árnason, Jill Hernandez, Anne Terwilliger, Robert Childs, Jeff Sauntry, Richard Power, Pietro Ruvolo, Del Ullian, Larry Degg, and Michael J. Cannon.

Who can leave out his publisher? Certainly not me. Rich O'Hanley has taken the time to discuss security issues with numerous organizations to understand what their needs are and then presented these findings to use. A great deal of our work here is a direct result of what Rich discovered that the industry wanted. Rich O'Hanley is not only the world's best editor and task master, but a good friend and source of knowledge. Thanks, Rich.

And finally, I extend a thank-you to my editors, Andrea Demby and Claire Miller. They take the time to put the raw manuscript into a logically flowing work. They sometimes have to ask me the same question more than once, but finally I grasp what needs to be done.

Chapter 1

Introduction

My introduction to risk analysis began in 1978 when I was an information systems security officer (ISSO) working for General Motors. The General Motors Systems Corporate Activity (GMISCA) group sponsored a two-day conference for their ISSOs. Worldwide, GM had nearly 150 people performing that activity and about half that number was in attendance. On the morning of the second day, a 90-minute session on risk analysis was scheduled. Because it was something that I needed to know about and had never done, I selected this session. The person giving the lecture was a Ph.D. candidate who did his undergraduate degree in mathematics. He was introduced and then addressed the audience for about two minutes; he then turned and faced the chalkboard and began to write numbers and formulas on the board. For the next 88 minutes he talked to the number and the numbers talked to him. He never turned to talk to the attendees until the end when he said, "And there you go." I turned to the person next to me and said that if this was risk analysis, I would rather drill my eye out with a hand auger.

I knew that we had audit comments on the need to do risk analysis, but no one seemed to know how to do it. Over the next few years I looked for books on the topic, and when I attended the Computer Security Institute's (CSI) annual conferences, I would visit the vendor exhibits and look at the products and consulting services available.

What I learned in my research was that risk analysis was a total mystery to me and to most others. Around 1988 I contacted CSI and asked if it had a class on risk analysis; the owner/director, John O'Mara, told me that risk analysis sounded like a great class and that I should put together a two-day class on the topic. I tried to make John understand that I needed to attend the class, and John said, "What better way is there to learn?" So off I went in search of answers to the question: What is risk analysis, and how does it get completed in a timely and efficient fashion?

What I learned as I began to prepare the class on risk analysis is that there are about as many ways to perform risk reviews (whatever you want to call them) as there are reasons to do them. From the Federal Information Processing Standards Publication (FIPS Pub) 65, "Guideline for Automatic Data Processing Risk Analysis," published by the National Bureau of Standards in August 1979, to the National Institute of Standards and Technology (NIST) Special Publication 800-30, "Risk Management Guide for Information Technology Systems," which is currently in draft form for revision A, there are many ways to perform risk analysis.

I am a teacher by training, with one of my majors in history. During different times our society looks to create myths and legends and will write rose-colored views of the events. After a while, debunkers will come along and shoot holes in the recordings of history and will present our heroes as just plain people. Risk analysis and assessment were initially created to answer questions based on formulas and equations. These approaches can work for some organizations, but business and industry need answers quickly. So, the goal of this book will be to present different concepts and ideas and show how they can be used. We will take those concepts and apply them to a process for risk analysis that will be quick and efficient. So somewhere between Parson Weems, who invented stories about George Washington, like chopping down the cherry tree or throwing a shilling across the Rappahannock, to Marcus Cunliffe, who wrote the debunking book *George Washington: Man and Myth*, we will present risk analysis in as balanced a manner as possible, and maybe you will not want to drill your eye out with a hand auger.

1.1 Frequently Asked Questions

To help set the tone for the remainder of this book, let us take a look at questions that normally arise when we discuss or teach risk mitigation techniques.

1.1.1 Why Should a Risk Assessment Be Conducted?

Management is charged with showing that due diligence is performed during decision-making processes for any enterprise. A formal risk assessment provides the documentation to prove that due diligence is performed. The output from the risk analysis and risk assessment processes will generally be used twice. The first time will be when decisions are made; for the risk analysis that means deciding whether to proceed on a new project, and for the risk assessment, what types of controls or safeguards need to be implemented. For risk assessment, the output will identify what countermeasures should be implemented or that management has determined that the best decision is to accept the risk.

The other time the results will be used is when the "spam hits the fan" — that is, when a problem arises and the organization must show the process it used to reach the decisions it did. The documentation created in the risk management processes will allow the organization to show who was involved, what was discussed, what was considered, and what decisions were made.

A risk management process also lets an enterprise take control of its own destiny. With an effective risk analysis process in place, only those controls and safeguards that are actually needed will be implemented. An enterprise will never again face having to implement a mandated control to be in compliance with audit requirements.

1.1.2 When Should a Risk Analysis Be Conducted?

A risk analysis should be conducted whenever money or resources are to be spent. Before starting a task, project, or development cycle, an enterprise should conduct an analysis of the need for the project. Understanding the concepts of risk analysis and applying them to the business needs of the enterprise will ensure that only necessary spending is done.

Additionally, there will never be the need to implement controls or safeguards unless they are actually needed. As risk management professionals, it is important to understand that there are no such items as security requirements or audit requirements. There are only business objectives or mission requirements. A proper risk management process will ensure that compensating controls are needed to ascertain that the business or mission of the enterprise is met.

1.1.3 Who Should Conduct the Risk Analysis and Risk Assessment?

Most risk management projects fail because the internal experts and subject matter experts are not included in the process. A process such as the Facilitated Risk Analysis and Assessment Process (FRAAP) takes advantage of the internal experts. No one knows your systems and applications or your business better than the people that develop and run them. Establishing a team of internal experts will ensure that the risk management process has those individuals with in-depth knowledge of the true workings of the business processes. No outsider can understand the nuances of your operations better than those people that must work with it and around it on a daily basis.

1.1.4 Who within the Organization Should Conduct the Risk Analysis and Risk Assessment?

If your organization is fortunate enough to have a project management office, then the facilitators from this group would be perfect for conducting the risk management processes. Because this book is directed at the information security profession, I would expect to see these professionals conduct the processes.

There are some groups that, because of their charters and responsibilities, would find a conflict of interest to lead or facilitate these processes. Applications development is a group that could have an impact on both risk analysis and risk assessment. Its job is to create applications and systems as quickly and efficiently as possible. So there could be an appearance of conflict of interest.

The audit staff and systems operations are two other groups that have charters of responsibility that would give an appearance of conflict of interest.

1.1.5 How Long Should a Risk Analysis or Assessment Take?

A risk analysis or assessment should be completed in days, not weeks or months. To meet the needs of an enterprise, the risk management process must be completed quickly with minimum impact on the employees' already busy schedule. The key process that we will discuss in this book, FRAAP, was created in response to the needs of the day-to-day workings of business and government agencies.

Time is a very precious commodity, and processes such as risk management must be structured to be fast and efficient. As you will see, if there is more time available, then there is no end to the different things that can be done. Most organizations, however, have little enough time to spare.

1.1.6 What Can a Risk Analysis or Risk Assessment Analyze?

These processes can be used to review any task, project, or idea. By learning the basic concepts of risk management, the organization can use it to determine if a project should be undertaken, if a specific product should be purchased, if a new control should be implemented, or if the enterprise is at risk from some threat.

1.1.7 What Can the Results of a Risk Management Tell an Organization?

The process can identify for the enterprise what the threats are and then establish a prioritization of these risks to allow management to concentrate on the biggest concerns.

The greatest benefit of a risk analysis is the determination of whether it is prudent to proceed. It allows management to examine all currently identified concerns, prioritize the level of vulnerability, and then to select an appropriate level of control or to accept the risk.

The goal of risk management is not to eliminate all risk. It is a tool to be used by management to reduce risk to an acceptable level.

1.1.8 Who Should Review the Results of a Risk Analysis?

A risk analysis is rarely conducted without a senior management sponsor. The results are geared to provide management with the information it needs to make informed business decisions. The results of a risk assessment are normally classified as confidential and are provided to only the sponsor and those deemed appropriate by the sponsor.

When working the risk analysis and risk assessment processes, it will be necessary to remind all employees that the information discussed in the processes is classified as confidential and may not be shared outside the risk management forum. For any third party taking part in the process, it will be necessary to execute a nondisclosure or confidentiality agreement to ensure the protection of information discussed.

1.1.9 How Is the Success of the Risk Analysis Measured?

The tangible way to measure success is to see a lower bottom line for cost. Risk assessment can assist in this process by identifying only those controls that need to be implemented.

Another way that the success of a risk analysis is measured is if there is a time when management decisions are called into review. By having a formal process in place that demonstrates the due diligence of management in the decision-making process, this kind of inquiring will be dealt with quickly and successfully.

1.2 Conclusion

The risk management process is a business process that supports management in its decision making. It allows the management owners of the assets to perform their fiduciary responsibility of protecting the assets of the enterprise in a reasonable and prudent manner. The process does not have to be a long, drawn-out affair. To be effective, risk analysis and risk assessment must be done quickly and efficiently.

Chapter 2

Risk Management

2.1 Overview

Risk management is the process that allows business managers to balance operational and economic costs of protective measures and achieve gains in mission capability by protecting business processes that support the business objectives or mission of the enterprise. For most of this book, we will concentrate on the impacts of risk in the information security (IS) and information technology areas of an organization. Risk management, however, is not restricted to the information technology and security realm. This is a business process that assists management in meeting its fiduciary duty to protect the assets of the organization.

Risk management is the total process used to identify, control, and minimize the impact of uncertain events. The objective of the risk management program is to reduce the risk of performing some activity or function to an acceptable level and obtain senior management approval.

Risk management is made up of four distinct processes: risk analysis, risk assessment, risk mitigation, and vulnerability assessment and controls evaluation (Table 2.1).

Senior management must ensure that the enterprise has the capabilities needed to accomplish its mission or business objectives. As we will see, senior management of a department, business unit, group, or other such entity is considered to be the *functional owner* of the enterprise's assets, and it is senior management's fiduciary duty to act in the best interest of the enterprise to implement reasonable and prudent safeguards and controls. Risk management is the tool that will assist in the task.

Table 2.1   Risk Management Terms

Term	Definition
Risk management	The total cost to identify, control, and minimize the impact of uncertain events. The objective of risk management is to reduce risk to an acceptable level. Support of this process by senior management is a demonstration of its due diligence.
Risk analysis	A technique to identify and assess factors that may jeopardize the success of a project or achieving a goal. This technique also helps define preventive measures to reduce the probability of these factors from occurring and identify countermeasures to successfully deal with these constraints when they develop.
Risk assessment	The computation of risk. Risk is a threat that exploits some vulnerability that could cause harm to an asset. The risk algorithm computes the risk as a function of the assets, threats, and vulnerabilities. One instance of a risk within a system is represented by the formula (asset * threat * vulnerability). The total risk for a network equates to the sum of all the risk instances.
Risk mitigation	The process in which an organization implements controls and safeguards to prevent identified risks from ever occurring, while at the same time implementing a means of recovery should the risk become a reality in spite of all efforts.
Vulnerability assessment and controls evaluation	Systematic examination of a critical infrastructure, the interconnected systems on which it relies, its information, or product to determine the adequacy of security measures, identify security deficiencies, evaluate security alternatives, and verify the adequacy of such measures after implementation.

2.2   Risk Management as Part of the Business Process

I do not care for the term *system development life cycle* (SDLC) with respect to risk management (Figure 2.1). The SDLC seems to have been structured to meet the needs of the information technology organization, and therefore anything associated with the SDLC must be an IT process. Risk management is a business process and all business decisions should have a business development life cycle (BDLC). The BDLC allows for those

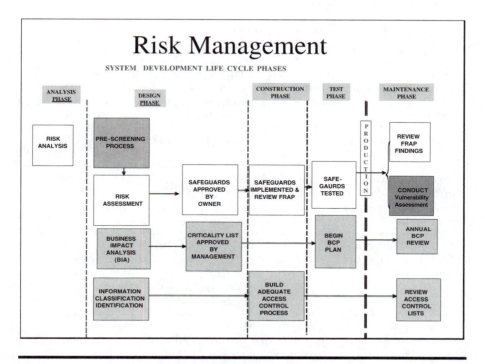

Figure 2.1 System development life cycle (SDLC).

elements that make up information technology development, but also takes into account normal business decisions. However, I will yield to the logic of the situation and continue with the concept of SDLC throughout this book.

Effective risk management must be totally integrated into the organization's system development life cycle. The typical SDLC has five phases, and they can be termed almost anything. Regardless of what the phases are labeled, they all have the same key concepts:

- Analysis
- Design
- Construction
- Test
- Maintenance

The National Institute of Standards and Technology (NIST) uses the following terms: initiation, development or acquisition, implementation, operation or maintenance, and disposal.

Table 2.2   SDLC vs. Risk Management

SDLC Phases	Risk Management Activities
Analysis — The need for a new system, application, or process and its scope is documented.	Analysis — Identified risks are used to support the development of system requirements, including security needs.
Design — The system or process is designed and requirements are gathered.	Design — Security needs lead to architecture and design trade-offs.
Development — The system or process is purchased, developed, or otherwise constructed.	Development — The security controls and safeguards are created or implemented as part of the development process.
Test — System security features should be configured, enabled, tested, and verified.	Test — Safeguards and controls are tested to ensure that decisions regarding risks identified are reduced to acceptable levels prior to movement to production.
Maintenance — When changes and updates are made to the system, the changes to hardware and software are noted and the risk analysis process is revisited.	Maintenance — Controls and safeguards are reexamined when changes or updates occur or on regularly scheduled intervals.

As the diagram points out, risk analysis is mapped throughout the SDLC. The first time risk analysis needs to be done is when there is a discussion on whether a new system or application of business process is required (Table 2.2).

2.3 Employee Roles and Responsibilities

Risk management is a management responsibility. To be successful, the risk management process must be supported by senior management and the concept of ownership of assets established. This concept is typically presented to the organization through the *asset or information classification policy*. Sample language for this portion of the policy might be similar to that shown in Table 2.3.

Employees have different roles, and these roles support the activities of the other roles and responsibilities. To establish a level of understanding through this book, let us examine typical roles found in an organization and what they are responsible for with regard to risk analysis and risk management (Table 2.4).

Table 2.3 Employee Responsibilities Example

Employees are responsible for protecting corporate information from unauthorized access, modification, destruction, or disclosure, whether accidental or intentional. To facilitate the protection of corporate information, employee responsibilities have been established at three levels: *owner, custodian,* and *user.*

Owner — The company manager of a business unit or office where the information is created, or the primary user of the information. Owners are responsible for:

Identifying the classification level of all corporate information within their organizational unit

Defining and implementing appropriate safeguards to ensure the confidentiality, integrity, and availability of the information resource

Monitoring safeguards to ensure their compliance and reporting situations of noncompliance

Authorizing access to those who have a business need for the information

Removing access from those who no longer have a business need for the information

Custodian — Employees designated by the owner to be responsible for protecting information by maintaining safeguards established by the owner.

User — Employees authorized by the owner to access information and use the safeguards established by the owner.

These are only examples of the types of roles and responsibilities found in a typical organization. It will be necessary to ensure that all employees have as part of their job description the concept of support of information security. The organization's *information classification* policy will also establish the key concepts of *owner, custodian,* and *user.*

For key positions such as Corporate Information Security Officer (CISO) and Information Security Administrator (ISA), in addition to a job description, it will be necessary to create and publish a charter to establish the goals and objectives for key assignments. A typical charter statement for security, management, and audit might include the language shown in Table 2.5.

2.4 Information Security Life Cycle

When implementing risk management, it will be necessary to view this process as part of the ongoing information security life cycle (Figure 2.2). As with any business process, the information security life cycle starts

Table 2.4   Typical Roles for Employees

Typical Role	Risk Management Responsibility
Senior management	Under the standard of due care, senior management is charged with the ultimate responsibility for meeting business objectives or mission requirements. Senior management must ensure that necessary resources are effectively applied to develop the capabilities to meet the mission requirements. It must incorporate the results of the risk analysis process into the decision-making process.
Chief information security officer (CISO)	This position was at one time called the chief information officer (CIO), but many organizations simply named their head of IT to this position, and therefore, the CIO has become the position known as the CIO.
	The CISO is responsible for the organization's planning, budgeting, and performance, including its information security components. Decisions made in this area should be based on an effective risk management program.
Resource owners	These are the business unit managers assigned as functional owners of organization assets; they are responsible for ensuring that proper controls are in place to address integrity, confidentiality, and availability of the information resources that they are assigned ownership. The term *owner* must be established in the asset classification policy.
	The managers (a.k.a. owners) are the individuals with the authority and responsibility for making cost–benefit decisions essential to ensure accomplishment of organization mission objectives. Their involvement in the risk management process enables the selection of business-orientated controls. The charge of being an owner supports the objective of fulfilling the fiduciary responsibility of management to protect the assets of the enterprise.
Information security professional	The security program manager is responsible for the organization's security programs, including risk management. The ISA has changed its designation because the designation *officer* is normally restricted to senior executives. The officers can be held personally liable if internal controls are not adequate.

Table 2.5   Sample Mission Statements

	Another important element found in most enterprisewide policy documents is a section on organizational responsibilities. This section is where the various mission statements of the enterprise organizations are resident, along with any associated responsibilities. For example:
Organization management	Officers and directors of the organization manage the assets of the organization in a prudent and diligent manner in accordance with the best interests of the customers, clients, employees, shareholders, regulatory agencies, and any other persons they represent.
Audit	Audit assesses the adequacy of and compliance with management, operating, and financial controls, as well as the administrative and operational effectiveness of organizational units.
Information security	Information security directs and supports the company and affiliated organizations in the protection of their information assets from intentional or unintentional disclosure, modification, destruction, or denial through the implementation of appropriate information security and business resumption planning policies, procedures, and guidelines.
Regulatory affairs	Regulatory affairs represents the organization's interests by initiating strategies and affecting enterprise relationships with the executive and legislative branches of the federal government, as well as with independent federal agencies. Regulatory affairs provides the organization with development, interpretation, and implementation of federal legislation and regulations.

with a risk analysis. Management is charged with showing that due diligence is performed during the decision-making process to proceed with any new task or project. A formal risk analysis provides the documentation that due diligence is performed.

Once the risk analysis is complete, the next step in the security life cycle is to conduct a risk assessment. As we have stated before, the results of a risk analysis or assessment will be used on two occasions: when a decision needs to be made and when a need arises to examine the decision-making process.

A risk assessment also allows an enterprise to take control of its own destiny. With an effective risk assessment process in place, only those controls and safeguards that are actually needed will be implemented. An

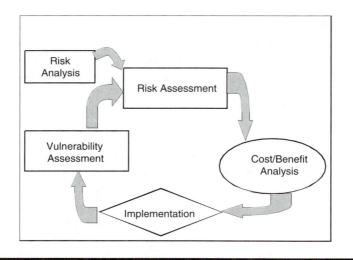

Figure 2.2   Information security life cycle.

enterprise will never again face having to implement a mandated control to be in compliance with audit requirements.

A risk analysis should be conducted whenever money or resources are to be spent. Before starting a task, project, or development cycle, an enterprise should conduct an analysis of the need for the project. Understanding the concepts of risk analysis and applying them to the business needs of the enterprise will ensure that only necessary spending is done.

Once a risk analysis has been conducted, it will be necessary to conduct a risk assessment to determine what threats exist to the project and business mission. These threats must be prioritized, and possible safeguards and controls must be selected. To be effective, a cost–benefit analysis to determine which controls will help mitigate the risk to an acceptable level at a cost the enterprise can afford must be part of this process. It is unwise to implement controls or safeguards just because they seem to be the right thing to do or because other enterprises are doing so. Each organization is unique, and the levels of revenue and exposure are different. By conducting a proper risk analysis, the controls or safeguards will meet the enterprise's specific needs.

Once the controls or safeguards have been implemented, it is appropriate to conduct an assessment to determine if the controls are working. In the information security profession, the term *vulnerability* has been defined as a condition of a missing or ineffectively administered safeguard or control that allows a threat to occur with a greater impact or frequency, or both. When conducting an Network Vulnerability Assessment (NVA), the team will assess existing controls, safeguards, and processes that are part of the network. This process, the assessment, will ensure that controls are effective and that they will remain so.

2.5 Risk Analysis Process

Risk analysis is a technique used to identify and assess factors that may jeopardize the success of a project or achieving a goal. Another term for this process is project impact analysis. This process will require a cost–benefit analysis be conducted. The cost–benefit process should incorporate the features and benefits of the asset or process under review.

Part of the review will examine the costs of the project. These costs include procurement and development; operation and maintenance, e.g., documentation development, user and infrastructure support training, and possible upgrades; and conversion or migration costs. All costs are examined in both dollars and staffing implications.

Although it is important to consider all of the elements of cost in deciding to move forward, procurement is just one variable. The cost of not moving forward with the new project must also be factored into the analysis process. What would be the impact to the enterprise if it was decided to delay or not approve the project? How would not moving forward impact the competitive advantage of the organization? How would this decision impact the ability to meet the mission of the enterprise? How would strategic business partners, suppliers, vendors, and other stakeholders be impacted?

Another important factor to consider in this process is the impact of regulatory compliance issues. The new project should, whenever possible, enhance regulatory requirements. Sometimes a new idea or concept is drafted by a department, such as marketing, and it gains support and management acceptance before the infrastructure, budget, and security personnel get the opportunity to perform a project impact analysis.

Whenever money or resources are to be spent, a risk analysis should be conducted. This will provide the business reasons that should be used to justify the decision to move forward. This is a way that management can demonstrate that due diligence has been performed. The output from the risk analysis process will be used twice. The first time is when decisions need to be made. Typically, the only other time the results would be examined is when the enterprise is being examined by a third party and management is asked to show its decision-making process.

For risk analysis and risk assessment, the need to demonstrate due diligence is an important factor. However, the overriding reason to conduct these processes is that it makes good business sense. The enterprise proceeds on certain paths based on need and the ability of the organization to meet those specific business or mission needs.

2.6 Risk Assessment

Risk assessment is the second process in the risk management life cycle. Organizations use risk assessment to determine what threats exist to a specific asset and the associated risk level of that threat. The threat prioritization (establishing the risk level) provides the organization with the information needed to select appropriate controls measures, safeguards, or countermeasures to lower the risk to an acceptable level.

As discussed earlier, the need to reduce a threat risk level to zero is counterproductive. Organizations must establish their threshold or concern and implement sufficient countermeasures to reduce the risk to a management-determined level.

As we examine the risk assessment portion of the risk management process, we will discuss six steps that will provide us with the three deliverables we need. Risk is a function of the probability that an identified threat will occur, and then the impact that the threat will have on the business process or mission of the asset under review. Each of the six steps will require the risk assessment team to explore their requirements and be as thorough as possible.

2.6.1 Step 1: Asset Definition

To be successful, this first step in the risk assessment process must be as thorough as possible. It will be difficult to conduct an accurate risk assessment if all of the team members do not have the same vision of what is to be reviewed.

During step 1, the risk assessment team leader and the owner are to define the process, application, system, or asset that is under review. The key here is to establish the boundaries of what is to be reviewed. Most failed projects come to grief because the scope of the project was poorly defined to begin with or because the scope was not managed well and was allowed to "creep" until it was out of control. If you are going to manage risk assessment as a project, then the asset definition must be looked upon as a scope statement. All of the elements that go into writing a successful scope statement should be used to define the asset and what will be expected from the risk analysis process.

As with any project, the deliverable from the asset definition step is to reach agreement with the owner on what the assessment is to review and all relevant parameters. The objective here is to put in writing a risk assessment statement of opportunity that consists of two elements: project statement and specifications.

For the project statement, identify the desired outcome. For example, "The team will identify potential threats to the asset under review and will prioritize those threats by assessing the probability of the threat occurring and the impact to the asset if the threat happened. Using the prioritized list of risks, the team will identify possible controls, counter-measures, and/or safeguards that can reduce the risk exposure to an acceptable level" (Presentation: "ISO 17799 A Minimum Standard for Maximum Security," Ross Fraser, March, 2002). This will become the risk assessment scope statement and provides the focus for the specifications.

Take enough time during the scope statement development to discuss and clarify the parameters of the project. Although these parameters will vary from project to project, the following items should be considered each time:

- *Purpose* — Fully understand the purpose of the project. What is the need driving the project? If the purpose is to correct a problem, identify the cause of the problem. A risk analysis has been per-formed that has decided that the project is to move forward. Review the results of this process to better understand the project's purpose.
- *Customer* — Your customer is the person or unit that has the need that this project is meant to fill. Determine who the real customer is and note other stakeholders.
- *Deliverables* — These are specific things that are to be delivered to the customer. In a risk assessment, the deliverables typically are:
  - Threats identified
  - Risk levels established
  - Possible controls identified
- *Resources* — What resources will be required to accomplish the project? Resources include:
  - Money
  - Personnel
  - Equipment
  - Supplies
  - Services
- *Constraints* — Identify those activities that could impact the deliv-erables of the project. Consider such things as:
  - Laws
  - Policies
  - Procedures
  - Resource limitations

- *Assumptions* — Identify those things that the project team believes to be true or complete:
  - Infrastructure risk assessment has been completed.
  - Baseline set of controls has been implemented.
- *Criteria* — Agree on specifically how the customer will evaluate the success of the project. What are the customer's criteria for the following elements of the project?
  - Timeliness
  - Cost
  - Quality

Criteria should be relevant and valid measures of how well the project accomplishes its stated purpose. You may need to help the customer clarify his true needs to ensure that the criteria to be used are valid indicators of project success.

2.6.2 Step 2: Threat Identification

We define a threat as an undesirable event that could impact the business objectives or mission of the business unit or enterprise. Some threats occur when existing controls that either were implemented incorrectly or have passed their usefulness now provide a weakness or threat to the infrastructure that can be exploited to circumvent the intended behavior of the control. This process is known as exploiting vulnerability.

A threat source is defined as any circumstance or event with the potential to cause harm to the asset under review. You will want to create as complete a list of threat sources as possible. Typically, there are three major categories of threat sources:

- *Natural threats* — Floods, earthquakes, tornadoes, landslides, avalanches, electrical storms, and other such events
- *Human threats* — Events that are either enabled by or caused by human beings, such as unintentional acts (errors and omissions) or deliberate acts (fraud, malicious software, unauthorized access). Statistically, the threat that causes the largest loss to information resources remains human errors and omissions
- *Environmental threats* — Long-term power outages, pollution, chemical spills, liquid leakage

To create a complete list of threats (Table 2.6), there are a number of different methods that can be used. These include developing checklists. Although I think checklists are important and need to be used, I must caution you that if used improperly, a checklist will impact the free flow of ideas and information. So use them to ensure that everything gets covered or identified, but do not rely on them available to complete the risk assessment process.

Another method of gathering threats is to examine historical data. Research what types of events have occurred and how often they have done so. Once you have the threat, it may be necessary to determine the annual rate of occurrence (ARO). This data can be obtained from a number of sources. For natural threats, the National Weather Center is a good place to get these rates of occurrence. For accidental human threats, an insurance underwriter will have these figures. For deliberate threats, consult local law enforcement or the organization's security force. For environmental threats, facilities management and the local power companies will have this information.

The method that I like best is brainstorming. I like to get a number of people (stakeholders) together and give them a structure to focus thought and then let them identify all of the threats they can think of. When brainstorming, there are no wrong answers. We want to ensure that all threats get identified. Once we have completed the information gathering, we will clean up duplicates and combine like threats.

2.6.3 Step 3: Determine Probability of Occurrence

Once a list of threats has been finalized and the team has agreed on the definitions of each threat, then it will be necessary to determine how likely that threat is to occur. The risk management team will want to derive an overall likelihood that indicates the probability that a potential threat may be exercised against the risk assessment asset under review. It will be necessary to establish definitions on probability and a number of other key terms.

The following is a sample definition of the probability or likelihood that a threat may occur:

- *Probability* — The likelihood that a threat event will occur
  - *High probability* — Very likely that the threat will occur within the next year
  - *Medium probability* — Possible that the threat may occur during the next year
  - *Low probability* — Highly unlikely that the threat will occur during the next year

When the team is preparing the definitions, it will want to ensure that the probability time frame meets the needs of the organization. When establishing the project scope statement, a review of the definitions is one of the tasks to be completed.

Table 2.6 Threat Table by Threat Source

Threat	Applicable Yes/No	Probability 1 = Low 2 = Medium 3 = High	Impact 1 = Low 2 = Medium 3 = High	Risk Level	Control Selected	New Risk Level
Natural Threat						
Electrical storm						
Ice storm						
Snowstorm/blizzard						
Major landslide						
Mudslide						
Tsunami						
Tornado						
Hurricane/typhoon						
High winds (70+ mph)						
Tropical storm						
Tidal flooding						
Seasonal flooding						
Local flooding						
Upstream dam/reservoir failure						

Sandstorm					
Volcanic activity					
Earthquake (2–4 on Richter scale)					
Earthquake (5 or more)					
Epidemic					
Human — Accidental					
Fire: Internal — minor					
Fire: Internal — major					
Fire: Internal — catastrophic					
Fire: External					
Accidental explosion — on site					
Accidental explosion — off site					
Aircraft crash					
Train crash					
Derailment					
Auto/truck crash at site					
Human error — maintenance					
Human error — operational					
Human error — programming					

Table 2.6   Threat Table by Threat Source (continued)

Threat	Applicable Yes/No	Probability 1 = Low 2 = Medium 3 = High	Impact 1 = Low 2 = Medium 3 = High	Risk Level	Control Selected	New Risk Level
Human error — users						
Toxic contamination						
Medical emergency						
Loss of key staff						
Human — Deliberate						
Sabotage/terrorism: external — physical						
Sabotage/terrorism: internal — physical						
Terrorism: biological						
Terrorism: chemical						
Bombing						
Bomb threat						
Arson						
Hostage taking						
Vandalism						

Labor dispute/strike						
Riot/civil disorder						
Toxic contamination						
Environmental						
Power flux						
Power outage – internal						
Power outage – external						
Water leak/plumbing failure						
HVAC failure						
Temperature inadequacy						
Telecommunications failure						
Toxic contamination						

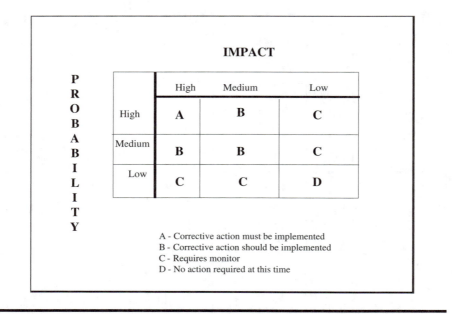

Figure 2.3   Probability–impact matrix example 1.

2.6.4 Step 4: Determine the Impact of the Threat

Once we have determined the probability of a threat occurring, it will be necessary to determine the impact that the threat will have on the organization. Before determining the impact value, it is necessary to ensure that the scope of the risk analysis has been properly defined. It will be necessary to ensure that the risk management team understands the objectives or mission of the asset under review and how it impacts on the organization's overall mission or objectives.

When determining the risk level (probability and impact), it will be necessary to establish the framework from which the evaluation is to occur (Figure 2.3). That is, how will existing controls impact the results? Typically, during the initial review or an assessment of infrastructure, the threats are examined as if there are no controls in place. This will provide the risk management team with a means of establishing a baseline risk level from which controls and safeguards can be identified and their effectiveness measured.

Although we make the assertion that no controls are in place, in the scope statement we will identify assumptions and constraints. These assumptions might include the concepts that a risk assessment has been performed on the supporting infrastructure elements and that appropriate controls have been implemented. This will mean that such an activity will have to have taken place or is scheduled to be done as soon as possible. By establishing these assumptions, the risk management team can focus on the threats and impacts related directly to the asset under review.

The results of the review of the probability and impact are the identification of a risk level that can be assigned to each threat. Once the risk level has been established, the team can identify appropriate actions. Steps 3 and 4 determine the likelihood that a given threat may occur and the magnitude of the impact should the threat occur. The risk level assessment process can be done again after a control has been selected. This will allow the team to determine if the selected control provides the desired reduction in the risk level.

The risk level process will require the use of a definition for impact as well as a matrix table that will allow the team to establish a risk level. The following is a sample definition for impact that can be used with the probability definition described above.

- *Impact* — The measure of the magnitude of loss or harm to the value of an asset
  - *High impact* — Shutdown of critical business unit that leads to a significant loss of business, corporate image, or profit
  - *Medium impact* — Short interruption of critical process or system that results in a limited financial loss to a single business unit
  - *Low impact* — Interruption with no financial loss

Another probability–impact matrix table could be created with the risk levels established as shown in Figure 2.4.

2.6.5 Step 5: Controls Recommended

After the risk level has been assigned, the team will identify controls or safeguards that could possibly eliminate the risk, or at least reduce the risk to an acceptable level. Remember that one of the goals of risk assessment is to document the organization's due diligence when making business decisions. Therefore, it will be important to identify all of the controls and safeguards that the team believes could reduce the risk to an acceptable level. By doing this, the team will be able to document all of the options that were considered.

There are a number of factors that need to be considered when recommending controls and alternative solutions. For instance, how effective is the recommended control? One way to determine the relative effectiveness is to perform the risk level process (probability and impact) to the threat with the control in place. If the risk level is not reduced to an acceptable point, then the team may want to examine another option.

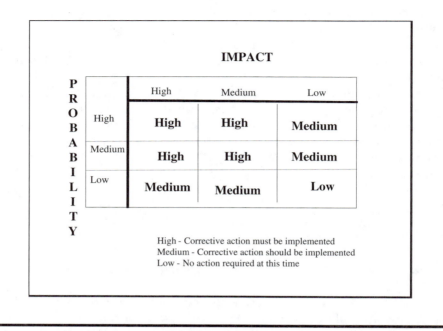

Figure 2.4   Probability–impact matrix example 2.

There may also be legal and regulatory requirements to implement specific controls. With so many new and expanding requirements mandated by government agencies, controlling boards, and laws, it will be necessary for the risk management team to be current on these requirements.

When selecting any type of control, it will be necessary to measure the operational impact to the organization. Every control will have an impact in some manner. It could be the expenditure for the control itself. It could be the impact of productivity and turnaround time. Even if the control is a new procedure, the effect on the employees must be reviewed and used in the determination on whether to implement.

A final consideration is the safety and reliability of the control or safeguard. Does the control have a track record that demonstrates that it will allow the organization to operate in a safe and secure mode? The overall safety of the organization's intellectual property is at stake. The last thing that the risk management team wants to do is implement a control that puts the enterprise at a greater risk.

The expenditure on controls must be balanced against the actual business harm. A good rule of thumb is that if the control costs more than the asset it is designed to protect, then the return on investment is probably going to be low. One way to identify a good "bang for the buck" is to identify each control and cross-reference it to all of the threats that could be mitigated by the implementation of that specific control. This process will provide the team with an initial idea of which control is most cost-effective.

To be effective, the risk analysis process should be applied across the entire organization. That is, all of the elements and methodology that make up the risk analysis process should be standard and all business units trained in its use. The output from the risk analysis will lead the organization to identify controls that should reduce the level of threat occurrence (Table 2.7).

Another way to map controls is by using some standard such as International Standards Organization (ISO) 17799 (Table 2.8). ISO 17799 is actually "a comprehensive set of controls comprising best practices in information security." It is essentially, in part (extended), an internationally recognized generic information security standard.

Its predecessor, BS7799-1, has existed in various forms for a number of years, although the standard only really gained widespread recognition following publication by ISO in December 2000. Formal certification and accreditation were also introduced around the same time.

The object of the controls list is to identify categories of controls that will lead the team to determine the specific control required. When developing your list, be sure to be thorough, but do not be so pedantic that the list of controls is similar to reading *War and Peace*.

2.6.6 Step 6: Documentation

Once the risk analysis is complete, the results need to be documented in a standard format and a report issued to the asset owner. This report will help senior management and the business owner make decisions on policy, procedures, budget, and systems and management change. The risk analysis report should be presented in a systematic and analytical manner that assesses risk so that senior management will understand the risks and allocate resources to reduce the risks to an acceptable level.

2.7 Cost–Benefit Analysis

To allocate resources and implement cost-effective controls, organizations, after identifying all possible controls and evaluating their feasibility and effectiveness, should conduct a cost–benefit analysis. This process should be conducted for each new or enhanced control to determine if the control recommended is appropriate for the organization. A cost–benefit analysis should determine the impact of implementing the new or enhanced control and then determine the impact of not implementing the control.

Table 2.7 Sample Controls List by IT Organization

Control Number	IT Group	Descriptor	Definition
1	Operations controls	Backup	Backup requirements will be determined and communicated to operations, including a request that an electronic notification be sent to the application system administrator stating that backups were completed. Operations will be requested to test the backup procedures.
2	Operations controls	Recovery plan	Develop, document, and test recovery procedures designed to ensure that the application and information can be recovered, using the backups created, in the event of loss.
3	Operations controls	Risk analysis	Conduct a risk analysis to determine the level of exposure to identified threats and identify possible safeguards or controls.
4	Operations controls	Antivirus	(1) Ensure LAN administrator installs the corporate standard antiviral software on all computers. (2) Training and awareness of virus prevention techniques will be incorporated into the organization information protection (IP) program.
5	Operations controls	Interface dependencies	Systems that feed information will be identified and communicated to operations to stress the impact to the functionality if these feeder applications are unavailable.
6	Operations controls	Maintenance	Time requirements for technical maintenance will be tracked and a request for adjustment will be communicated to management if experience warrants.
7	Operations controls	Service level agreement	Acquire service level agreements to establish level of customer expectations and assurances from supporting operations.

8	Operations controls	Maintenance	Acquire maintenance and supplier agreements to facilitate the continued operational status of the application.
9	Operations controls	Change management	Production migration controls, such as search and remove processes, to ensure data stores are clean.
10	Operations controls	Business impact analysis	A formal business impact analysis will be conducted to determine the asset's relative criticality with other enterprise assets.
11	Operations controls	Backup	Training for a backup to the system administrator will be provided and duties rotated between them to ensure the adequacy of the training program.
12	Operations controls	Backup	A formal employee security awareness program has been implemented and is updated and presented to the employees at least on an annual basis.
13	Operations controls	Recovery plan	Implement a mechanism to limit access to confidential information to specific network paths or physical locations.
14	Operations controls	Risk analysis	Implement user authentication mechanisms (such as firewalls, dial-in controls, secure ID) to limit access to authorized personnel.
15	Application controls	Application control	Design and implement application controls (data entry edit checking, fields requiring validation, alarm indicators, password expiration capabilities, checksums) to ensure the integrity, confidentiality, and availability of application information.
16	Application controls	Acceptance testing	Develop testing procedures to be followed during applications development and during modifications to the existing application that include user participation and acceptance.
17	Application controls	Training	Implement user programs (user performance evaluations) designed to encourage compliance with policies and procedures in place to ensure the appropriate utilization of the application.

Table 2.7 Sample Controls List by IT Organization (continued)

Control Number	IT Group	Descriptor	Definition
18	Application controls	Training	Application developers will provide documentation, guidance, and support to the operations staff (operations) in implementing mechanisms to ensure that the transfer of information between applications is secure.
19	Application controls	Corrective strategies	The development team will develop corrective strategies such as reworked processes, revised application logic, etc.
20	Security controls	Policy	Develop policies and procedures to limit access and operating privileges to those with business need.
21	Security controls	Training	User training will include instruction and documentation on the proper use of the application. The importance of maintaining the confidentiality of user accounts, passwords, and the confidential and competitive nature of information will be stressed.
22	Security controls	Review	Implement mechanisms to monitor, report, and audit activities identified as requiring independent reviews, including periodic reviews of user IDs to ascertain and verify business need.
23	Security controls	Asset classification	The asset under review will be classified using enterprise policies, standards, and procedures on asset classification.
24	Security controls	Access control	Mechanisms to protect the database against unauthorized access, and modifications made from outside the application, will be determined and implemented.
25	Security controls	Management support	Request management support to ensure the cooperation and coordination of various business units.

26	Security controls	Proprietary	Processes are in place to ensure that company proprietary assets are protected and that the company is in compliance with all third-party license agreements.
27	Security controls	Security awareness	Implement an access control mechanism to prevent unauthorized access to information. This mechanism will include the capability of detecting, logging, and reporting attempts to breach the security of this information.
28	Security controls	Access control	Implement encryption mechanisms (data, end to end) to prevent unauthorized access to protect the integrity and confidentiality of information.
29	Security controls	Access control	Adhere to a change management process designed to facilitate a structured approach to modifications of the application, to ensure appropriate steps and precautions are followed. Emergency modifications should be included in this process.
30	Security controls	Access control	Control procedures are in place to ensure that appropriate system logs are reviewed by independent third parties to review system update activities.
31	Security controls	Access control	In consultation with facilities management, facilitate the implementation of physical security controls designed to protect the information, software, and hardware required of the system.
32	Systems controls	Change management	Backup requirements will be determined and communicated to operations, including a request that an electronic notification that backups were completed be sent to the application system administrator. Operations will be requested to test the backup procedures.
33	Systems controls	Monitor system logs	Develop, document, and test recovery procedures designed to ensure that the application and information can be recovered, using the backups created, in the event of loss.
34	Physical security	Physical security	Conduct a risk analysis to determine the level of exposure to identified threats and identify possible safeguards or controls.

Table 2.8 Controls List Using ISO 17799

Control Number	ISO 17799 Section	Class[a]	Control Description
1		Risk assessment (2)	Conduct an accurate and thorough assessment of the potential risks and vulnerabilities to the confidentiality, integrity, and availability of information resources.
2	Security policy	Policy (3.1)	Develop and implement an information security policy.
3	Organizational security	Management information security forum (4.1)	Establish a corporate committee to oversee information security. Develop and implement an information security organization mission statement.
4	Organizational security	Security of third-party access (4.2)	Implement a process to analyze third-party connection risks and implement specific security standards to combat third-party connection risks.
5	Organizational security	Security requirements in outsourcing contracts (4.3)	Ensure the security requirements of the information owners have been addressed in a contract between the owners and the outsource organization.
6	Asset classification and control	Accounting of assets (5.1)	Establish an inventory of major assets associated with each information system.
7	Asset classification and control	Information classification (5.2)	Implement standards for security classification and the level of protection required for information assets.

8	Asset classification and control	Information labeling and handling (5.2)	Implement standards to ensure the proper handling of information assets.
9	Personnel security	Security in job descriptions (6.1)	Ensure that security responsibilities are included in employee job descriptions.
10	Personnel security	User training (6.2)	Implement training standards to ensure that users are trained in information security policies and procedures, security requirements, business controls, and correct use of IT facilities.
11	Personnel security	Responding to security incidents and malfunctions (6.3)	Implement procedures and standards for formal reporting and incident response action to be taken on receipt of an incident report.
12	Physical and environmental security	Secure areas (7.1)	Implement standards to ensure that physical security protections exist, based on defined perimeters through strategically located barriers throughout the organization.
13	Physical and environmental security	Equipment security (7.2)	Implement standards to ensure that equipment is located properly to reduce risks of environmental hazards and unauthorized access.
14	Physical and environmental security	General controls (7.3)	Implement a clear desk/clear screen policy for sensitive material to reduce risks of unauthorized access, loss, or damage outside normal working hours.
15	Communications and operations management	Documented operating procedures (8.1)	Implement operating procedures to clearly document that all operational computer systems are being operated in a correct, secure manner.

Table 2.8 Controls List Using ISO 17799 (continued)

Control Number	ISO 17799 Section	Class[a]	Control Description
16	Communications and operations management	System planning and acceptance (8.2)	Implement standards to ensure that capacity requirements are monitored, and future requirements projected, to reduce the risk of system overload.
17	Communications and operations management	Protection from malicious software (8.3)	Implement standards and user training to ensure that virus detection and prevention measures are adequate.
18	Communications and operations management	Housekeeping (8.4)	Establish procedures for making regular backup copies of essential business data and software to ensure that it can be recovered following a computer disaster or media failure.
19	Communications and operations management	Network management (8.5)	Implement appropriate standards to ensure the security of data in networks and the protection of connected services from unauthorized access.
20	Communications and operations management	Media handling and security (8.6)	Implement procedures for the management of removable computer media such as tapes, disks, cassettes, and printed reports.
21	Communications and operations management	Exchanges of information and software (8.7)	Implement procedures to establish formal agreements, including software escrow agreements when appropriate, for exchanging data and software (whether electronically or manually) between organizations.
22	Access control	Business requirements for system access (9.1)	Implement a risk analysis process to gather business requirements to document access control levels.

Control Number	ISO 17799 Section	Class[a]	Control Description
23	Access control	User access management (9.2)	Implement procedures for user registration and deregistration access to all multiuse IT services.
24	Access control	User responsibility (9.3)	Implement user training to ensure users have been taught good security practices in the selection and use of passwords.
25	Access control	Network access control (9.4)	Implement procedures to ensure that network and computer services that can be accessed by an individual user or from a particular terminal are consistent with business access control policy.
26	Access control	Operating system access control (9.5)	Implement standards for automatic terminal identification to authenticate connections to specific locations.
27	Access control	Application access control (9.6)	Implement procedures to restrict access to applications system data and functions in accordance with defined access policy and based on individual requirements.
28	Access control	Monitoring system access and use (9.7)	Implement audit trails that record exceptions and other security-relevant events that produce and maintain to assist in future investigations and in access control.
29	Access control	Remote access and telecommuting (9.8)	Implement a formal policy and supporting standards that address the risks of working with mobile computing facilities, including requirements for physical protection, access controls, cryptographic techniques, backup, and virus protection.

Table 2.8 Controls List Using ISO 17799 (continued)

Control Number	ISO 17799 Section	Class[a]	Control Description
30	Systems development and maintenance	Security requirements of systems (10.1)	Implement standards to ensure that analysis of security requirements is part of the requirement analysis stage of each development project.
31	Systems development and maintenance	Security in application systems (10.2)	Implement standards to ensure that data that is input into applications systems is validated to ensure that it is correct and appropriate.
32	Systems development and maintenance	Cryptography (10.3)	Implement policies and standards on the use of cryptographic controls, including management of encryption keys, and effective implementation.
33	Systems development and maintenance	Security of system files (10.4)	Implement standards to exercise strict control over the implementation of software on operational systems.
34	Systems development and maintenance	Security in development and support environments (10.5)	Implement standards and procedures for formal change management process.

Control Number	ISO 17799 Section	Class[a]	Control Description
35	Business continuity management	Aspects of business continuity planning (11.1)	Implement procedures for the development and maintenance of business continuity plans across the organization.
36	Compliance	Compliance with legal requirements (12.1)	Implement standards to ensure that all relevant statutory, regulatory, and contractual requirements are specifically defined and documented for each information system.
37	Compliance	Reviews of security policy and technical compliances (12.2)	Implement standards to ensure that all areas within the organization are considered for regular review to ascertain compliance with security policies and standards.

[a] The numbers in parentheses are the matching section numbers found in ISO 17799.

Remember that one of the long-term costs of any control is the requirement to maintain its effectiveness. It is therefore necessary to factor this cost into the benefit requirement of any control. When performing a cost–benefit analysis, it will be necessary to consider the cost of implementation based on some of the following:

- Costs of implementation, including initial outlay for hardware and software
- Reduction in operational effectiveness
- Implementation of additional policies and procedures to support the new controls
- Cost of possibly hiring additional staff or, at a minimum, training existing staff in the new controls
- Cost of education support personnel to maintain the effectiveness of the control

2.8 Risk Mitigation

Risk mitigation is a systematic methodology used by senior management to reduce organizational risk. Once the risk assessment has been conducted (threats identified, risk levels established, controls chosen), management can use various risk mitigation techniques to complete the process. Risk mitigation can be achieved through a number of different methods. We will identify and discuss the six most common methods of risk mitigation:

- *Risk assumption* — After examining the threats and determining the risk level, the team's findings lead management to determine that it is the best business decision to accept the potential risk and continue operating. This is an acceptable outcome of the risk assessment process. If, after completing the risk assessment process, management decides to accept the risk, then it has performed due diligence.
- *Risk alleviation* — Senior management approves the implementation of the controls recommended by the risk management team that will lower the risk to an acceptable level.
- *Risk avoidance* — This is where after performing the risk assessment, management chooses to avoid the risks by eliminating the process that could cause the risks. For example, foregoing certain functions or enhancements to systems or applications because the risk assessment results lead management to conclude that to proceed, the organization would be placed at too great of an exposure.

- *Risk limitation* — To limit the risk by implementing controls that minimize the adverse impact of a threat. This is the standard process that is used when a risk assessment is completed. After identifying threats, establishing the risk level, and selecting reasonable and prudent controls, management is limiting risk exposure.
- *Risk planning* — This is a process where it is decided to manage risk by developing an architecture that prioritizes, implements, and maintains controls.
- *Risk transference* — Here management transfers the risk by using other options to compensate for a loss, such as purchasing an insurance policy.

Whichever risk mitigation technique is used, the business objectives or mission of an organization must be considered when selecting any of these techniques.

2.9 Final Thoughts

Practically no system or activity is risk-free, and not all implemented controls can eliminate the risk that they are intended to address. The purpose of risk management is to analyze the business risks of a process, application, system, or other asset to determine the most prudent method for safe operation. The risk assessment team reviews these assets with the business objectives as their primary consideration. We do not want, nor can we use, a control mechanism that reduces risk to zero. A security program that has as its goal 100 percent security will cause the organization to have 0 percent productivity.

The risk assessment process has two key objectives: to implement reasonable and prudent controls and to document management's due diligence. As security professionals, we are aware that our goal is to provide support for the organization and to ensure that management objectives are met. By implementing an effective risk management and risk assessment process, this objective will be met and embraced by our user community.

Chapter 3

Risk Assessment Process

3.1 Introduction

The dictionary defines *risk* as "someone or something that creates or suggests a hazard." In today's business environment, it is one of the many costs of doing business or providing a service. Information security (IS) and audit professionals know and understand that nothing ever runs smoothly for very long. Any manner of internal or external hazard or risk can cause a well-running organization to loose competitive advantage, miss deadlines, or suffer embarrassment. As such, management is looking to us to provide the processes that allow it to perform a systematic review of risk, threats, hazards, and concerns and provide cost-effective measures to lower risk to an acceptable level.

3.2 Risk Assessment Process

To be effective, the risk assessment process must be accepted as part of the business process of the enterprise. The risk management professional looks to ensure that the analysis and assessment processes support the business objectives or mission of the organization. For years I have been trying to help security and audit professionals understand that security or audit requirements are not what the business needs. There are only business or mission recommendations or solutions. Remember, part of the success of a process is its acceptance by the user community. Trying to mandate requirements to managers can be counterproductive. An effective risk assessment process will search for the business needs of the enterprise and will work with the business owners to identify safeguards to meet those needs.

To be successful, the needs of the customer must be identified and met. Every time the risk assessment is to be conducted, the risk management professional must meet with the client to determine what is to be reviewed, what kinds of risk elements are to be examined, and what the client needs as a deliverable or results from the process.

For an information security professional, most of the focus of the risk assessment process revolves around the information security triad of integrity, confidentiality, and availability of information resources. As we discussed before, the only inhibiting factor in risk assessment is what you can conceive of to conduct a risk assessment against. These are only initial examples of what can be examined by an effective risk analysis process. Throughout the book we will review a number of risk assessment methods and critique them. By looking at different methods, you will be able to build a risk assessment process that will meet your organization's specific needs.

According to *Systems Management* magazine, top IS project managers were asked what functional capability they most needed to be successful; the number one answer was *risk management*. Projects often have involuntary controls or requirements imposed on them. The owner and project leader do not recognize or understand the need for the seemingly arbitrary set of controls, and therefore do not understand the need. As a result, the project manager is often surprised by negative consequences, and the project sponsor suffers unmet expectations.

The risk assessment process must be geared to support the business or mission of the enterprise. Many times, owners are told that certain controls are being implemented because the controls are audit requirements or security requirements. As we discussed, there are only business or mission requirements. Our job is to help the owner find business-friendly controls or countermeasures.

The role of security (whether physical or information) is to assist management in meeting its fiduciary responsibility to adequately protect the assets of the enterprise. With capital assets, it is easy to see that stealing property affects the enterprise's ability to conduct business. So, now we must help management to identify intellectual property and implement effective, cost-efficient safeguards.

3.3 Information Is an Asset

Every enterprise has to establish its own set of requirements for the protection of information assets. These are typically documented through an information classification policy and handling standards. The individual safeguards will differ depending on sensitivity and criticality of the information resource. Therefore, the goal of an enterprisewide information security program and risk assessment process is to determine the threat impact to information assets based on:

- *Integrity* — The information is as intended without inappropriate modification or corruption
- *Confidentiality* — The information is protected from unauthorized or accidental disclosure
- *Availability* — Authorized users can access applications and systems when required to perform their jobs

It may be necessary to create a more specific definition or example of each of these elements to provide the team with a better frame of reference from which to work (Table 3.1).

The process for classifying information needs to be well defined, and a methodology to assist the users in determining the level of classification must be implemented as part of the risk management process. Later, we will use qualitative risk assessment methods to demonstrate how a user-friendly classification process can be created. To assist the information risk management process, it will be necessary to have the users visualize the elements that make up the value of the information asset. These might include some or all of the following:

- The cost of producing the information
- The value of the information on the open market
- The cost of reproducing the information if destroyed
- The benefit the information brings to the enterprise in meeting its business objectives or mission
- The repercussion to the enterprise if the information was not readily available
- The advantage it would give to a competitor if it could use, change, or destroy the information
- The cost to the enterprise if the information was released, altered, or destroyed
- The loss of client or customer confidence if the information was not held and processed securely
- The loss of public credibility and embarrassment if the information was not secure

The value of a particular information resource must be determined by the business manager owner where the information resource is created or by the primary user of that resource. This is a process that cannot be

Table 3.1   Review Element Definitions

Review Element	Definition
Loss of integrity	System and data integrity refers to the requirement that information be protected from improper modification. Integrity is lost if unauthorized changes are made to the data or the system either intentionally or accidentally. If the loss of system or data integrity is not corrected, continued use of the contaminated system or corrupted data could result in inaccuracy, fraud, or erroneous decisions. Also, violation of integrity may be the first step in a successful attack against system availability or confidentiality.
Loss of availability	If a mission-critical system is unavailable to its end users, the organization's mission may be affected. Loss of system functionality and operational effectiveness may result in loss of productive time, therefore impeding the end users' performance of their tasks in supporting the organization's mission.
Loss of confidentiality	System and data confidentiality refers to the protection of information from unauthorized disclosure. The impact of unauthorized disclosure of confidential information can range from the jeopardizing of nonpublic, personal private information to loss of competitive advantage or trade secret information. Unauthorized, unanticipated, or unintentional disclosure could result in loss of public confidence, competitive advantage, organization embarrassment, or legal or regulatory action.

discharged to the information security staff or to audit or to any other third party; it must remain with the business unit.

3.4 Risk Assessment Methodology

The risk assessment process consists of four elements: asset scoped, threats identified, risk level established, and possible controls selected. In Chapter 1 we discussed creating a project scope statement to define the asset that is to be the subject of the review.

As a review, what is an asset? An accountant might say that an asset is anything of value. However, many times the asset in question is a tangible piece of property that can be seen. However, the physical assets are not the only assets that must be protected. Assets can be divided into two major headings:

- *Physical* — Those items that can be seen
- *Logical* — The intellectual property of the enterprise

Other classification levels might include people, physical and environmental, telecommunications, and hardware, software, data, and information. Another list might include topics such as hardware, software, data, and information and people and procedures. All too often, management tends to focus on the enterprise's physical assets. Although important, the intellectual assets of an organization are often more valuable and harder to protect than the physical assets.

As we have seen, the proper definition of the asset to be reviewed in the risk assessment process is vital to the success of the process. The ability to precisely identify what a specific asset is cannot be overemphasized.

We will now review the remaining three elements of the risk assessment process.

3.4.1 Threat Identification

After you have identified the asset that needs to be protected, you must begin to look for and identify threats to that asset. What then is a threat? Based on the context in which it is used, threat can mean a number of things, none of them typically good. It is normally looked upon as an "intent to do harm to someone or something." According to Webster, a threat is "an indication of an impending undesirable event" or, my favorite, "an expression of intention to inflict evil, injury, or damage."

There can be an unlimited number of threats that can be of concern to your enterprise. Any number of typical or common threats can be identified, such as fire, flood, or fraud. It is very important to consider all threats, no matter how unlikely they may seem. Later, in the risk level process, we can weed out those threats that have little or no possibility of occurring. As a starting point, you want to consider those threats that might actually impact your organization.

When attempting to identify potential threats, it might prove beneficial to create scenarios that will help the team expand its search pattern. You will want to examine circumstances or events that could cause harm to the asset under review or to the mission or business objectives of the organization.

As we discussed in Chapter 1, there are three common sources for threats, and they can be classified as natural, human, or environmental. Remember that human is divided into two subcategories: accidental and deliberate.

When searching for threats, it is important to consider all potential sources or scenarios that could lead to an impact on the organization. Try not to overlook the obvious. For example, you may have a data center located in Mesa, AZ. The idea of a natural flood may be dismissed by the team as too remote a likelihood to consider. However, an environmental threat such as a broken main could quickly flood the data center and cause severe damage to the assets. So be sure to examine the source of each threat — natural, human, or environmental — before dismissing it.

As we have mentioned before, the human threat must be viewed through intentional acts, such as deliberate attacks by malicious persons or disgruntled employees, or unintentional acts, such as negligence and errors. A deliberate attack can be an attempt to gain unauthorized access to a system or application either by password guessing or cracking or by using a Post-it Note attached to the workstation to remember the access codes.

You will want to include discussions on what would motivate a threat source to act. Remember, motivation is pretty much limited to the human source. Although I have many times thought that Mother Nature had it in for me when I had to work outside, I am fairly certain that these acts were not deliberately aimed at me. It may help to put together a table (see Table 3.2) for the team members to facilitate discussion.

3.4.1.1 Elements of Threats

When examining threats, experts identify three elements that are associated with threat:

- *Agent* — The catalyst that performs the threat. The agent can be human, machine, or nature.
- *Motive* — Something that causes an agent to act. These actions can be either accidental or intentional. Based on the elements that make up an agent, the only motivating factor that can be both accidental and intentional is human.
- *Results* — The outcome of the applied threat. For the information security profession, the results normally lead to a loss of access, unauthorized access, modification, disclosure, or destruction of the information asset.

During the risk assessment process it will be necessary to identify as many threats as possible. There are a number of ways that this can be accomplished. The first way may be to review current risk management textbooks and develop a list of possible threats.

Identifying a threat is just the first part of the analysis phase. It will be necessary to determine just how vulnerable your enterprise is to that threat. There are a number of factors that will impact a threat. In fact,

Table 3.2 Threat Sources

Source	Motivation	Threat
External hacker	Challenge Ego Game playing	System hacking Social engineering Dumpster diving
Internal hacker	Deadline Financial problems Disenchantment	Trapdoor Fraud Poor documentation

Cracker	Destruction of
	  information
	Monetary gain
	Unauthorized data
	  alteration
		Spoofing
		System intrusion
		Impersonation
		Denial of service attack

Terrorist (environmental)	Revenge Greenmail Strident cause	System attack Social engineering Letter bombs Viruses Denial of service
Poorly trained employees	Unintentional errors Programming errors Data entry errors	Corruption of data Malicious code introduced System bugs Unauthorized access

there are nearly as many factors affecting the threat and its impact to your enterprise as there are threats.

Your geographical location can have an impact to the threat model. If you located in the Midwest, then some natural threats will not be part of your areas of concern. There are very few dust storms in Lincoln, NE. Although Detroit and the northern states and cities are used to handling ice and snow, just the threat of an inch of snow can send southern cities into a panic. Beyond the natural threats, geography can also impact the infrastructure supporting your enterprise. The northeastern United States has too many people and businesses for the existing support infrastructure. The telecommunications, power, electricity, and roads are stretched to their capacity, and any additional impact can and often does cause problems.

The facility that your enterprise is housed in can impact threats. Depending on the age of the building, it can be either an asset or a threat. Do not get confused by thinking that only newer construction is safe. In many instances the older structures are able to withstand some pretty impressive happenstance. Examine the construction of the complex and determine if there is an active fire suppression system installed and tested.

Who you share the facility with and who your neighbors are can affect the level or vulnerability the threat is to your enterprise. During a recent physical security review, the seven-story office building was typical when it came to security officers in the lobby, additional level of access for restricted areas, and a fire suppression system that is tested. The biggest threat we found to the enterprise was the fact that it shared its building with noncompany law enforcement agencies.

Other factors that might impact the level of vulnerability include those listed in Table 3.3.

3.4.1.2 Threat Occurrence Rates

Once assets and threats have been identified, it will be necessary to establish some link between the two. One of the most basic forms of risk analysis is a process known as an annual loss exposure (ALE). The ALE takes the value (V) of an asset and then uses the likelihood (L) of a threat occurrence in a formula to calculate the ALE:

$$V \times L = ALE$$

Getting and understanding the likelihood of an occurrence is going to take some work. For natural threats, local weather centers and the National Weather Center track the number of occurrences of specific weather threats during the calendar year. The risk management team will need to research these findings and then develop a table. This table can be an average based on the number of occurrences divided by the number of years. Or you can track the number of occurrences over a 5-year period and develop a rate of occurrence, with the lowest number at one end of the range and the highest number at the other.

For all other types of threats, it will be necessary to do additional research. For criminal activities, the risk management team can look to local law enforcement, the FBI, and state agencies. Each entity keeps a log of the number of times a specific activity has occurred within its jurisdiction. This information, along with the information gathered by your internal audit and security staffs, will provide the rates of occurrence found through the weather bureaus.

For some threats, it may be necessary to contact your enterprise's insurance company to see if it has information that it can share with you. Do not forget to review the system incident logs to determine errors, omissions, hardware failure, software bugs, and other types of system-related threats.

Once you have done your legwork, you may use something like Table 3.4 to show annual rates of occurrence.

Table 3.3 Threat Impacts

Impacts to Threats	Concern
Information sensitivity	What kinds and type of information does your enterprise generate?
Employee emergency training	Have employees been trained to respond to emergency incidents? Are there procedures in place that will assist employees during an emergency?
Protection and detection features	Are there additional asset protection features in place? Can the enterprise detect when a threat is happening?
Employee morale	Are employees unusually dissatisfied? Is there unrest within the ranks?
Local economic conditions	Is the surrounding area economically deprived?
Visibility	Is your organization a high-profile company or agency?
Redundancies	Are there backup systems in place?
Proficiency level of employees	Are employees properly trained?
Written procedures	Are there written desk procedures in place? Are these procedures used to train backup personnel?
Employee security awareness	Do employees attend annual security awareness sessions?
Past prosecutions	Has the enterprise ever sought relief in the courts for attacks on its assets? Has information been turned over to law enforcement for criminal prosecution?

The ALE would work like this: You have a $3 million data center located in a flood area. A major flood that would destroy the data center occurs once every 100 years.

> Value = $3 million
> Likelihood = Once every 100 years (using the table above, L = 0.01)
> $3 million × 0.01 = $30,000

Table 3.4 Rates of Occurrence

Rate of Occurrence	Fractional Equivalent	Multiplier Factor
Never	0	0.0
Once in 300 years	1/300	0.00333
Once in 200 years	1/200	0.005
Once in 100 years	1/100	0.01
Once in 50 years	1/50	0.02
Once in 25 years	1/25	0.04
Once in 5 years	1/5	0.20
Once in 2 years	1/2	0.50
Yearly	1/1	1.0
Twice a year	1/.5	2.0
Once a month	12/1	12.0
Once a week	52/1	52.0
Once a day	365/1	365.0

Insurance companies use the ALE to assist them in determining what kind of premium they should charge. For the risk management professional, this form of risk analysis is often misleading. The loss if a flood occurs is not $30,000, but actually $3,000,000. Among the problems with using the ALE method is the inability to predict how soon a threat will occur.

Once the threat list has been reviewed, consolidated, and edited, it will be necessary to establish a risk level for each threat. We will examine that process next.

3.4.1.3 Risk Level Determination

Once a list of threats has been finalized, it will be necessary to determine how likely that threat is to occur. The risk assessment team will want to derive an overall likelihood that indicates the probability that a potential threat may be exercised against the risk assessment asset under review. When establishing probability levels, it will be necessary to include governing factors such as motivation from the source of the threat and the existence of current controls.

When examining the threat, there are two key ways to assess the probability and impact. The first method is to establish probability without consideration for existing controls. This method is typically used when

Table 3.5   Probability Level Definitions

Probability Level	Definition
High	The threat source is highly motivated and has sufficient capability, and controls are inadequate to keep the threat from being exercised.
Medium	The threat source is motivated and capable, but controls are in place that may impede the successful exercise of the threat.
Low	The threat source lacks motivation or capability, or controls are in place to prevent, or at least significantly impede, the threat from being exercised.

conducting an initial risk assessment for an enterprise infrastructure resource such as a network segment, platform, or information security program. This method will give the team a baseline of exposure levels from which to build the control program.

The other method is to examine the risk level by taking into account existing controls. This will allow the team to examine existing controls and establish a risk level based on how effective the existing controls are. This method is typically used when examining a specific local area network (LAN), application, or subnet.

The likelihood the organization is susceptible to a specific threat is typically described as high, medium, or low (Table 3.5).

Once the probability that a threat might occur has been determined, the impact that the threat will have on the organization must be addressed. Before determining the impact value, it is necessary to ensure that the scope of the risk assessment has been properly defined. It will be necessary to ascertain that the risk assessment team understands the objectives or mission of the asset under review and how it impacts on the organization's overall mission or objectives. Before beginning the impact analysis, it is necessary to obtain the following:

- *Asset mission* — This was accomplished as part of the project scope statement. The scope statement must be discussed with the team at the start of the risk assessment process.
- *Information sensitivity* — To conduct a successful risk assessment, everyone must know the sensitivity of the information that will be handled by the asset under review. We will be discussing this process in the chapter on prescreening (Chapter 6).
- *Asset criticality* — How important is this asset to the mission of the organization? It will be necessary to conduct a business impact analysis (BIA) on the asset to determine its relative criticality. We will be discussing these processes later in the book.

Again, when determining the impact, the team needs to know how existing controls are to be considered. The scope statement will include the establishment of assumptions and constraints. These assumptions might include the concepts that a risk assessment has been performed on the supporting infrastructure elements and that appropriate controls have been implemented. This will mean that such an activity has already taken place or is scheduled to be done as soon as possible. By establishing these assumptions, the risk management team can focus on the threats and impacts related directly to the asset under review.

Some tangible impacts can be measured quantitatively in lost revenue, cost of repairing the system, or the level of effort required to correct problems caused by a successful threat occurrence. Other impacts, the intangible ones such as loss of public confidence, loss of creditability, and damage to the organization's reputation, cannot be measured in specific units, but must be qualified in terms of high, medium, and low impacts (Table 3.6).

Once the team has established the probability level and the impact level, it will be able to assign a risk level to the threat. This can be done by creating the type of risk level matrix we discussed in Chapter 1 (Figure 3.1). Try to keep the levels as clear and concise as possible.

3.4.1.4 Controls and Safeguards

After the risk level has been assigned, the team will identify controls or safeguards that are in place or could be put in place to possibly eliminate the risk, or at least reduce the risk to an acceptable level. One of the goals of risk assessment is to document the organization's due diligence when making business decisions. Therefore, it will be important to identify as many controls and safeguards as possible that could reduce the risk exposure level. By doing this, the team will be able to document all of the options that were considered.

There are a number of factors that need to be considered when recommending controls and alternative solutions. For instance, how effective is the recommended control? One way to determine the relative effectiveness is to perform the risk level process (probability and impact) to the threat with the identified control in place. If the risk level is not reduced to an acceptable point, then the team may want to examine another option.

There may also be legal and regulatory requirements to implement specific controls. With so many new and expanding requirements mandated by government agencies, controlling boards, and laws, it will be necessary for the risk management team to be current on these requirements.

Table 3.6 Impact Level Definitions

Impact Level	Definition
High	The loss of confidentiality, integrity, or availability could be expected to have severe or catastrophic adverse effects on organizational operations, assets, or individuals.
	Severe degradation or loss of mission capability to an extent and duration that the organization is not able to perform its primary functions
	Results in major damage to the organization's assets
	Results in major financial loss
	Results in severe or catastrophic harm to individuals, involving loss of life or serious life-threatening injuries
Medium	The loss of confidentiality, integrity, or availability could be expected to have serious adverse effects on organizational operations, assets, or individuals.
	Significant degradation in mission capability to an extent and duration that the organization is able to perform its primary functions, but the effectiveness is reduced
	Results in significant damage to the organization's assets
	Results in significant financial loss
	Results in significant harm to individuals, but not loss of life or serious injuries
Low	The loss of confidentiality, integrity, or availability could be expected to have limited adverse effects on organizational operations, assets, or individuals.
	Degradation in mission capability to an extent and duration that the organization is able to perform its primary functions, but the effectiveness is reduced
	Results in minor damage to the organization's assets
	Results in minor financial loss
	Results in minor exposure to harm

When selecting any type of control, it will be necessary to measure the operational impact to the organization. Every control will have an impact in some manner. It could be the expenditure for the control itself. It could be the impact of productivity and turnaround time. Even if the control is a new procedure, the effect on the employees must be reviewed and used in the determination of whether to implement.

A final consideration is the safety and reliability of the control or safeguard. Does the control have a track record that demonstrates that it

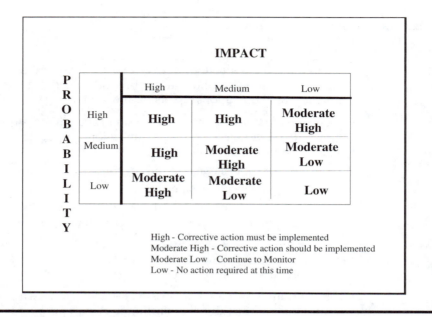

Figure 3.1 Risk level matrix table.

will allow the organization to operate in a safe and sound mode? The overall safety of the organization's intellectual property is at stake. The last thing that the risk assessment team will want to do is to implement a control that puts the enterprise at a greater risk.

The expenditure on controls must be balanced against the actual business harm. A good rule of thumb is that if the control costs more than the asset it is designed to protect, then the return on investment is probably going to be low. One way to identify a good return on investment is to identify each control and cross-reference it to all of the threats that could be mitigated by the implementation of that specific control. This process will provide the team with an initial idea of which control is most cost-effective.

Therefore, the goal of this step in the risk assessment process is to analyze the controls that have been implemented or are planned for implementation (Table 3.7). Security controls encompass the use of technical and nontechnical methods. The technical controls are safeguards that are incorporated into computer hardware, software, or firmware. These would include access control mechanisms, identification and authentication processes, encryption tools, and intrusion detection software. Nontechnical controls are management and operational controls such as policies, procedures, standards, personnel security, and environmental control mechanisms.

Table 3.7 Control Categories Example 1

Security Category	Control
Management	Risk assessment
	Security planning
	System and service acquisition procedures
	Control vulnerability assessment
	Processing authorization
Operational	Personnel security
	Physical and environmental controls
	Continuity planning
	Configuration management
	Hardware and software maintenance
	System integrity
	Media protection
	Incident response
	Security awareness program
Technical	Identification and authentication
	Logical access control
	Audit trails and logs
	Communication protection
	System protection

The control categories for both technical and nontechnical control methods can be further classified as avoidance, assurance, detection, and recovery. The team should concentrate on controls that will allow the mission of the enterprise to function while providing an adequate level of protection. It may be prudent to establish a list of possible controls in each of the layers that will help the enterprise meet its business objectives.

- *Avoidance controls* — Proactive safeguards that attempt to minimize the risk of accidental or intentional intrusions.
- *Assurance controls* — Tools and strategies employed to ensure the ongoing effectiveness of the existing controls and safeguards.

Table 3.8   Control Categories Example 2

Control Category	Control
Avoidance	Encryption and authentication
	System security architecture
	Facilitated risk analysis process
	Information awareness program
	Information security program
	Interruption prevention
	Policies and standards
	Public key infrastructure
	Secure application architecture
	Secure communications plans
Assurance	Application security review
	Standards testing
	Penetration testing
	Periodic perimeter scans
	Vulnerability assessment
Detection	Intrusion detection
	Remote intrusion monitoring
Recovery	Business continuity planning
	Business impact analysis
	Crisis management planning
	Disaster recovery planning
	Incident response procedures
	Investigation tools

■ *Detection controls* — Techniques and programs used to ensure early detection, interception, and response for security breaches.
■ *Recovery controls* — Planning and response services to rapidly restore a secure environment and investigate the source of the breaches.

Examples of controls and safeguards for each of the security layers include those listed in Table 3.8.

During this step, the risk assessment team will determine the security controls generally based on existing security architecture, some regulatory requirement, a business standard, or a combination of all three. As we discussed in Chapter 1, Information Technology: Code of Practice for Information Security Management (ISO 17799) is a good basis for establishing a set of controls.

There are other sources for standards, and each year risk assessment teams receive new regulations discussing the need to protect information and information processing assets. Other sources might include some of the following:

- "Security Technologies for Manufacturing and Control Systems" (ISA-TR99.00.01-2004)
- "Integrating Electronic Security into Manufacturing and Control Systems Environment" (ISA-TR99.00.02-2004)
- Federal Information Processing Standards Publications (FIPS Pubs)
- National Institute of Standards and Technology
- CobiT® Security Baseline
- Health Insurance Portability and Accountability Act (HIPAA)
- The Basel Accords
- Privacy Act of 1974
- Gramm–Leach–Bliley Act (GLBA)
- Sarbanes–Oxley Act (SOX)
- "Information Security for Banking and Finance" (ISO/TR 13569)
- Federal Financial Institutions Examination Council (FFEIC) examination guidelines

When a new set of standards or controls is introduced, I try to map them to an established industry standard such as ISO 17799. This allows me to be certain that any new item is assimilated into the controls list and that items are not duplicated. By doing this, management is given the opportunity to see that the new standards or industry requirements have already been addressed in the existing practices of the organization.

First, I map out the new requirements such as HIPAA, as in Table 3.9. After mapping out the new standards, I map them to the organization's existing control standards or to ISO 17799. That might look like Table 3.10.

In the Information Security Architecture there are four layers of controls: avoidance, assurance, detection, and recovery. Or you can create a set of controls that map to the enterprise such as operations, applications, systems, security, etc. Mapping to some standard such as the international standard for information security, ISO 17799, or the Gramm–Leach–Bliley Act are other options (Table 3.11).

Table 3.9 HIPAA Controls List

Category	Control	Classification	HIPAA Control Description
Security Management Process			Implement policies and procedures to prevent/detect.
1	Risk analysis	Required	Conduct an accurate and thorough assessment of the potential risks and vulnerabilities to the confidentiality, integrity, and availability of electronically protected health information (EPHI).
2	Risk management	Required	Implement security measures sufficient to reduce risks and vulnerabilities to a reasonable and appropriate level.
3	Sanction policy	Required	Apply appropriate sanctions against workforce members who fail to comply with the security policies and procedures of the covered entity.
4	Information system activity review	Required	Implement procedures to regularly review records of information systems activity.
Assigned Security Responsibility			Identify the security official who is responsible for the development and implementation of the policies and procedures.
5	Privacy officer	Required	Identify a single person responsible for the development and implementation of the policies and procedures supporting HIPAA compliance.

Administrative Safeguards			Implement policies and procedures to ensure that all members of the organization's workforce have appropriate access to EPHI, and to prevent those workforce members who are not authorized to have access under the information access management standard from obtaining access to electronic health information.
6	Authorization/ supervision	Addressable	Implement procedures for the authorization and supervision of workforce members who work with EPHI or in locations where it might be accessed.
7	Workforce clearance procedure	Addressable	Implement procedures to determine that the access of a workforce member to EPHI is appropriate.
8	Termination procedure	Addressable	Implement procedures for terminating access to EPHI when the employment of a workforce member ends or as required by access authorization policies.
Information Access Management			Implement policies and procedures for authorizing access to EPHI.
9	Isolate healthcare clearinghouse functions	Required	If a covered entity (CE) operates a healthcare clearinghouse, it must implement policies and procedures to protect the EPHI maintained by the clearinghouse from unauthorized access by the larger organization.
10	Access authorization	Addressable	Implement policies and procedures for granting access to EPHI, for example, through access to a workstation, transaction, program, process, or other mechanism.

Table 3.9 HIPAA Controls List (continued)

Category	Control	Classification	HIPAA Control Description
11	Access establishment and modification	Addressable	Implement policies and procedures that, based on the entity's access authorization policies, establish, document, review, and modify a user's right of access to a workstation, transaction, program, or process.
Security Awareness and Training			Implement a security awareness and training program for all members of the workforce, including management.
12	Security reminders	Addressable	Periodic security reminders.
13	Protection from malicious software	Addressable	Procedures guarding against, detecting, and reporting malicious software.
14	Log-in monitoring	Addressable	Procedures to monitor log-in attempts and report discrepancies.
15	Password management	Addressable	Procedures to create, change, and safeguard passwords.
Security Incident Procedures			Implement policies and procedures to address security incidents.
16	Response and reporting	Required	Identify and respond to suspected or known security incidents; mitigate to the extent practicable harmful effects of the security incidents that are known to the CE; document security incidents and their outcomes.

Contingency Plan				Establish (and implement as needed) policies and procedures for responding to an emergency or other occurrence that damages systems that contain EPHI.
	17	Data backup	Required	Establish and implement procedures to create and maintain retrievable exact copies of EPHI.
	18	Disaster recovery plan	Required	Establish (and implement as needed) procedures to restore any loss of data.
	19	Emergency mode operations plan	Required	Establish (and implement as needed) procedures to enable continuation of critical business processes to ensure access to EPHI and provide for adequate protection of EPHI while operating in emergency mode.
	20	Testing and revision procedures	Addressable	Implement procedures for periodic testing and revision of contingency plans.
	21	Applications and data criticality	Addressable	Assess the relative criticality of specific applications and data in support of other contingency plan components.
Evaluation	22			Perform a periodic technical and nontechnical evaluation, based initially upon the security rule standards, and subsequently in response to environmental or operational changes affecting the security of EPHI, that establishes the extent to which a CE's security policies and procedures meet the requirements.
Business Contracts	23			A CE may permit a business associate (BA) to create, receive, maintain, or transmit EPHI on its behalf only if the CE obtains satisfactory assurances that the BA will appropriately safeguard the information.

Table 3.9 HIPAA Controls List (continued)

Category	Control	Classification	HIPAA Control Description
Physical Safeguards			
Facility Access Control			Implement policies and procedures to limit physical access to EPHI systems and the facilities in which they are housed, while ensuring that properly authorized access is allowed.
24	Contingency operations	Addressable	Establish (and implement as needed) procedures that allow facility access in support of restoration of lost data under the disaster recovery plan and emergency mode operations plan in the event of an emergency.
25	Facility security plan	Addressable	Implement policies and procedures to safeguard the facility and the equipment therein from unauthorized physical access, tampering, and theft.
26	Access control and validation procedures	Addressable	Implement procedures to control and validate a person's access to facilities based on his role or function, including visitor control, and control access to software programs for testing and revision.
27	Maintenance records	Addressable	Implement policies and procedures to document repairs and modifications to the physical components of a facility that are related to security.
Workstation Use			Implement policies and procedures that specify the proper functions to be performed, the manner in which those functions are to be performed, and the physical attributes of the surroundings of a specific workstation or class of workstation that can access EPHI.
28	Workstation security	Standard	Implement physical safeguards for all workstations that access EPHI to restrict access to authorized users.

#		Standard	
29	Device and media control		Implement policies and procedures that govern the receipt and removal of hardware and electronic media that contain EPHI into and out of a facility, and the movement of these items within a facility.
30	Disposal	Required	Implement policies and procedures to address the final disposition of EPHI and the hardware or electronic media on which it is stored.
31	Media reuse	Required	Implement procedures for removal of EPHI from electronic media prior to reuse.
32	Accountability	Addressable	Maintain a record of the movement of hardware and software and any person responsible for movement.
33	Data backup and storage	Addressable	Create a retrievable, exact copy of EPHI, when needed, prior to moving equipment.
Technical Safeguards			
Access Control			Implement technical policies and procedures for electronic information systems that maintain EPHI to allow access only to those persons or software programs that have been granted access rights as specified.
34	Unique user identification	Required	Assign a unique name or number for identifying and tracking user identity.
35	Emergency access procedure	Required	Establish (and implement as needed) procedures for obtaining necessary EPHI during an emergency.
36	Automatic log-off	Addressable	Implement electronic procedures that terminate an electronic session after a predetermined time of inactivity.

Table 3.9 HIPAA Controls List (continued)

Category	Control	Classification	HIPAA Control Description
37	Encryption and decryption	Addressable	Implement a mechanism to encrypt and decrypt EPHI.
38	Audit controls	Standard	Implement hardware, software, and procedural mechanisms that record and examine activity in information systems that contain or use EPHI.
39	Integrity	Standard	Implement policies and procedures to protect EPHI from improper alteration or destruction.
40	Authentication	Standard	Implement procedures to verify that a person or entity seeking access to EPHI is the one claimed.
41	Transmission security	Standard	Implement technical security measures to guard against unauthorized access to EPHI that is being transmitted over an electronic communications network.
42	Business associate contracts	Standard	The contract between the CE and its BA must meet the following requirements, as applicable: A CE is not in compliance if it knew of a pattern of activity or practice of the BA that constituted a material breach or violation of the BA's obligation under the contract, unless the CE took reasonable steps to cure the breach or end the violation, and if such steps were unsuccessful to (A) terminate the contract, if feasible; or (B) report the problem to the secretary of HHS, if not.

Policies and Procedures			
43	Documentation	Standard	Implement reasonable and appropriate policies and procedures to comply with the standards, implementation specifications, and other requirements.
44	Time limit	Required	Maintain the policies and procedures required by the security rule in writing, which may be electronic, and if an action, activity, or assessment is required to be documented, maintain a written record, which may be electronic.
45	Availability	Required	Retain the documentation required by the security rule for six years from the date of its creation or the date when it was last in effect, whichever is later.
46	Updates	Required	Make documentation available to those persons responsible for implementing the procedures to which the documentation pertains.
			Review documentation periodically and update as needed, in response to environmental and operational changes affecting the security of the EPHI.

Table 3.10   Mapping HIPAA to ISO 17799 Standards

ISO 17799 Section	Control[a]	HIPAA
	Risk assessment (2)	Risk analysis (required)
Security policy	Policy (3.1)	Isolate healthcare clearinghouse functions (required)
		Integrity (standard)
Organizational security	Management information security forum (4.1)	Risk management (required)
		Sanction policy (required)
		Privacy officer (required)
Organizational security	Security of third-party access (4.2)	Business associate contracts (standard)
Organizational security	Security requirements in outsourcing contracts (4.3)	Audit controls (required)
Asset classification and control	Accounting of assets (5.1)	Inventory all assets
Asset classification and control	Information classification (5.2)	Information is an asset and the property of the enterprise
Asset classification and control	Information labeling and handling (5.2)	
Personnel security	Security in job descriptions (6.1)	
Personnel security	User training (6.2)	
Personnel security	Responding to security incidents and malfunctions (6.3)	
Physical and environmental security	Secure areas (7.1)	Workstation security (standard)
Physical and environmental security	Equipment security (7.2)	
Physical and environmental security	General controls (7.3)	

Table 3.10   Mapping HIPAA to ISO 17799 Standards (continued)

ISO 17799 Section	Control[a]	HIPAA
Communications and operations management	Documented operating procedures (8.1)	Response and reporting (required) Emergency mode operations plan (required) Transmission security (standard)
Communications and operations management	System planning and acceptance (8.2)	
Communications and operations management	Protection from malicious software (8.3)	
Communications and operations management	Housekeeping (8.4)	Data backup (required)
Communications and operations management	Network management (8.5)	
Communications and operations management	Media handling and security (8.6)	Device and media control (standard) Media reuse (required)
Communications and operations management	Exchanges of information and software (8.7)	
Access control	Business requirement for system access (9.1)	Risk analysis (required)
Access control	User access management (9.2)	Authentication (standard)
Access control	User responsibility (9.3)	
Access control	Network access control (9.4)	
Access control	Operating system access control (9.5)	Emergency access procedure (required)

Table 3.10   Mapping HIPAA to ISO 17799 Standards (continued)

ISO 17799 Section	Controlª	HIPAA
Access control	Application access control (9.6)	Unique user identification (required)
Access control	Monitoring system access and use (9.7)	
Access control	Remote access and telecommuting (9.8)	
Systems development and maintenance	Security requirements of systems (10.1)	Risk analysis
Systems development and maintenance	Security in application systems (10.2)	
Systems development and maintenance	Cryptography (10.3)	
Systems development and maintenance	Security of system files (10.4)	
Systems development and maintenance	Security in development and support environments (10.5)	
Business continuity management	Aspects of business continuity planning (11.1)	Data backup (required) Disaster recovery plan (required) Emergency mode operations plan (required)
Compliance	Compliance with legal requirements (12.1)	
Compliance	Reviews of security policy and technical compliances (12.2)	Information system activity review (required) Audit controls (required)

ª The numbers in parentheses are the matching section numbers found in ISO 17799.

Table 3.11 Mapping ISO 17799, HIPAA, GLBA, and SOX

ISO 17799 Section	Control[a]	HIPAA	GLBA	Sarbanes–Oxley
	Risk assessment (2)	Risk analysis (required)	Assess risk	Assess current internal controls
Security policy	Policy (3.1)	Isolate healthcare clearinghouse functions (required) Integrity (standard)	Board approves written policy and program	Policies and procedures must support effective internal control of assets
Organizational security	Management information security forum (4.1)	Risk management (required) Sanction policy (required) Privacy officer (required)	Involve the board of directors Assign specific responsibilities	Corporation management is responsible for ensuring internal controls are adequate
Organizational security	Security of third-party access (4.2)	Business associate contracts (standard)	Contract clauses meet guidance objectives	
Organizational security	Security requirements in outsourcing contracts (4.3)	Audit controls (required)	Report program effectiveness to board	Management must report on internal controls' effectiveness
Asset classification and control	Accounting of assets (5.1)	Inventory all assets	Implement policies to evaluate sensitivity of customer information	Identify all assets of the corporation

Table 3.11 Mapping ISO 17799, HIPAA, GLBA, and SOX (continued)

ISO 17799 Section	Control[a]	HIPAA	GLBA	Sarbanes–Oxley
Asset classification and control	Information classification (5.2)	Information is an asset and the property of the enterprise	Implement standards and procedures to protect customer information	Information is an asset and the property of the enterprise
Asset classification and control	Information labeling and handling (5.2)		Implement standards	
Personnel security	Security in job descriptions (6.1)		Background check on certain positions	
Personnel security	User training (6.2)		Train staff to implement program	
Personnel security	Responding to security incidents and malfunctions (6.3)		Incident response program	
Physical and environmental security	Secure areas (7.1)	Workstation security (standard)	Implement physical access restrictions	
Physical and environmental security	Equipment security (7.2)			
Physical and environmental security	General controls (7.3)			

Communications and operations management	Documented operating procedures (8.1)	Response and reporting (required) Emergency mode operations plan (required) Transmission security (standard)	Implement measures to protect against information destruction or damage				
Communications and operations management	System planning and acceptance (8.2)						
Communications and operations management	Protection from malicious software (8.3)						
Communications and operations management	Housekeeping (8.4)	Data backup (required)	Protect information destruction or loss				
Communications and operations management	Network management (8.5)						
Communications and operations management	Media handling and security (8.6)	Device and media control (standard) Media reuse (required)					

Table 3.11 Mapping ISO 17799, HIPAA, GLBA, and SOX (continued)

ISO 17799 Section	Control[a]	HIPAA	GLBA	Sarbanes–Oxley
Communications and operations management	Exchanges of information and software (8.7)			
Access control	Business requirement for system access (9.1)	Risk analysis (required)	Risk assessment required	
Access control	User access management (9.2)	Authentication (standard)	Authorized access only	
Access control	User responsibility (9.3)		Train users	
Access control	Network access control (9.4)			
Access control	Operating system access control (9.5)	Emergency access procedure (required)	Implement incident response program	
Access control	Application access control (9.6)	Unique user identification (required)		
Access control	Monitoring system access and use (9.7)		Monitoring systems and intrusion detection	
Access control	Remote access and telecommuting (9.8)			
Systems development and maintenance	Security requirements of systems (10.1)	Risk analysis	Risk assessment	Assess effectiveness of internal control

Systems development and maintenance	Security in application systems (10.2)			
Systems development and maintenance	Cryptography (10.3)		Assess encryption requirements	
Systems development and maintenance	Security of system files (10.4)			
Systems development and maintenance	Security in development and support environments (10.5)			
Business continuity management	Aspects of business continuity planning (11.1)	Data backup (required) Disaster recovery plan (required) Emergency mode operations plan (required)	Implement measures to protect against loss, destruction, or damage of information	
Compliance	Compliance with legal requirements (12.1)			
Compliance	Reviews of security policy and technical compliances (12.2)	Information system activity review (required) Audit controls (required)	Report findings annually to board	Management must report on internal controls' effectiveness

[a] The numbers in parentheses are the matching section numbers found in ISO 17799.

3.4.1.5 Cost–Benefit Analysis

To allocate resources and implement cost-effective controls, organizations, after identifying all possible controls and evaluating their feasibility and effectiveness, should conduct a cost–benefit analysis. This process should be conducted for each new or enhanced control to determine if the control recommended is appropriate for the organization. A cost–benefit analysis should determine the impact of implementing the new or enhanced control, and then determine the impact of not implementing the control.

One of the long-term costs of any control is the requirement to maintain its effectiveness. It is therefore necessary to factor these costs into the benefit received from any control. When performing a cost–benefit analysis, it is necessary to consider the cost of implementation based on some of the following:

■ Costs of implementation, including initial outlay for hardware and software
■ Reduction in operational effectiveness
■ Implementation of additional policies and procedures to support the new controls
■ Cost of possibly hiring additional staff or, at a minimum, training existing staff in the new controls
■ The cost of education support personnel to maintain the effectiveness of the control

3.4.1.6 Documentation

Once the risk assessment is complete, the results need to be documented in a standard format and a report issued to the asset owner. This report will help senior management make decisions on policy, procedures, budget, and systems and management change. The risk assessment report should be presented in a systematic and analytical manner that assesses risk so that senior management will understand the risks and allocate resources to reduce the risk to an acceptable level.

3.5 Final Thoughts

Practically no system or activity is risk-free, and not all implemented controls can eliminate the risk that they are intended to address. The purpose of risk management is to analyze the business risks of a process, application, system, or other asset to determine the most prudent method for safe operation. The risk assessment team reviews these assets with the business objectives as their primary consideration. A security program that has as its goal 100 percent security will cause the organization to have 0 percent productivity.

The risk assessment process has two key objectives: to implement only those controls necessary and to document management's due diligence. As company representatives, we must be aware that the goal is to provide support for the mission of the company. By implementing an effective risk management and risk assessment process, this objective will be met and embraced by our constituents.

Chapter 4

Quantitative versus Qualitative Risk Assessment

4.1 Introduction

There are as many different styles and types of risk analysis as there are enterprises trying to run them. In the 2003 Computer Security Institute's *Buyer's Guide* there were 26 different ads for risk analysis products, software, and consulting services. The organizations that are most satisfied with their risk analysis process are those that have defined a relatively simple process that can be adapted to various business units and involve a mix of individuals with knowledge of business operations and technical aspects of the systems or resources being analyzed.

In conducting the risk assessment, consideration should be given to the advantages and disadvantages of quantitative and qualitative assessments. The main advantage of the qualitative style of risk assessment is that it prioritizes the risks and identifies areas for immediate action and improvement. The disadvantage of qualitative risk assessment is that it does not provide specific quantifiable measurements of the magnitude of the impacts, therefore making a cost–benefit analysis of recommended controls more difficult (Table 4.1).

The major advantage of quantitative risk assessment (Table 4.2) is that it provides a measurement of the impacts' magnitude, which can be used

Table 4.1   Qualitative Risk Assessment Attributes

Minimally quantified estimates
Exposure scale ranking estimates
Easier to conduct than quantitative risk assessment

Table 4.2   Quantitative Risk Assessment Attributes

Quantified estimates of impact, threat frequency, safeguard effectiveness and cost, and probability
Powerful aid to decision making
Difficult to conduct

in the cost–benefit analysis of recommended controls. The disadvantage is that, depending on the numerical ranges used to express the measurement, the meaning of the quantitative risk assessment may be unclear, requiring the results to be interpreted in a qualitative manner. Additional factors often must be considered to determine the magnitude of the impact. These may include, but are not limited to:

- An estimate of the frequency of the threat occurrence rate over a specified period, usually in one-year increments
- An approximate cost for each occurrence of the threat
- A weighted factor based on a subjective analysis of the relative impact of a specific threat

In 1998 the Government Accounting Office (GAO) visited the organizations that were previous winners of the Computer Security Institute's Information Security Program of the Year Award. Its task was to identify best practices. It found that "organizations that are most satisfied with their risk analysis procedures are those that have defined a relatively simple process that can be adapted to various organizational units and involve a mix of individuals with knowledge of business operations and technical aspects of the enterprise's systems and security controls" (Government Accounting Office, May 1998, Executive Guide for Information Security Management, GAO/AIMD 98-68).

OMB's 1996 revision of Circular A-130, Appendix III, recognizes that federal agencies have had difficulty in performing effective risk assessments.... For this reason, the revised circular eliminates a long-standing federal requirement for formal risk assessments. Instead, it promotes a risk-based approach and suggests that, rather than trying to precisely measure risk, agencies should focus on generally assessing and managing risks.

4.2 Quantitative and Qualitative Pros and Cons

Each process has its advantages and disadvantages. The best way to determine which assessment style is best for your organization is to map out the benefits and pitfalls of each. Typically, you would want to do something like the list in Table 4.3.

Qualitative risk analysis provides for a systematic examination of threats and risks and for a review of proposed countermeasures and safeguards to determine the best cost–benefit for implementation. By establishing a quality risk management team, this subjective analysis can rely on the expertise of the enterprise's internal experts. The entire process is subjective in nature, and therefore the team must be properly screened and populated with knowledgeable personnel.

Qualitative risk analysis is a technique that can be used to determine the level of protection required for applications, systems, facilities, or other enterprise assets. During the systematic review of threats the team will be able to establish the probabilities of threats occurring, the impact of loss if the threats do occur, and how well the safeguards or countermeasures designed to reduce the risks to an acceptable level will work. The qualitative methodology attempts only to prioritize the various risk elements in subjective terms.

The remainder of this book will be spent on examining the qualitative risk assessment process. We will finish with the Facilitated Risk Analysis and Assessment Process (FRAAP). So, for all you fans of quantitative risk assessment, you may want to look elsewhere for answers.

4.3 Qualitative Risk Assessment Basics

The first of the methods that we will examine is a 10-step procedure that creates a qualitative risk assessment process from project planning to the final report. Each of the steps builds upon the previous step. We examine three baseline qualitative risk assessment processes. By examining these three processes, you will be able to see from where the impetuous for the Facilitated Risk Analysis and Assessment Process came.

We will examine a number of qualitative risk assessment processes, each one giving you input into how to create your own specific process. As you become comfortable with completing the risk assessment process, you will learn that it is necessary to be flexible in the process elements.

Table 4.3   Quantitative and Qualitative Risk Assessment Pros and Cons

Quantitative Risk Assessment	Qualitative Risk Assessment
Advantages	**Advantages**
The results are based substantially on independently objective processes and metrics.	Calculations are simple.
Great effort is put into asset value definition and risk mitigation.	It is not necessary to determine monetary value of asset.
Cost–benefit assessment effort is essential.	It is not necessary to quantify threat frequency.
Results can be expressed in management-specific language.	It is easier to involve nonsecurity and nontechnical staff.
	It provides flexibility in process and reporting.
Disadvantages	**Disadvantages**
Calculations are complex.	It is very subjective in nature.
Historically, it only works well with a recognized automated tool and associated knowledge base.	Limited effort is required to develop monetary value for targeted assets.
There is a large amount of preliminary work.	There is no basis for the cost–benefit analysis of risk mitigation.
It is not presented on a personnel level.	
Participants cannot be coached easily through the process.	
It is difficult to change directions.	
It is difficult to address out-of-scope issues.	

By being exposed to a number of different successful risk assessment processes, you will be able to alter your processes to meet the specific needs of each client.

Most risk assessment processes require a business impact analysis (BIA) to determine relative criticality of the resource, application, system, or business process. We will examine that process in Chapter 9. Whenever you begin a risk assessment project, it will be important to identify in the project scope statement if the BIA has been conducted and whether the information or data has been classified as to its sensitivity.

4.3.1 Step 1: Develop a Scope Statement

Every successful project begins with a definition of what is to be accomplished. For risk assessment, this will involve describing what is to be examined. This could be a physical environment, such as a data center; a specific system, such as a UNIX system supporting research and development; a processing entity, such as the corporate wide area network (WAN) or a subsection of the network, such as the payroll administration local area network (LAN); or a specific application, such as accounts payable.

In creating a statement of work or a scope statement, it is customary to begin with identifying the sponsor. This is normally the owner of the application, system, data, or process. The owner is typically described as the management person responsible for the protection of the asset in question. In most organizations, the sponsor is not an information technology (IT) person.

To limit the possibility of scope creep, it will be necessary to establish the boundaries on what is to be examined. An application that uses the corporate network to pass data is within the scope of a normal risk analysis. However, conducting a corporate analysis of the security of the Internet may be counterproductive. Keep the focus on those processes for which the organization can effect change.

The scope statement will next want to address the overall objectives of the analysis. For information security, these objectives are normally the impact of threats on the integrity, confidentiality, and availability of information processed by specific applications or systems. Consider the types of information security challenges facing your organization, and use this to define the objectives.

When conducting a risk analysis, it will be necessary to state the concerns as to how they impact the business objectives or the mission of the organization, and not how they impact security objectives. Proper controls are implemented because there is a strong business need, not so that the business unit will be in compliance with security requirements. Keep the business of the organization foremost in the discussions during the risk analysis process.

4.3.2 Step 2: Assemble a Quality Team

It is essential that properly qualified and competent personnel be selected to become members of the Qualitative Risk Assessment (QRA) team. Many information security professionals attempt to conduct the risk assessment either alone or just with other members of the security group. To be effective, the risk assessment process must have representatives from all of the departments and areas that have a vested interest or stake in the asset under review.

I was recently at a client's site and was asked to help them address an issue on the reluctance of most of the departments to pay for an intrusion detection system (IDS). A risk assessment had been conducted and the results identified the IDS as necessary, and that it should be implemented as quickly as possible. However, over the last nine months there was a major push back from all departments to implement the IDS. I went over the risk assessment process with them:

- *Step 1: Project scope statement* — Yes. They had it and showed it to me.
- *Step 2: Assemble a quality team* — Yes and no. They had identified the stakeholders, but the risk assessment team consisted of only information security and audit.

The problem with their process was an inadequate team, and this caused the controls selected to be rejected.

To be successful, make certain that all stakeholders are invited and that the team has as broad a representation as possible. The team should consist of at least those items listed in Table 4.4.

The functional owner and the users of the asset are the most important members of this team. It will be their expertise that we will want to tap to identify user-related problems. It will be the responsibility of the owner to make any final decisions.

The systems analysts are those individuals that are able to converse in a bilingual manner. That is, they can speak in business and IT. Many times the business people tell the IT people what is wanted and needed and the requirements get lost in the language barrier. The systems analysts are able to provide interpretation for both groups.

The infrastructure groups of system and applications programming, database administration, operations, telecommunications, and networks have to be part of the process to provide insight into how the environment is set up and what controls are already in place.

Physical and information security provide the risk assessment team with the view from the people that are charged with protecting the assets of the organization. The facilities management people are normally responsible for business continuity planning (BCP) and can provide input into this key area.

If controls are going to impact employees, then human resources must be part of the team. If the organization has union-represented employees, then the labor relations staff must be part of the team.

Regulatory affairs and corporate communications (formally public relations) should be part of the team if the areas that they are responsible for may be impacted by the risk assessment asset under review.

Table 4.4   Possible Risk Assessment Team Members

Possible Team Member	Crucial	Support
Functional owners	Yes	
System users	Yes	
Systems analysis	Yes	
Applications programming	Yes	
Database administration	Yes	
Auditing (if appropriate)		Yes
Physical security		Yes
Facilities management	Yes	
Telecommunication	Yes	
Network administration	Yes	
Legal (if necessary)		Yes
Regulatory affairs		Yes
Corporate communications		Yes
Human resources		Yes
Labor relations		Yes
Processing operations management	Yes	
Systems programming	Yes	

Finally, there are three groups that should be invited with a word of caution. The first of these is senior management. It is important for the senior executive in charge of the asset under review be there to kick off the meeting. However, after the preliminary introductions and after the scope statement has been reviewed, the executive should leave. The problem with having senior executives present is that they have a tendency to impact the free flow of information. Many employees are unwilling to discuss shortcomings in a process if management can hear what is being discussed.

The other group that may cause uneasiness when discussing problems is the audit staff. Although this concern is almost always unfounded, some employees have a hard time discussing anything in front of the audit team. This is because they feel that anything they say can and will be used against them at a later time. If there is a good working relationship with the audit team and the development team, then these concerns will evaporate.

Select the team members from those employees with the experience to give good working knowledge of how the processes work and what can be expected in the way of support. The quality in qualitative risk assessment comes from the team. A knowledgeable team will provide quality results.

4.3.3 Step 3: Identify Threats

Members of the risk assessment team will determine which threats can cause harm to the asset under review. This can be done by a number of different ways. One way is to provide a list of threats, like the one we discussed in this chapter, and have the team members choose those that they feel apply to the current situation. The problem with checklists is that some teams will get to the end of the list and believe that they have identified all possible threats. When using a list, be sure to get the team to try to determine what other threats may be appropriate.

Once the list is complete, the team will have to develop the proper definitions for each threat. Although this may be time-consuming for the first one or two risk analysis processes, once the list has been developed and field-tested, it can be used for every risk analysis. It will be necessary to create a threat definitions list and use it for each of the risk assessment projects. A typical list of threat definitions might look like the one shown in Table 4.5.

As discussed above, there are drawbacks to using definitions and a list of threats. To combat this, the team can brainstorm ideas. One way of doing this is to have the team members use Post-it Notes or have a scribe write down the ideas on a flip chart. These threat ideas would then be reviewed by the team members and all duplicates would be deleted and like threats combined. You may want the team to think of only integrity risks or threats first, and then go on to confidentiality issues, and finally on to availability threats. Or you can have them identify natural hazards, and then accidental, and finally deliberate threats. The key in brainstorming is to get as many threats as possible out of each category.

Once all applicable threats have been identified, they are entered into the Risk Factor Determination Worksheet (Table 4.6).

4.3.4 Step 4: Prioritize Threats

Once the threats have been entered into the Risk Factor Determination Worksheet, the team will determine how often each of the identified threats is likely to occur. Because this is a qualitative risk assessment, the frequencies are expressed as low to high and can be given a numeric value by applying the factors listed in Table 4.7.

Table 4.5   Threat Definitions

Threat Source	Threat	Definition
Natural		
	Air pollution	The soiling of the atmosphere by contaminants to the point that injury may be caused to health, property, or plant or animal life, or the use and enjoyment of the outdoors may be prevented.
	Blizzard	A severe weather condition characterized by low temperatures, winds of 35 mph or greater, and sufficient falling and blowing snow in the air to frequently reduce visibility to π miles or less for a duration of at least three hours. A severe blizzard is characterized by temperatures near or below 10°F, winds exceeding 45 mph, and visibility reduced by snow to near zero.
	Earthquake	A sudden, transient motion or trembling of the earth's crust, resulting from the waves in the earth caused by faulting of the rocks or by volcanic activity.
	Hurricane	The name for a tropical cyclone with sustained winds of 74 mph (65 knots) or greater in the North Atlantic Ocean, Caribbean Sea, Gulf of Mexico, and eastern North Pacific Ocean. This same tropical cyclone is known as a typhoon in the western Pacific and a cyclone in the Indian Ocean.
	Ice storm	A severe weather condition characterized by falling freezing precipitation. Such a storm forms a glaze on objects, creating hazardous travel conditions and utility problems.
	Lightning	A sudden and visible discharge of electricity produced in response to the buildup of electrical potential between cloud and ground, between clouds, within a single cloud, or between a cloud and surrounding air.

Table 4.5   Threat Definitions (continued)

Threat Source	Threat	Definition
	Sandstorm	A strong wind carrying sand particles through the air. They are low-level occurrences, usually only 10 feet in height to not more than 50 feet above the surface. Due to the frequent winds created by surface heating, they are most predominant during the day and die out in the night. Visibility is reduced to between 5/8 and 6/16 statute mile, and if less than 5/16, then the storm is considered a heavy sandstorm.
	Surge	The increase in seawater height from the level that would normally occur if there were no storm. Although the most dramatic surges are associated with hurricanes, even smaller low-pressure systems can cause a slight increase in the sea level if the wind and fetch is just right. It is estimated by subtracting the normal astronomic tide from the observed storm tide.
	Tornado	A violently rotating column of air in contact with and extending between a convective cloud and the surface of the earth. It is the most destructive of all storm-scale atmospheric phenomena. They can occur anywhere in the world given the right conditions, but are most frequent in the United States in an area bounded by the Rockies on the west and the Appalachians on the east.
	Yellow snow	Snow that is given golden or yellow appearance by the presence of pine or cypress pollen in the vicinity.
Environmental		
	Electrical disturbance	A momentary fluctuation in the electrical power source, consisting of a voltage surge (peak), voltage dip, or interruptions of less than a half hour.

Table 4.5 Threat Definitions (continued)

Threat Source	Threat	Definition
	Electrical interruption	A long-term disruption in the electrical power source, usually greater than a half hour.
	Emanation	The inadvertent emanation or transmission of data signals from components of computers, computer peripherals, and word processors, which may be recorded by monitoring equipment.
	Fire	A conflagration affecting information systems through heat, smoke, or suppression agent damage. This threat category can be further broken down into minor, major, and catastrophic.
	Hardware failure	A unit or component failure sufficient enough to cause delays in processing or monetary loss to the enterprise.
	Liquid leakage	A liquid inundation from sources other than a flood. Examples of this include burst or leaking pipes, and the accidental discharge of sprinklers.
	Software error	Any extraneous or erroneous data in the operating system or applications program that results in processing errors, data output errors, or processing delays.
	Telecommunications interruption	Any communications unit or component failure sufficient to cause interruptions in the data transfer via telecommunications between computer terminals, remote or distributed processors, and the host computing facility.
Human — Deliberate		
	Alteration of data	An intentional modification, insertion, or deletion of data, whether by authorized users or not, which compromises the auditing process, recoverability, availability, confidentiality, or integrity of the information produced, processed, controlled, or stored by the information processing systems.

Table 4.5   Threat Definitions (continued)

Threat Source	Threat	Definition
	Alteration of software	An intentional modification, insertion, or deletion of operating system or application system programs, whether by an authorized user or not, which compromises the auditing process, efficiency, recoverability, availability, confidentiality, or integrity of information, programs, the system, or resources controlled by the computer systems.
	Bomb threat	A notification of the existence of an explosive device at a facility, whether true or not.
	Disclosure	The unauthorized or premature intentional release of proprietary, classified, company confidential, personal, or otherwise sensitive information.
	Employee sabotage	A deliberate action taken by an employee, group of employees, or nonemployee(s) working together with an employee(s) to disrupt enterprise operations.
	Fraud	A deliberate unauthorized manipulation of hardware, software, or information with the intent of financial gain for the perpetrator.
	Strike	An organized employee action (union or not, legal or not) designed to halt or disrupt normal business operations. Strikes can be categorized as unfair labor practice, economic, or unprotected strikes.
	Theft	The unauthorized appropriation of hardware, software, media, computer supplies, or data of a classified nature, but included in the disclosure category.
	Unauthorized use	An unauthorized use of computer equipment or programs. Examples of this include the running of personal programs such as games, inventories, and browsing other files.
	Vandalism	The malicious and motiveless destruction or defacement of property.

Table 4.5   Threat Definitions (continued)

Threat Source	Threat	Definition
Human — Accidental		
	Alteration of data	An accidental modification, insertion, or deletion of data or information stored on the system.
	Alteration of software	The accidental modification, insertion, or deletion of operating system or application system programs or portions of code supporting the production systems.
	Disclosure	The accidental release or proprietary, classified, company confidential, personal, or otherwise sensitive information.
	Operator/user error	An accidental, improper, or otherwise ill-chosen act by an employee that results in processing delays, equipment damage, lost data, or modified data.

Table 4.6   Risk Factor Determination Worksheet

Threat	Threat Probability	Threat Impact	Risk Factor

Table 4.7   Threat Probability Priorities

Low	Low to Medium	Medium	Medium to High	High
1	2	3	4	5

Table 4.8   Probability Factor Definitions

Probability Factor	Definition
Low	Extremely unlikely that threat will occur during the next 12 months
Low to medium	Unlikely that threat will occur during the next 12 months
Medium	Possible that threat will occur during the next 12 months
Medium to high	Likely that threat will occur during the next 12 months
High	Highly likely that threat will occur during the next 12 months

Each team member will enter the value that his experience or statistical data tells him is the probability of a threat occurrence happening. If the team member has no knowledge of a threat probability, then he leaves this field blank and moves on to the next threat. It will be necessary to establish what each category means so that the team members will be working with the same definitions of threat occurrence. The team should be given a set of definitions similar to the ones listed in Table 4.8.

The members can do this task independently and then average the findings, or each team as a whole can review each threat one at a time and reach consensus.

Another way to express the threat occurrence rate is the probability of occurrence. This is very similar to the annual occurrence rate charts we discussed previously. However, the difference here is that we are not trying to find an absolute numerical probability, but to rely more on the knowledge of the team. This is why the makeup of the team is very important. It is their experience that will allow this process to move forward at a more rapid rate than if the risk assessment required stopping until each threat could be mathematically calculated. In qualitative risk analysis, the trade-off is for faster, pretty good results, rather than expending large amounts of resources trying to find the perfect answer.

Once the probability of occurrence has been determined, those figures are recorded in the "Threat Probability" column, as shown in Table 4.9.

4.3.5 Step 5: Threat Impact

At this point, members of the team are to estimate the loss impact if the threat were to occur. Step 4 was to determine the probability of the threat occurring; this step is to determine the impact to the asset under review if the specific threat were to occur. To make certain that the results are as complete as possible, the team will have to decide before the impact

Table 4.9 Threat Probability Assignments

Threat	Threat Probability	Threat Impact	Risk Factor
Electrical disturbance	5		
Deliberate disclosure	3		
Fraud	4		
User input error	5		

Table 4.10 Impact Probabilities

Low	Low to Medium	Medium	Medium to High	High
1	2	3	4	5

review is done whether the threats are to be examined with or without existing controls in place. Typically, if the risk assessment is conducted against an infrastructure component (platform, network segment, or telecommunications), the threat is examined as if no controls are in place. For applications, systems, or business processes, the review will take existing controls into consideration.

The team will then approach each threat as it did in the previous step. Working either independently or as a group, the team will compute the threat impact and enter that value into the proper place on the Threat Determination Worksheet.

If the team decides to work independently, it will then be necessary to provide discussion time once the averages are calculated. If one team member ascribed a value at either end of the scale and the average comes out at the other end, then there should be some discussion to ensure consensus. The same table as that used in step 4 will be used in this step (Table 4.10).

Each team member will enter the value that his experience or statistical data tells him is the impact to the business or mission should the threat occur. If the team member has no knowledge of a threat, then he should leave this field blank and move on to the next threat. It will be necessary to establish what each category means so that the team members will be working with the same definitions of threat occurrence. The team should be given a set of definitions similar to those in Table 4.11.

The threat impact averages or consensus values are then entered into the "Threat Impact" column in Table 4.12.

Table 4.11   Impact Probability Definitions

Impact Factor	Definition
Low	Single work group or department affected; little or no impact to the business process
Low to medium	One or more departments affected; slight delay in meeting mission objectives
Medium	Two or more departments or a business unit affected; four- to six-hour delay in meeting mission objectives
Medium to high	Two or more business units affected; one- to two-day delay in meeting mission objectives
High	Entire mission of the enterprise affected

Table 4.12   Threat Impact Value Assignments

Threat	Threat Probability	Threat Impact	Risk Factor
Electrical disturbance	5	2	
Deliberate disclosure	3	3	
Fraud	4	3	
User input error	5	2	

4.3.6 Step 6: Risk Factor Determination

During this step, the team will add the threat priority and threat impact values together to achieve the risk factor for each identified threat. The risk factors will range from a low of 2 to a high of 10 (Table 4.13).

After all of the risk factors have been calculated, the team will have to identify possible controls or safeguards for any threat that obtained a risk factor of 6 or higher.

No enterprise has sufficient resources to examine all risks regardless for their risk factors. Therefore, it will be necessary to determine which risk factors will be identified for further review. Those with a value of 4 or 5 should be monitored on a regular basis to ensure the risk factor does not rise to an unacceptable level. The threats with a risk factor of 3 or below do not require action at this time.

Table 4.13   Risk Factor Calculations

Threat	Threat Probability	Threat Impact	Risk Factor
Electrical disturbance	5	2	7
Deliberate disclosure	3	3	6
Fraud	4	3	7
User input error	5	2	7

4.3.7 Step 7: Identify Safeguards and Controls

In this step, the team will analyze the identified threats with a high risk factor and select technical, administrative, and physical controls that will offer a cost-effective, acceptable level of protection to the asset under review. The model for information protection objectives has been established as consisting of four layers: avoidance, assurance, detection, and recovery:

■ Avoidance controls are proactive safeguards that attempt to minimize the risk of accidental or intentional intrusions.
■ Assurance controls are tools and strategies employed to ensure the ongoing effectiveness of the existing controls and safeguards.
■ Detection controls are techniques and programs used to ensure early detection, interception, and response for security breaches.
■ Recovery controls are planning and response services to rapidly restore a secure environment and investigate the source of the breaches.

The team should concentrate on controls that will allow the mission of the enterprise to function while providing an adequate level of protection. It may be prudent to establish a list of possible controls in each of the layers that will help the enterprise meet its business objectives.

Examples of controls and safeguards for each of the security layers include those listed in Table 4.14.

In addition to the controls discussed above, some threats might require a physical safeguard or some combination of the controls. The team is to consider additional safeguards and countermeasures and determine the cost for implementing and maintaining the proposed controls. The team is to enter its recommended safeguard and its associated cost in the "Possible Safeguard" and "Safeguard Cost" columns of the worksheet (Table 4.15).

Table 4.14 Control Categories Using Information Security Model

Control Category	
Avoidance	Encryption and authentication
	System security architecture
	Facilitated risk analysis process
	Information awareness program
	Information security program
	Interruption prevention
	Policies and standards
	Public key infrastructure
	Secure application architecture
	Secure communications plans
Assurance	Application security review
	Standards testing
	Penetration testing
	Periodic perimeter scans
	Vulnerability assessment
Detection	Intrusion detection
	Remote intrusion monitoring
Recovery	Business continuity planning
	Business impact analysis
	Crisis management planning
	Disaster recovery planning
	Incident response procedures
	Investigation tools

It may be beneficial to list all safeguards considered and rank them according to the team's recommendation (Table 4.15). This will allow management to see what was considered and what the team is recommending as the cost-effective safeguard. It is also possible that one safeguard may reduce the risk exposure of more than one threat, thus increasing its cost-effectiveness.

Table 4.15   Threat Worksheet with Safeguards

Threat	Threat Probability	Threat Impact	Risk Factor	Possible Safeguard	Safeguard Cost
Electrical disturbance	5	2	7	Uninterruptible power supply (UPS) system	$38,000
				Surge suppressors	$25 per machine
Deliberate disclosure	3	3	6	Information handling standards	45 staff hours to create
				Employee awareness program	20 hours to develop presentation, 1 hour for each employee to attend
Fraud	4	3	7	Access control lists	Software on installed
				Audit logs	Capability exists with system
User input error	5	2	7	Edit checking	8 additional hours of programming per application

4.3.8 Step 8: Cost–Benefit Analysis

This is probably the most important step of any risk assessment process. Every control will cost something to the enterprise. The cost might be money to purchase and install the control. It might be human resources to develop and implement controls, such as policies and standards, or it might be as simple as turning on an audit trail. In each incident, the way the enterprise does business will be altered. Another way to look at this is that the culture of your organization will be changed. It will be necessary to provide awareness sessions for employees for changes to the work process.

As we examine other forms of risk assessment you will be shown a number of ways to do a cost–benefit analysis. During this step 8, the analysis should be very thorough to ensure that the safeguards recommended for implementation meet the business objectives and provide an adequate level of asset protection. Because we are using qualitative risk analysis, it may be necessary to conduct step 6 over again. That is, review the impact of the threat with the proposed control in place. There should be a significant reduction impact value before the control is accepted.

The analysis process should identify those safeguards that offer the maximum amount of protection at a minimum cost. In other words, it is always best to implement controls that will affect more than one threat. This is known as getting more bang for the buck. You will see in Chapter 6, on the Facilitated Risk Analysis and Assessment Process, that one of the most important report forms sent to the client is a cross-reference listing of each identified control and all of the threats that this control would help elevate.

4.3.9 Step 9: Rank Safeguards in Recommended Order

Once the cost–benefit analysis has been performed, the team should list the controls in order of recommendation for selection by the asset owner. Because resources are limited, management will be relying on the team to provide it with adequate information. The team will need to determine how the priority order will be presented. It may choose how many threats a safeguard can control, or it may choose a dollar level, an impact on productivity, or whether the safeguard can be developed internally or will require third-party assistance.

The key to developing the priority list is to determine what works best within your enterprise and then working to meet those objectives. The location of the priority listing will become part of the risk assessment report and should be referenced in the executive overview section of the report. There should be a discussion on how the team arrived at its priority ranking. Include enough detail to ensure that management can make an informed decision.

The team must understand that management may decide to accept the risk. The process of risk assessment is to ensure that management has performed its due diligence. As part of this process, management needs to have a documented cost–benefit analysis to ensure that it has the information required to make informed business decisions.

4.3.10 Step 10: Risk Assessment Report

The results of the risk assessment process must be presented to management in the form of a report. The report will serve two purposes: to report the findings and to serve as a historical document. Once completed, the risk assessment process will allow management to implement the controls and safeguards that it deems to be sufficient to meet the enterprise's business objectives. This is the overriding reason that organizations implement risk assessment as part of the design phase of a project development methodology or the system development life cycle.

However, it is the historical element of the risk assessment process that is often the most important. Having a well-documented process to decision making and having a library of reports that chronicle this process will provide management with the support it needs to show that it has lived up to its fiduciary responsibility to protect the assets of the enterprise.

For many organizations, the only time the risk assessment report will ever see the light of day is when some third party is attempting to determine how decisions were made. By issuing a report that contains, at a minimum, the elements we will discuss in this section, the enterprise will have documentation to defend its position.

A sample table of contents might include the following:

- *Introduction*
- *Background* — Detail why the risk analysis process was undertaken and the business reasons leading to the commitment of resources to complete the risk assessment.
- *Assess the scope statement* — Include the actual scope statement and explain how it was determined that this would be the project or asset to be reviewed. A review of how the risk assessment met the deliverables identified in the scope statement is also part of this discussion. If any elements were not completed or dropped from the original scope, an explanation should also be included.
- *Explanation of approach* — Chronicle the approach used for the risk assessment process. Include a brief outline of the steps and the expected deliverables from each step.

- *Executive overview* — In one or two pages, discuss the entire process and findings. Include as part of this overview a reference to the appendix that lists the team members. Make certain that the executive overview clearly states the findings of the team and the risk assessment process in particular.

- *Threat identification* — Discuss the process used to identify threats, issues, concerns, risks, etc. Also include how the threats were categorized. This would include a review of the categories identified by the team as the ones to be used in the review and how this was determined. Typically, for an information security risk analysis, the categories will be availability, confidentiality, and integrity. Be sure to include all definitions. This is important for all threats as well as categories. As a historical document, it will be necessary to include a clear picture of the team's thinking or state of mind at the time of the review.

- *Risk factor determination* — During this phase, the team determined the probability that a specific threat might occur and its impact on the enterprise if it does occur. In the report, identify the definition of probability or vulnerability and impact. Discuss the process used and how the risk determination factors were established. Although the team strives for consensus, sometimes it cannot be reached. This would be the place to put any discussion on threat priority disagreement.

- *Safeguard identification* — It will be necessary to be very thorough in discussing how the team determined what safeguards were available and how the recommendation was reached. Management will want to know who was contacted to determine what was available. The "who" would include any benchmarking that was conducted. One of the ways to sell a recommendation to management is to tell it what others in your industry are doing. Include information on any research that was conducted with groups such as the Gartner Group, Meta, Giga, or other industry advisor organizations.

- *Cost–benefit analysis* — Management's acceptance of the findings and recommendations will depend on how well the team's cost–benefit analysis is understood. It will be important, then, to ensure that the report identifies the process used and how it takes into consideration the business objectives of the enterprise.

- *Safeguard recommendations* — The final, and probably most important, element is the team's recommendations. The recommendations can include the control to be implemented, the control alternative, or whether to accept the risk as the most beneficial course of action.

■ *Appendix* — There will be a number of items that will need to be recorded as part of the historical documents that support the risk analysis. Recommended appendices include:
  – Team members
  – Definitions
  – Threats by priority order
  – Research reports

The risk assessment report is a confidential document and its access should be restricted to a limited group determined by the owner of the asset under review. Although there may be a team that conducted the risk analysis process, the report belongs to the sponsoring manager.

4.3.11 Summary

Qualitative risk assessment is among the easiest methodologies to perform; it is also the most subjective. The quality of the risk assessment results produced are in direct correlation to the professionalism and knowledge of the team assembled and the objectivity of the process facilitator. The results achieved by a professionally led team, utilizing this form of methodology, is as valid as those realized through the utilization of more labor-intensive and time-consuming quantitative processes.

The next qualitative risk assessment process that we will examine uses tables to help the team determine values for tangible and nontangible losses. We will use this concept later when we discuss business impact analysis.

4.4 Qualitative Risk Assessment Using Tables

This next qualitative risk assessment process was presented by Gareth Davies at a Southeast Michigan Computer Security Special Interest Group meeting in 1991 in the Detroit area. This process takes the standard ideas discussed in the first qualitative risk assessment process and modifies the approach to include the use of tables. This version was designed to overcome identified shortcomings in traditional risk analysis. In particular, these developers needed to address nontangible as well as tangible threats. Although creating a value for a tangible asset is fairly easy, creating a common methodology to handle both types of loss requires a different approach. This method uses a scoring system to enable financial risks to be compared to nonfinancial risks. This process will allow teams to take secondary impacts into consideration.

Instead of 10 steps, this process uses 3 stages (asset valuation, risk evaluation, and risk management) that map fairly well to the process we just reviewed. As we review different risk analysis processes, it will be necessary to remember that each methodology begins with the same two processes: identify the asset (create a scope statement) and assemble a quality team.

As part of the initial scope statement phase, it will be necessary to identify the functional owner of the asset. This individual or group of individuals will act on behalf of the enterprise to manage the asset and make the decisions necessary to ensure the asset is properly protected from unauthorized use, access, disclosure, or destruction. The functional owner is normally identified as the senior management individual within the business unit or department where the asset is created, or is the primary user of the asset. This concept is typically found in an organization's information classification policy.

Where an asset is shared across a number of departments, it is recommended that those departments determine who will act as their spokesperson. Most enterprises that employ this form of decision-making process will rotate the responsibility annually. That way the needs of the many will be properly weighed against the needs of the few.

In addition to what asset is to be reviewed, it will be necessary to determine what business or control impacts will be assessed, that is, whether the risk assessment will examine threats to availability, confidentiality, and integrity or impacts to disclosure, modification, unavailability, or destruction. The risk assessment can be used to investigate any element of the business process or mission of the enterprise. It is during the scope statement deliverables that these questions need to be answered. It will be necessary for the risk assessment facilitator and the functional owner to agree on the definitions of each of these elements. Additionally, it will be necessary for them to agree on the definitions of probability and impact.

The functional owner will sponsor the risk assessment, provide the resources for the effort, decide the safeguards that are to be implemented, and keep control of the risk assessment report.

Asset identification will take on a number of different approaches, but they will all lead to the same result: the asset to be reviewed has been identified and a project scope statement has been drafted. As we discussed in the previous examples, the scope statement is the most important element of the risk assessment process. It will ensure that the specific asset is properly identified and that all team members will have a clear understanding of what is to be reviewed.

The other consistent process in every methodology is the assembly of the team. It will be necessary to ensure that the team is a good representation of a cross section of the business enterprise and all stakeholders.

As discussed above, the important members are the owner and the users of the asset under review. It is strongly recommended that the team be made up of personnel that have been with the enterprise long enough to know how things work and where there might be problems. It is not necessary to have a specific level of employees; what is important is that the employees have sufficient knowledge to provide their insights into how things can go wrong and what needs to be done to correct them.

Once the scope statement is finalized and the definitions agreed upon, and the team has been assembled, stage 1 of this risk assessment can begin.

4.4.1 Stage 1: Asset Valuation (BIA)

After the initial steps have been completed (project scope statement) and the team has been assembled, the first task will be to determine what the impact would be to the enterprise if the asset under review was compromised. In this example, this risk assessment team will use a series of tables to help the team identify the impact of various threats.

The values found in the tables are the results of meetings with various departments and business units to get their expert input into what would constitute a level of loss for the enterprise. For example, the values in the Financial Losses table (Table 4.16) represent what the financial staff indicated are the thresholds of concern. When you meet with your support staff, it may be easier to get them to establish the high and low thresholds.

Table 4.16   Financial Losses

Financial Loss	Valuation Score
<$2000	1
$2001 to $15K	2
$15,001 to $40K	3
$40,001 to $100K	4
$100,001 to $300K	5
$300,001 to $1M	6
>$1M but <$3M	7
>$3M but <$10M	8
>$10M but <$30M	9
>$30M	10

Typically, four or five values work best. To establish the low-end threshold, the internal experts might want to consider what level of loss or impact would require the enterprise to make some minor form of correction. At the other end of the spectrum is the value when the enterprise would be in extremely serious trouble. Once the two ends are determined, you can work to develop the number of gradations needed to meet your specific objectives.

As you can see, this table has 10 values. That may be too fine a gradation for your enterprise, and I normally recommend a limit of four or five thresholds in each category. The more choices available to the team members, the greater the possibility is for confusion.

In the risk assessment process, the team will be asked to assign a value to specific categories based on tables developed through discussions with the departments responsible for those activities. The process that we will review in this chapter is only an example of what can be done. The tables can be modified (as you will see in the discussion on business impact analysis), as can the elements to be reviewed, to meet your specific needs (Table 4.17).

Using a matrix like the one in Table 4.18, the team will enter its scores for each of the categories selected. As in the previous risk assessment, either the team can discuss each entry and reach consensus before entering a score, or the process can allow for individual scores that are then averaged. If the latter is used, it will be necessary to provide time for discussion to reach a final consensus.

Using the tables developed by the team with assistance from the various supporting units, the team will complete the worksheet to determine a value for the asset under review. The key in this process is to identify any assets where compromise would cause a value of X. It will be the responsibility of the team and management to identify exactly what X will be; in most instances, it will be a threshold that causes management to wince.

Table 4.19 contains an example for the asset valuation for nonpublic, personal customer information handled and processed by the GLBA Bank & Trust of Ibid, UT.

Once these assets have been properly valued, the team will present its findings to the sponsoring entity. This acts as a checkpoint that the process is functioning as it is intended to and that management is ready to authorize stage 2 of the risk assessment.

4.4.2 Stage 2: Risk Evaluation

During the risk evaluation stage, the team will establish threats that may impact the assets and then assess the probability and impact of the threats.

Table 4.17 Qualitative Risk Assessment Values

Financial Loss	Cost of Disruption	Extent of Legal Implication	Value to Competitor	Corporate Embarrassment	Valuation Score
<$2000	<$2000	<$5K	Less than $50,000	Embarrassment restricted to within the project or work site	1
$2001 to $15K	$2001 to $15K			Embarrassment spread to other work areas of operating group or division	2
$15,001 to $40K	$15,001 to $40K			Embarrassment spread throughout the enterprise	3
$40,001 to $100K	$40,001 to $100K	>$5K but <$10K	Between $50K and $100K		4
$100,001 to $300K	$100,001 to $300K	>$10K but <$50K	Between $100K and $10M	Public made aware through local press coverage	5
$300,001 to $1M	$300,001 to $1M				6
>$1M but <$3M	>$1M but <$3M			Adverse national press	7
>$3M but <$10M	>$3M but <$10M	>$50K but <$1M, and CISO liable for prosecution	Over $10M		8
>$10M but <$30M	>$10M but <$30M				9
>$30M	>$30M	>$1M and company officers and directors liable for prosecution		Stock price impacted	10

Table 4.18 Qualitative Risk Assessment Asset Valuation Worksheet

	Financial Loss	Disruption	Legal Implication	Loss of Competitive Advantage	Corporate Embarrassment	Overall Score
Disclosure						
Modification						
Unavailability						
Destruction						

Table 4.19 Asset Valuation Example

	Financial Loss	Disruption	Legal Implication	Loss of Competitive Advantage	Corporate Embarrassment	Overall Score
Disclosure	2	—	5	4	5	4
Modification	—	—	5	—	5	5
Unavailability	—	6	1	—	5	4
Destruction	6	6	5	4	5	5

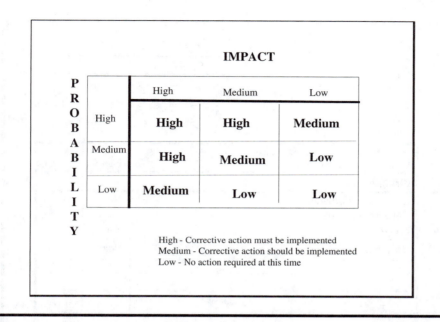

Figure 4.1   Threat evaluation matrix.

As we discussed in previous chapters, the identification of threats can be done any number of ways. The key is to create a list of as many concerns, issues, threats, etc., as possible. Trying to develop a complete list is the most important task in this stage of the risk assessment.

Once the list of threats is complete, the team will rate the threat according to the probability of occurrence and the impact the threat would cause to the asset or mission of the enterprise. As we discussed in the previous sections and chapters, it will be necessary to establish clear definitions of:

■ Exactly what each threat is
■ What probability of occurrence means
■ What the impact to the asset or mission means

Also as previously discussed, it will be necessary to have the definitions for probability and impact, as well as the definitions for high, medium, and low for each.

In this risk assessment example, the team will use the worksheet shown in Figure 4.1 to assign the appropriate risk level score. The team can discuss each threat individually and then determine the specific score, or the members can score each threat and then average the results. In the latter case, there must be enough time for the members to discuss differences in individual scoring.

Risk Level Worksheet

	Disclosure	Modification	Unavailability	Destruction	Vulnerability Score	
Asset Under Review: Non-public, Personal customer information	4	5	4	5	Without Control	With Control
Threats:						
Electrical disturbance					Medium	
Deliberate disclosure					High	
Fraud					Medium	
User input error					Medium	

Figure 4.2 Vulnerability Analysis Worksheet.

If a threat is not applicable to the asset under review, then the team is to enter a value of N/A on the Vulnerability Analysis Worksheet (Figure 4.2), as opposed to assigning a value of 1.

The scores from the asset valuation process will allow the team to identify those assets that could cause an impact to the enterprise mission if they were compromised. Because most organizations do not have unlimited resources, this process will allow the team to concentrate its efforts on those assets that have real impact.

It is usually best to examine the threat without regard to existing controls and then perform a second review taking into consideration existing controls. When performing the second process, it will be necessary to identify the control that will counter the threat. This is usually done by identifying the threat (fire) and then the control (fire suppression system). This total will then be entered into the last column of the Vulnerability Analysis Worksheet.

Once those assets have been identified, the threat evaluation process will allow the team to identify threats to those assets and then determine the vulnerability the enterprise has to those threats. These two stages lead to the final process, the identification of controls that can be implemented to lower the vulnerability to the threat to a management-acceptable level.

4.4.3 Stage 3: Risk Management

The most important element of any risk assessment process is the recommendations of controls and safeguards that will help mitigate the threat or vulnerability level to the asset under review. Using the totals from stage 1, the team has identified those assets that are mission critical to the enterprise. With the scores from stage 2, the team has identified the threats that expose the enterprise and its assets to an unacceptable level of concern. As in the first process we discussed in this chapter, the team will be charged with making recommendations to the sponsor.

The team will document existing countermeasures and map the risk level analysis results to the levels of exposure with the safeguards in place. Once that has been completed, the team will concentrate on those threats for which there are no existing countermeasures identified. It is here that management will want the team to provide leadership and recommendations.

Countermeasures must be shown to provide a cost-effective level of control while still allowing the enterprise to meet its mission or business objectives. The countermeasures may act in one of four ways:

■ Reduce the likelihood that the threat will occur
■ Reduce the impact if the threat were to occur
■ Detect the threat if it does occur
■ Provide the means to recover if the threat were to occur

The team will have to recommend to management what countermeasures appear to be most effective and which ones can control more than one threat. Once the report is completed, the team will have to document the results and obtain final sponsor sign-off. This will normally complete the risk analysis process, but there are two more activities that will make the process more complete.

The report will normally identify the individual or department that is responsible for implementation of the countermeasure. Included in this identification process is the expected implementation date. There should be steps taken to ensure that some level of follow-up is conducted to make certain that the countermeasures are implemented in a timely manner. The review of the implementation process is normally conducted by the audit staff.

The final element of an effective risk assessment process is scheduling the next review of the asset. Nothing within an enterprise remains constant, so it will be necessary to schedule a follow-up assessment. This process should be scheduled every 18 months to 2 years. Using the initial risk assessment as a baseline, the enterprise will be able to mark its improvement of protecting assets.

4.4.4 Summary

The second qualitative risk assessment process used tables to help the team establish levels of loss for tangible and nontangible issues. This process has laid the groundwork for the creation of an effective BIA process, which is discussed in Chapter 9.

By establishing a quality team, the results of the risk assessment process can be used by the organization as a clear picture of where the current liabilities are and which threats need to be addressed quickly.

The next process that we will examine brings in the final element needed to complete the groundwork for the FRAAP.

4.5 The 30-Minute Risk Assessment

In July 1992, the Computer Security Institute's *Alert* published an article on Dan Erwin's interesting twist on qualitative risk assessment under review. Dan has determined that it is the role of the security specialist and project leaders to be the facilitators of the risk assessment process. The process of *information security risk analysis* (ISRA) is a not difficult concept for the layperson to grasp; however, to ensure that the ISRA process is completed in a timely and efficient manner, a trained facilitator is required.

4.5.1 Overview

The ISRA is a formal methodology that is used by a system designer, manager, or security analyst to identify security concerns, develop an action plan, analyze costs, and assign responsibilities. The process allows a facilitator to perform a subjective risk assessment on a specific system, application, or other corporate asset. The ISRA involves the system users from the very beginning by requiring them to voice their concerns and choose effective controls.

The ISRA should be part of the system development life cycle feasibility phase and cost–benefit studies of new systems. It can also be used on existing systems prior to major updates, during periods of change, or as required by management.

4.5.2 Objectives

As with most security-related processes from the mid-1980s on, the ISRA is to identify undesirable or unauthorized events, concerns, risks, threats, etc., not in terms of their effect on information security, but in terms of their effect on the business process or mission of the enterprise.

The function of information security can be defined by three objectives:

- *Data integrity* — The prevention of unauthorized or undesirable modification or destruction of data/information or source code.
- *Data sensitivity* — The prevention of unauthorized or undesirable disclosure of information.
- *Data availability* — The prevention of the loss of accessibility of data or system services.

Many controls will be effective in meeting all three objectives. However, some controls are specific to one objective and may even be detrimental on other objectives. The risk assessment matrix will help the user, designer, or security specialist choose the most appropriate and cost-effective controls.

When using the ISRA process, it is also useful to assess what risks are being protected from:

- *Accidental acts* — Undesirable acts (errors and omissions).
- *Deliberate acts* — Unauthorized acts (fraud and misuse).

4.5.3 ISRA Matrix

Combine the three security objectives and the two security risks to form a matrix (Figure 4.3). This matrix can then be used to facilitate a discussion that will lead to the identification of the threats. Controls can be identified based on the threats. Care must be taken not to define controls until the threats have been identified. This will ensure that only threat-based controls are applied.

4.5.4 The ISRA Process

To perform an ISRA, the facilitator assembles the internal experts of the system or asset being assessed. For example, if the project required the company to install a LAN in a sales office, then the team must involve someone from the sales staff, someone from clerical, the functional management team, a LAN technical expert, someone from hardware or software support, and a representative from information security.

The facilitator doing the ISRA need not be an expert in the system being studied. His role is to pose questions, provide background information, and gently nudge those present to participate. It is important for the facilitator to appear to remain neutral at all times.

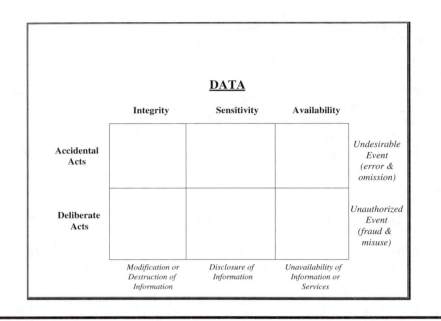

Figure 4.3   Risk assessment matrix.

As discussed in the other qualitative risk analysis processes, the team is the most important element in a quality risk assessment process. The choosing of the right people is critical to the success of the process. If the right people are in the room, they will know what the threats are and what controls are acceptable. Because this is a subjective assessment, the answers derived from the process are only as good as the people who gave them.

A brainstorming technique is used to prompt the participants to identify risks using the matrix. The matrix is posted on flip charts, and each box is filled out concentrating on one element at a time. The participants are asked to identify threats to their data based on the asset being studied.

For example, if the asset being studied is "much of the data processed by this system is being moved from a mainframe to a client–server-based application," what are the threats associated with this change? Box by box, this opportunity is reviewed and the threats are listed.

Each attendee is asked to identify at least three things that could cause his data to be modified or destroyed accidentally, due to the change to the system that is being studied. The threats are written on a flip chart for the participants to view (Figure 4.4). The process is repeated for the other headings until the matrix is filled. When all six categories have been reviewed, the team reviews the lists, makes any modifications or enhancements, and then does a reality check. This list of threats is now complete and the team will turn its attention to possible controls.

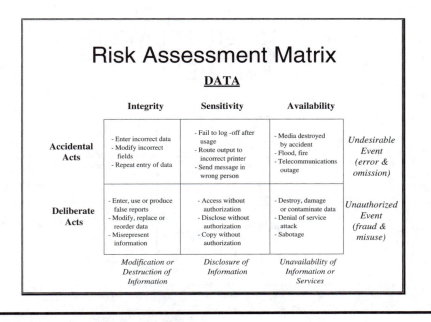

Figure 4.4   ISRA threats identified.

There is no attempt to calculate the probability and impact to determine the risk level. It is the team's experience that determines if a threat is of sufficient concern to keep it on the list.

4.5.5 *Threat-Based Controls*

Once the threats are fully identified, the team can select controls (safeguards, standards, rules, etc.) that can best protect against the specific risk. By using this method, there is almost always a choice of controls. This means the owner can choose the control that best suits his way of doing business or his personal preference. Once the controls that meet business needs are identified, a cost–benefit analysis is done to help choose the most cost-effective controls.

In most cases, there is no need to quantify the risk level, only the cost of the various controls. For example, if the threat is that someone might steal a computer, the controls list might include:

- An armed guard
- A watchdog
- A surveillance camera
- A locked door
- A list of replacement suppliers

Risk Assessment Matrix

Control Suggestions

	Integrity	Sensitivity	Availability	
Accidental Acts	•Edit checking •Desk checking •Checks and balances	•Access control •Segregation of duties •Physical security	•Backup •System design •Redundancies	*Undesirable Event (error & omission)*
Deliberate Acts	•Passwords •Sign on (unique UserID) • Audit trails	•Passwords •Sign on •Waste disposal •Storage procedures •ACLs	•Offsite storage •Disaster plan •Physical security •Emergency procedures	*Unauthorized Event (fraud & misuse)*
	Modification or Destruction of Information	*Disclosure of Information*	*Unavailability of Information or Services*	

Figure 4.5   Risk assessment matrix with control suggestions.

Most team members and the owner know the basic value of the threat without doing a lot of calculations to determine that a guard dog in the computer room may not be the answer. The question is then which of the other choices work best and which can the enterprise afford.

A control has to be implemented to eliminate or lower to an acceptable level of risk each threat that was identified (Figure 4.5). It should be noted that one control can often impact a number of threats. There is often more than one control that will impact the same threat; in such an instance, it is best to list all possible controls. The team should not be limited in controls that it may select. Technology-based controls are no better than non-technology-based controls. The decision of which control is best must be made by the owner and based on what works best for his business needs. This approach forces the team into a cost–benefit mode and ensures that a $2000 solution is not applied to a $5 problem.

4.5.6 Documentation

When the session is complete, the security staff will create a document detailing the results of the process and presenting security's conclusions on the existing controls. The risk assessment document will also include an action plan detailing corrective activities to be taken. The action plan will include the time frame to complete the activities and what organization has the responsibility to implement the new or updated controls. The document should include the following topics:

- Project scope statement.
- A description of the change and its effect on security.
- Risk assessment process.
  - Describe specific threats to the enterprise's information assets with regard to:
    - Data integrity
    - Data sensitivity
    - Data availability
- Description of the existing controls.
- Identification of controls selected to supplement existing controls or new controls.
  - For new controls, identify:
    - What they are
    - Who will implement them
    - When the implementation will be complete
- Identification of threats that appear to have no logical countercontrol mechanism. This would be those threats where the most cost-effective control is to accept the risk or where there is no current control available. This process identifies those threats as out of control.

4.5.7 Out-of-Control Process

The risk assessment process cannot solve all of an organization's problems. The threats that cannot be controlled or that the organization cannot afford to control must be documented for the owner's review and approval of this noncompliant or out-of-control condition. These out-of-control processes are then taken to senior management for action or endorsement. Security officers must be willing to accept management's decision to accept controls that present an acceptable level of control.

4.5.8 Final Notes

Trade-offs must sometimes be made between business objectives and security. These trade-offs need not always be resolved in favor of security, but only management can make that informed decision and then accept the risk.

Accidents, errors, and omissions account for more losses than deliberate acts. Nearly 65% of information losses are caused by errors and omissions. Of all problems and threats, 70% of the attacks come from internal sources. Therefore, controls that reduce the potential for harmful effects from accidents are also a first step toward reducing the opportunities for fraud and misuse. Security against deliberate acts can only be achieved if a potential perpetrator believes there is a definite probability of being detected.

4.6 Conclusion

Qualitative risk assessment is a process that allows an organization to evaluate tangible and intangible threats to the assets of the organization. It provides for a logical and consistent method to review threats and their impacts to the assets under review. The three methods we reviewed in this chapter are the building blocks that we will use to review other methods in the following chapters.

In the next chapter we will examine additional forms of qualitative risk assessment. Each one will provide you with additional tools that you will need to create a risk assessment process tailored to meet your organization's specific needs. In Chapter 6 we will discuss the most widely used qualitative risk assessment process — the FRAAP. Later in the book we will use the methods we just discussed to create prescreening and business impact analysis methodologies. The qualitative risk assessment process can also be used to assist organizations in the adoption of an information classification policy. We will present two classification methodologies using qualitative risk assessment.

Chapter 5

Other Forms
of Qualitative
Risk Assessment

5.1 Introduction

To date, no one risk assessment technique will satisfy the needs of every organization. In this chapter we will review a number of qualitative risk assessment techniques, which, combined with the material presented so far, will provide you with several alternatives from which you will be able to build your own specific risk assessment process.

Using the different risk assessment techniques, we will be better able to reinforce the process used when performing a risk assessment. There is a logical progression of activities that we will identify through the use of these risk assessment examples.

During this chapter we will examine four different risk analysis processes:

- Hazard impact analysis
- Threat analysis
- Questionnaires
- Single-time loss algorithm

5.2 Hazard Impact Analysis

The hazard impact analysis (HIA) was developed by the Federal Emergency Management Administration (FEMA) and the Michigan State Police to determine the hazards (or threats) a physical site is susceptible to and how vulnerable the site is to that threat. The process examines the hazards that we have identified in the natural threat source category. The HIA will determine the impact of these hazards to staff, property, and business. The process lends itself to those organizations attempting to establish controls where limited resources are available and people and property may be at risk.

To review, the standard risk assessment process is to:

1. Assemble the internal experts (the risk assessment team).
2. Develop a scope statement or risk assessment opportunity statement.
3. Agree on the definitions.
4. Ensure the team understands the process.
5. Conduct the risk assessment.

It is important that these steps be followed regardless of what risk assessment process is used or created by your organization. The output of the risk assessment process may be suspect if these steps are not followed.

As we have discussed before, after the scope statement is completed and the team is assembled, it will be necessary to identify threats to the asset under review. This can be done any number of ways; for our example, we will use the list of natural threats discussed in Chapter 3 (Table 5.1).

5.2.1 Hazard Impact Analysis Process

Once the threats have been identified and all of the terms defined, the team will examine each threat using the worksheet shown in Figure 5.1.

In column 1 the team will enter the types of threats:

■ Fire
■ Flood
■ Tornado
■ Virus
■ Fraud
■ Electrical outage
■ Bomb threat

Table 5.1 Hazard Impact Analysis Threat List

Hazard Impact Analysis — Natural Threats
Electrical storm
Ice storm
Snowstorm/blizzard
Major landslide
Mudslide
Tsunami
Tornado
Hurricane/typhoon
High winds (70+ mph)
Tropical storm
Tidal flooding
Seasonal flooding
Local flooding
Upstream dam/reservoir failure
Sandstorm
Volcanic activity
Earthquake (2–4 on Richter scale)
Earthquake (5 or more)
Epidemic

Once those are entered, the team will score the probability of occurrence through either group discussion and consensus or working individually and averaging the scores. As we have discussed before, it will be necessary to have definitions of probability and impact already established. These definitions must also include a breakdown of the high, medium, and low terms.

The higher the number entered into column 2, the higher the probability that the threat will occur. The team will want to concentrate only on the threat and probability at this time; the impact portion will be reviewed separately.

After the probability has been established, the team will look at impacts. These are divided into three categories and should be viewed as if there are no controls in place:

■ Human
■ Property
■ Business

Each impact category is to be assessed separately, so it is probably better to review all human impact elements and then move over to property and finally business (Figure 5.2). The controls will come into

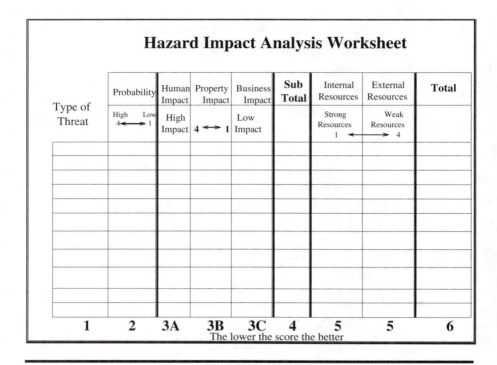

Figure 5.1   Hazard Impact Analysis Worksheet.

play later. Once the impacts have been scored, the threat totals will be added up and that figure will be entered into the subtotal column. A threat with a subtotal between 10 and 16 should be given extra attention.

The component to be reviewed is resources or controls that are available either internally or externally. Note that these are reversed from the impact numbers. The team will want to identify existing internal controls that can help reduce the impact. It will be a two-step approach: identify the safeguard resource, and then determine its effectiveness in fighting the impact.

For example, in the threat of a tornado, internal resources that could reduce the impact might be evacuation plans, evacuation drills, a warning system (PA systems, alarm), or physical security staff monitoring weather bulletins. If there are internal controls in place, then the team will have to enter their value into column 5.

External controls for this scenario might include local tornado warning alarms, local weather bureau alerts, and building location (Figure 5.3). These two totals are then added to the subtotal value (remember, they are reversed values — stronger is lower and weaker is higher). If there are no internal or external resources, then the value is 4.

Hazard Impact Analysis Worksheet

Type of Threat	Probability High ⟵⟶ Low 4 ⟵⟶ 1	Human Impact High Impact	Property Impact 4 ⟷ 1	Business Impact Low Impact	Sub Total	Internal Resources Strong Resources 1 ⟵	External Resources Weak Resources ⟶ 4	Total
Tornado	1	4	4	4	13			
Virus (benign)	4	1	1	2	7			
Electrical interruption	3	1	3	1	8			
1	**2**	**3A**	**3B**	**3C**	**4**	**5**	**5**	**6**

The lower the score the better

Figure 5.2   Hazard Impact Analysis Worksheet with probability and impact totals.

The key in working with the HIA process is common sense. A tornado hitting your building is a very low probability, but if it does hit, then the impact could be very high. So look for controls that will help, but they must be in line with cost requirements. Save the budget for those threats that have a higher probability and impact. Look at the recent virus attacks; few have been destructive, but they have been so persistent that the cleanup costs are now tagged in the billions.

The methodology is used to reinforce the risk assessment process. First, identify the threats. After all of the threats have been identified, the team will examine the probability of the threat occurring. Once the probability has been established, the team will examine the impacts to people, business, and property. Finally, the team will address controls, looking first to those controls that are available internally, and then to those that are available for external resources.

5.2.2 Paralysis by Analysis

The process of risk assessment can become bogged down by the inclusion of too much detail. You must be able to find a happy medium between

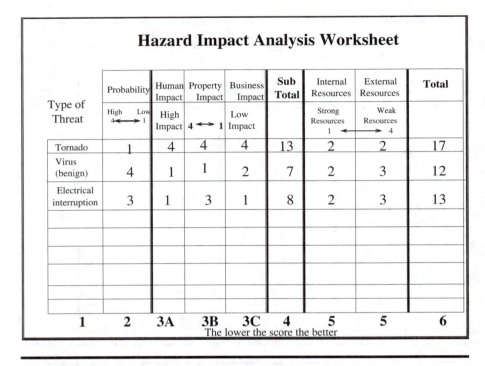

Figure 5.3 Hazard Impact Analysis Worksheet — complete.

too little and too much information. This is not easy. By its very nature, analysis will generate huge quantities of information. When attempting to determine the probability and impact, try to keep the objective in mind. Often, the risk assessment process bogs down because the team deviates from the standard risk assessment methodology and attempts to work the process before the preliminary steps are complete.

5.3 Questionnaires

Another method of risk assessment is the development of owner-completed questionnaires. Questionnaires can be developed to meet a specific resources requirement or can be used to review a broader area. An important key to developing an effective risk assessment questionnaire is to remember the audience. Who will be filling out the forms? Will it be auditors, security administrators, or managers? The language used in the questionnaires must be scaled to meet the requirements of the intended audience. Also, the number of questions must be limited. If the questionnaire is too long or in-depth, the user community will ignore it or do a poor job of completing the form.

Typically, a series of 20 questions per topic should be the limit. This is not a hard-and-fast rule, but the goal of a questionnaire is to get the user community to complete the document. When I worked for a large multinational corporation, the information security program was given 20 questions each year. We would normally divide the questions into 10 that usually remained constant and 10 that were used to assess the topic we were stressing that year.

5.3.1 Risk Assessment Questionnaire Process

Each question will be reviewed by the user to determine if the business unit or department is in compliance with an existing enterprise policy, procedure, standard, or other regulation. Each question must identify the document it references. If the question references a specific policy, then either the policy name or number, or both, should be included in the question, for example:

> A corporate information officer (CIO) has been named and is responsible for implementing and maintaining an effective information protection (IP) program (Sarbanes–Oxley Act, Federal Sentencing Guidelines for Criminal Activities).

The questionnaire is designed to determine if the business unit is in compliance with each question. If the reviewer answers yes, the business is in compliance; then, in the comments section, the reviewer is to enter what methods were used to determine that the unit was in compliance with the question. If the reviewer answers no, then the comments section is used to identify the steps that are to be taken to move the unit into compliance, and by what date.

The date column is the date that the question was reviewed, and the initials are those of the reviewer (the individual who made the yes/no determination).

On the final page of each questionnaire section, the business unit manager is required to sign. This is a way to ensure that the results have been reviewed with senior management. A typical questionnaire might look something like the one in Table 5.2.

The Computer Security Institute (CSI) has prepared the Information Protection Assessment Kit (IPAK), a self-administered test intended to help an organization determine how well its information protection program is doing. The questionnaire was developed through the efforts of industry experts such as John O'Leary, CSI director of education; Cheri Jacoby, partner with PricewaterhouseCoopers, LLP; Dan Erwin, information security specialist at Dow Chemical, retired; Fred Trickey, Yeshiva University; Tom Peltier, Peltier and Associates; Mike Gregorio, Coca-Cola Company;

Table 5.2 Sample Questionnaire

Information Protection Question	Compliance Yes/No	Comments	Date	Initials
A corporate information officer (CIO) has been named and is responsible for implementing and maintaining an effective information protection (IP) program.				
The IP program supports the business objective or mission statement of the organization.				
An enterprisewide IP policy has been implemented.				
An individual has been assigned as the corporate IP coordinator, and overall responsibility for the IP program implementation has been assigned.				
The IP program is an integral element of sound management practices.				
IP is identified as a separate and distinct budget item (approximately 1 to 3 percent of the overall ISO budget).				
Senior management is aware of the business needs for an effective IP program and is committed to support its success.				
An effective risk analysis process has been implemented to assist management in identifying potential threats, probability of threat occurrence, and possible countermeasures.				
IP controls are based on cost–benefit analysis utilizing risk analysis input.				

Table 5.2 Sample Questionnaire (continued)

Information Protection Question	Compliance Yes/No	Comments	Date	Initials
IP responsibilities and accountability for all employees with regard to IP are explicit.				
Each business unit, department, agency, etc., has designated an individual responsible for implementing the IP program for that organization.				
The IP program is integrated into a variety of areas both within and outside the computer security field.				
Comprehensive IP policies, procedures, standards, and guidelines have been created and disseminated to all employees and appropriate third parties.				
An ongoing IP awareness program has been implemented for all organization employees.				
A positive, proactive relationship with the audit staff has been established.				
Employees have been made aware that their activities may be monitored.				
An effective program to monitor IP program-related activities has been implemented.				
Employee compliance to IP-related issues is an annual appraisal element.				

Table 5.2 Sample Questionnaire (continued)

Information Protection Question	Compliance Yes/No	Comments	Date	Initials
The system development life cycle addresses IP requirements during the initiation or analysis (first) phase.				
The IP program is reviewed annually and modified as necessary.				

and Charles Cresson Wood, Baseline Software. The IPAK is available through CSI for a nominal fee.

5.3.2 Summary

Questionnaires are used prior to when a risk assessment is scheduled. This allows the facilitator to get an overview of the level of controls currently in place. The questionnaire is also used when assessment resources are limited and a facilitator is not available. This process, coupled with a prescreening methodology, can help an organization when resources are stretched.

5.4 Single Time Loss Algorithm

John O'Leary, CSI director of the education resource center, introduced the concept of the single time loss algorithm (STLA) for risk analysis. This process takes some of the elements of quantitative risk analysis and adds some qualitative aspects.

Mr. O'Leary uses his background in mathematics to express the variables of a threat in a formula. The structure of this process is very similar to that of the methods we have examined so far. It requires that the key elements of risk analysis be done:

■ Assemble the internal experts (the risk analysis team).
■ Develop a scope statement or risk analysis opportunity statement.
■ Agree on the definitions.
■ Identify the threats.
■ Identify the requirements to recovery from the threat.

This risk analysis process will require two brainstorming sessions: one to identify and prioritize the threats and another to identify the recovery elements. The latter session may take longer than the first. For a threat like an earthquake, a completed algorithm might look something like the following:

$$(\text{Total asset value} + \text{contingency implementation costs} + \text{data reconstruction costs}) \times 0.25 + \text{cost of 1-week delay} = \text{STL}$$

The formula takes the value of the asset and adds that to the cost of implementing the business contingency plan plus the cost of a data reconstruction. The determination of data reconstruction will include many factors, such as the availability of backup media, the staff available to process the jobs, the new media to copy the backup to, and the time to do all of these tasks. The 0.25 figure is the annual rate of occurrence (which we discussed in Chapter 2). Finally, the cost of one week's delay is added to these figures to give an STL total. The team will have to establish what a single day's loss to the enterprise might be. One way to do that is to take the annual revenues and divide that figure by 260 (the typical number of working days in a year), and this will give you a ballpark figure on daily losses (Table 5.3).

The algorithm represents those elements that would be necessary to recover a specific asset or resource if a certain threat was to occur. The formulas can be used in two ways. The team can actually develop values for each element and work the formula, which might be a difficult task, or the team can use the complexity of the formulas to help it prioritize the threats and identify where safeguards will provide the most benefits.

5.5 Conclusion

Which risk analysis process will work best for you and your organization? Only you will be able to determine that. Before you can make this decision, it will be necessary to examine as many as possible. In this chapter we presented variations on qualitative risk analysis themes. The keys to each process are the same:

1. Assemble the internal experts (the risk analysis team).
2. Develop a scope statement or risk analysis opportunity statement.
3. Agree on the definitions.
4. Ensure the team understands the process.
5. Conduct the risk analysis.

Table 5.3 Single Time Loss Algorithm

Natural Threats	
Earthquake	(Total asset value + contingency implementation costs + data reconstruction costs) × 0.25 + cost of 1-week delay = STL
Flooding	(Total asset value + contingency implementation costs + data reconstruction costs) × 0.10 + cost of 1-week delay = STL
Hurricane	Cost of 3-day delay = STL
Landslide	(Total asset value + contingency implementation costs + data reconstruction costs) × 0.05 + cost of 1-week delay = STL
Lightning	(Total asset value + contingency implementation costs + data reconstruction costs) × 0.20 + cost of 1-week delay = STL
Sandstorm	Cost of 3-day delay = STL
Snow/ice	Cost of 1-day delay = STL
Tornado	Cost of 3-day delay = STL
Tsunami	(Total asset value + contingency implementation costs + data reconstruction costs) × 0.10 + cost of 1-week delay = STL
Volcanic eruption	Cost of 3-day delay = STL
Windstorm	Cost of 1-day delay = STL
Accidental Threats	
Disclosure	Value of sensitive data + cost to recover organizational credibility + cost of potential lawsuits + cost of potential lost business + cost of potential rework to compensate for disclosed data = STL
Electrical disturbance	Cost of data reconstruction + cost of 1-day delay × 0.5 = STL
Electrical interruption	Cost of data reconstruction + cost of hardware replacement + cost of 1-day delay = STL
Emanation	Value of sensitive data + cost to recover organizational credibility + cost of potential lawsuits + cost of potential lost business + cost of potential rework to compensate for disclosed data = STL

Table 5.3 Single Time Loss Algorithm (continued)

Environmental failure	Cost of 1-day delay = STL
Fire	This category is broken down into several subcategories:
Minor fire in computer room	(Value of owned and leased assets and facilities of the highest valued computer room + 50 percent of contingency implementation costs + a proportional percentage of installed utilities value + 50 percent of data reconstruction costs) × 0.10 + cost of 1-day delay × 0.5 = STL
Major fire in computer room	(Value of owned and leased assets and facilities of the highest valued computer room + 50 percent of contingency implementation costs + a proportional percentage of installed utilities value + 50 percent of data reconstruction costs) × 0.10 + cost of 1-week delay × 0.5 = STL
Minor fire in media library	(Total asset value of the library + a proportional percentage of installed utilities value) × 0.05 + cost of 1-day delay = STL
Major fire in media library	(Total asset value of the library + a proportional percentage of installed utilities value) × 0.05 + cost of 3-day delay = STL
Catastrophic fire	Total asset value of the data center + contingency implementation costs + data reconstruction costs + cost of 2-week delay = STL
Hardware failure	Total number of computer processing hours lost per YY (year): number of occurrences per year × average hourly CPU cost + cost of data recovery + STL
Liquid leakage	Total asset value × 0.01 + cost of 3-day delay = STL
Deliberate Threats	
Alteration of data	Cost of data recovery + cost of YY-day delay = STL
Alteration of software	Cost of software recovery + cost of data recovery + cost of YY-day delay = STL
Bomb threat	Cost of lost work hours + cost of 1-day delay = STL
Disclosure	Value of sensitive data + cost to recover organizational credibility + cost of potential lawsuits + cost of potential lost business + cost of potential rework to compensate for disclosed data = STL

Table 5.3   Single Time Loss Algorithm (continued)

Employee sabotage	Value of computer center assets and utilities and facilities × 0.05 + 50 percent of contingency implementation costs + cost of 1-week delay = STL
Fraud	Cost of data reconstruction resulting from database manipulation + loss from fraudulent action itself + cost of legal action + cost of YY-day delay in selected application processing = STL
Strike	Cost of YY-day delay = STL
Unauthorized use of system	Cost of Y (number) hours of CPU time = STL
Vandalism	Value of computer center assets and utilities and facilities × 0.05 + 50 percent of contingency implementation costs + cost of 3-day delay = STL

In the next chapter we will examine the Facilitated Risk Analysis and Assessment Process (FRAAP), and after that, three variations on this process, to help you prescreen applications, conduct business impact analysis, and information category classification.

Risk assessment is a process that will have to be dynamic to meet the changing needs of your organization. It is designed to be flexible and provide each organization with the ability to customize it to meet specific needs. The goal of this chapter was to reinforce the five steps of risk assessment.

We also discussed the process that each risk assessment procedure must follow. After steps 1 through 4 are complete, the team will:

1. Identify threats.
2. Determine the probability that the threat will occur.
3. Establish the impact to the organization were the threat to occur.
4. Identify controls (either existing or ones to implement) that will reduce the risk to an acceptable level.

When time restrictions limit the number of risk assessments that can be conducted, or there is a need to establish the current baseline set of controls that are in existence, a questionnaire may be beneficial. The questions must be geared toward the intended and generally free from technical, audit, or legal jargon.

Chapter 6

Facilitated Risk Analysis and Assessment Process (FRAAP)

6.1 Introduction

Most enterprises are attempting to manage the same types of threats that face every other organization. With the changing business culture, successful security professionals have had to modify the process of responding to new threats in the high-profile, ultraconnected business environment.

Even with the change of focus, today's organizations must still protect the integrity, confidentiality, and availability of information resources they rely on. Although there is an increased interest in security by senior management, the fact remains that the business of the enterprise is business. An effective security program must assist the business units by providing high-quality reliable service in helping them protect the enterprise's assets.

6.2 FRAAP Overview

The Facilitated Risk Analysis and Assessment Process (FRAAP) has been developed as an efficient and disciplined process for ensuring that information security-related risks to business operations are considered and documented. The process involves analyzing one system, application, platform, business process, or segment of business operation at a time. By convening a team of internal subject matter experts, the FRAAP will rely on the organization's own people to complete the risk assessment process. These experts include the business managers who are familiar with mission needs of the asset under review and the infrastructure staff who have a detailed understanding of potential system vulnerabilities and related controls. The FRAAP sessions follow a standard agenda and are facilitated by a member of the project office or information security staff. The facilitators are responsible for ensuring that the team members communicate effectively and adhere to the project scope statement.

The FRAAP is divided into three phases: pre-FRAAP, FRAAP session, and post-FRAAP. During the FRAAP session, the team will brainstorm to identify potential threats to the integrity, confidentiality, and availability of information resources. The team will then establish a prioritization of threats based on the threat probability and relative impact. The effects of such impacts on business operations and broadly categorize the threats according to their risk level or priority level.

The team does not usually attempt to obtain or develop specific numbers for the threat likelihood or annual loss estimates unless the data for determining such factors is readily available. Instead, the team will rely on its general knowledge of threats and vulnerabilities obtained from national incident response centers, professional associations and literature, and the members' own experiences.

When assembling the team, it is the experience that allows the members to believe that additional efforts to develop precisely quantified risks are not cost-effective because:

- Such estimates take an inordinate amount of time and effort to identify and verify or develop.
- The risk documentation becomes too voluminous to be practical.
- Specific loss estimates are generally not needed to determine if a control is needed.

After identifying the threats and establishing the relative risk level for each threat, the team identifies controls that could be implemented to reduce the risk, focusing on the most cost-effective controls. Unlike the 30-minute risk analysis, the team will use a common set of controls designed to address various types of threats. Ultimately, the decision as to what controls are needed lies with the asset owner. It is the owner who will take into account the nature of the sensitivity information resource and its criticality to business operations and the control cost.

The team's conclusions as to what threats exist, what their risk levels are, and what controls are needed are documented for the business owner to use in developing an action plan to implement necessary controls.

Once the FRAAP session is complete, the security professional can assist the business owner in determining which controls are cost-effective and meet business needs. Once each threat has been assigned a control measure or has been accepted as a risk of doing business, the senior business manager and participating technical expert sign the completed document. The document and all associated papers are owned by the business unit sponsor and are retained for a period to be determined by the records management procedures (usually seven years).

Each risk analysis process is divided into three distinct sessions:

- The pre-FRAAP meeting normally takes about an hour and includes the business owner, project leader, scribe, and facilitator.
- The FRAAP session takes approximately four hours and includes 15 to 30 people, though sessions with as many as 50 and as few as 4 people have occurred.
- Post-FRAAP is where the results are analyzed and the management summary report is completed. This process can take up to five workdays to complete.

During the rest of this chapter we will examine why the FRAAP was developed, what each one of the three phases entails, and what are the deliverables from each phase.

6.3 Why the FRAAP Was Created

Prior to the development of the FRAAP, risk assessment was often perceived as a major task that required the enterprise to hire an outside consultant and could take weeks, if not months, to complete. The risk assessment process has often been shrouded in mystery, with it frequently seeming like elements of voodoo were being used. The final report sometimes looked as though the name of your organization was simply edited into a standard report template.

By hiring outside consultants, the expertise of the in-house staff was often overlooked and the results produced were not acceptable to the business unit manager. Additionally, with the old process, business managers, who were not part of the risk assessment process, found that they did not understand the recommended controls, did not want the recommended controls, and often worked to undermine the control implementation process.

What was needed was a risk assessment process that:

- Is driven by the business managers
- Takes days instead of weeks or months

- Is cost-effective
- Uses in-house experts

The FRAAP meets all of these requirements and adds another: it can be conducted by someone with limited knowledge of a particular system or business process, but with good facilitation skills.

The FRAAP is a formal methodology developed through understanding the previously developed qualitative risk assessment processes and modifying them to meet current requirements. It is driven by the business side of the enterprise and ensures that controls selected enable the business owners to meet their mission objectives. With the FRAAP, controls are never implemented to meet audit or security requirements. The only controls selected focus on the business need.

The FRAAP was created with an understanding that the internal resources had limited time to spend on such tasks. By holding the information-gathering session to four hours, the subject matter experts (SMEs) are more likely to participate in the process. Using time as a critical factor, the FRAAP addresses as many risk assessment issues as possible. If there is more time, then there are more tasks that can be performed. During this chapter we will present the FRAAP in its plain vanilla form. After the basics, we will present the variations that can be incorporated. Many of these variations will require additional time.

By involving the business units, the FRAAP uses them to identify risks and threats. Once the resource owner is involved in identifying threats, he generally sees the business reason of why implementing cost-effective controls to help limit the exposure is necessary. The FRAAP allows the business units to take control of their resources. It allows them to determine what safeguards are needed and who will be responsible for implementing those safeguards.

The results of the FRAAP are a comprehensive set of documents that will identify threats, prioritize those threats into risk levels, and identify possible controls that will help mitigate those threat risk levels.

The FRAAP provides the enterprise with a cost-effective action plan that meets the business needs to protect enterprise resources while conducting business. Most importantly, with the involvement of the business managers, the FRAAP provides a supportive client or owner who believes in the action plan.

6.4 Introducing the FRAAP to Your Organization

As with any new process, it is always best to conduct user awareness sessions to acquaint employees before the process is rolled out. It will be necessary to explain what the FRAAP is, how it works, and how it will help the businesspeople meet their specific objectives.

6.4.1 Awareness Program Overview

To be successful, the awareness program should take into account the needs and current levels of training and understanding of the employees and management. There are five keys to establishing an effective awareness program:

- Assess current level of risk assessment understanding.
- Determine what the managers and employees want to learn.
- Examine the level of receptiveness to the security program.
- Map out how to gain acceptance.
- Identify possible allies.

To assess the current level of risk assessment understanding, it will be necessary to ask questions of the audience. Although some employees may have been part of a risk assessment in the past, most employees have little firsthand knowledge of risk assessment. Ask questions such as why they believe there is a need for risk assessment. Listen to what the employees are saying and scale the training sessions to meet their specific needs. In the awareness field, one size or plan does not fit everyone.

Work with the managers and supervisors to understand what their needs are and how the risk assessment process can help them. It will become necessary for you to understand the language of the business units and to interpret their needs. Once you have an understanding, you will be able to modify the presentation to meet these special needs. No single awareness program will work for every business unit. There must be alterations and a willingness to accept suggestions from nonsecurity personnel.

Identify the level of receptiveness to the risk assessment process. Find out what is accepted and what is meeting with resistance. Examine the areas of noncompliance and try to find ways to alter the program if at all possible. Do not change fundamental risk assessment precepts just to gain unanimous acceptance; this is an unattainable goal. Make the process meet the greater good of the enterprise and then work with pockets of resistance to lessen the impact.

The best way to gain acceptance is to make employees and managers partners in this process. Never decree a new control or policy to the employee population without involving them in the decision-making process. This will require you to do your homework and understand the business process in each department. It will be important to know the peak periods of activity in the department and what the managers' concerns are. When meeting with the managers, be sure to listen to their concerns and be prepared to ask for their suggestions on how to improve the program. Remember, the key here is to partner with your audience.

Finally, look for possible allies. Find out which managers support the objectives of the risk assessment process and those that have the respect of their peers. This means that it will be necessary to expand the area of support beyond risk management and the audit staff. Seek out business managers that have a vested interest in seeing this program succeed. Use their support to springboard the program to acceptance.

A key point in this entire process is to never refer to the risk assessment process or the awareness campaign as "my program." The enterprise has identified the need for risk assessment, and you and your group are acting as the catalysts to moving the process forward. When discussing the process with employees and managers, it will be beneficial to refer to it as their risk assessment process or "our process." Make them feel that they are key stakeholders in this process.

Involve the user community and accept their comments whenever possible. Make the risk assessment process their process. Use what they identify as important in the awareness program. By having them involved, the risk assessment process truly becomes theirs and they are more willing to accept and internalize the results.

6.4.2 Introducing the FRAAP

The FRAAP is a formal methodology for risk assessment that is driven by the owner. Each FRAAP session is called by the owner and the team members are invited by the owner. The concept of what constitutes an owner is normally established in the organization's information classification policy. The policy generally addresses three concepts, as shown in Table 6.1.

The concept may seem difficult to internalize because the organization owns all of its assets. In this instance, the term *owner* is establishing management's responsibility for protecting intellectual property. Many times when I am teaching I am told that some organizations cannot use that term. It is the concept of management acting on behalf of the organization that is important. Management is charged with a fiduciary responsibility to protect the assets of the organization. The two key elements that make up this responsibility are:

- *Duty of loyalty* — Any decision regarding enterprise assets must be made in the best interest of the enterprise.

Table 6.1 Employee Responsibility Definitions

Employees are responsible for protecting corporate information from unauthorized access, modification, destruction, or disclosure, whether accidental or intentional. To facilitate the protection of corporate information, employee responsibilities have been established at three levels: owner, custodian, and user.

Owner: Company management of the organizational unit where the information resource is created, or management of the organizational unit that is the primary user of the information resource. Owners have the responsibility to:

Establish the classification level of all corporate information within their organizational unit

Define appropriate safeguards to ensure the confidentiality, integrity, and availability of the information resource

Monitor safeguards to ensure they are properly implemented

Authorize access to those who have a business need for the information

Delete access for those who no longer have a business need for the information

Custodian: Employees designated by the owner to be responsible for maintaining the safeguards established by the owner.

User: Employees authorized by the owner to access information and use the safeguards established by the owner.

■ *Duty of care* — Management must implement reasonable and prudent controls to safeguard the enterprise's assets.

As you can see, the risk assessment process assists management in meeting its obligations to protect the assets of the organization. By being an active partner in the risk assessment process, management, when acting in the owner capacity, gets the opportunity to see what threats are lurking around the business process. The FRAAP allows the owner, then, to identify where control weaknesses are and to develop an action plan to remedy the risks in a cost-effective manner.

The results of the FRAAP are a comprehensive risk assessment document that has the threats, risk levels, and controls documented. It also includes an action plan created by the owner with action items, responsible entities identified, and a time frame for completion established. The FRAAP assists management in meeting its obligation to perform due diligence.

The FRAAP is conducted by a trained facilitator. This individual will lead the team through the identification of threats, the establishment of a risk level by determining probability and impact, and then the selection of possible safeguards or controls. Because of qualitative risk assessment's subjective nature, it will be the responsibility of the facilitator to lead the team into different areas of concern to ensure as many threats as possible are identified.

Instead of concentrating on establishing audit or security requirements, the facilitator ensures that the risk assessment process examines threats that might impact the business process or the mission of the enterprise. This ensures that only those controls and countermeasures that are truly needed and cost-effective are selected and implemented.

6.4.3 Facilitation Skills

Facilitation of a FRAAP requires the use of a number of special skills. These skills can be improved by attending special training and by facilitating. The skills required include the ability to do the following.

6.4.3.1 Listen

This is having the ability to be responsive to verbal and nonverbal behavior of the attendees. In today's society, the ability to listen is a lost art. Instead of a dialogue, we participate in parallel monologues. The best way to picture how we function is to imagine the world as a big token ring. When someone has the token, they speak. While they are speaking, the rest of us are in quiet mode. It looks like we are listening, but we are really preparing to receive the token and start talking.

Recently I heard an interview on National Public Radio where the author was discussing this very activity. He used as an example a fellow employee sitting down at the lunch table and telling his coworkers that his wife is dying of cancer. Another employee responds, "I had an aunt that died of cancer." This is not dialogue; this is a parallel monologue. The employee did not respond to the first employee's comment; he opened a second line of discussion.

As a facilitator, it will be necessary to give team members your undivided attention when they begin to discuss a specific threat. As a facilitator, you will generally be thinking ahead to remember who the next speaker is, and other questions will run through your mind. You will have to fight this natural tendency and concentrate on what is being said to you.

As a personal example, I worked for a company where one of my peers would ask a question of someone during a meeting. Halfway through the answer she would ask, "Can you start over? I wasn't paying attention."

She was busy preparing her next question and forgot to listen to the response.

By paraphrasing the threat responses, you will be better able to concentrate on the team member's comment, and this will help the scribe capture the threat description.

6.4.3.2 Lead

This is getting the FRAAP session started and encouraging discussion while keeping the team focused on the topic at hand.

We have all been in meetings when someone other than the discussion leader took over. Make sure that as the facilitator you do not relinquish the role of leader. The owner has asked you to lead the session and to keep it on track. By being prepared to do the job, there will be little chance for someone else to try and take over the risk assessment session.

6.4.3.3 Reflect

This is repeating ideas in fresh words or for emphasis. This will allow two things to occur. First, the facilitator will be better able to concentrate on the threat being discussed. Repeating the comment in different words requires the facilitator to understand what is being said and to put the comment into precise phrases. Second, this process will assist the scribe in correctly gathering the comments.

6.4.3.4 Summarize

This is being able to pull themes and ideas together. Many times the team members will give long explanations about the issue that they believe warrants investigation. They will embellish the information and search for the correct words. By being able to weed out the extraneous information and summarizing the remarks into one or two sentences, the FRAAP will move along more efficiently.

6.4.3.5 Confront

This is being able to feed back opinions, reacting honestly to input from the team and taking harsh comments and turning them into positive statements. As with any meeting, some people come with an agenda. It could be that they believe that they are too busy and do not have time for such foolishness, or that someone on the team may have wronged them recently. Whatever the cause, some team members will be caustic and acerbic. Do not get sucked into their state of mind. Try to remind them that the team owner asked for them to attend because they had knowledge that will help the owner make intelligent decisions. If all else fails, at the break discuss the situation with the owner, and if necessary, tell the person that he or she can leave.

6.4.3.6 Support

This is creating a climate of trust and acceptance. This is sort of like the old TV show *Family Feud*. On that show the host (facilitator) would say "good answer" even if the response was totally out of line. The goal was to make everyone feel important and that they were part of the team. As the FRAAP facilitator, that will be your job. Following the *Family Feud* analogy to its logical end, it probably is not necessary to kiss each of the team members when they give their first threat response.

6.4.3.7 Crisis Intervention

This is helping to expand a person's vision of options or alternatives and to reinforce action points that can aid in resolving any conflict or crisis. Some team members will not understand what is going on and what all of these negative threats are going to do to the overall project. Even after the FRAAP or whatever risk assessment process you use has become part of the business culture, some employees may not be aware of what it is intended to do.

At the beginning of each FRAAP session, remind the team that the risk analysis was completed and that the project has been approved. The risk assessment is conducted to identify threats to the successful implementation of the project and to identify safeguards or countermeasures that will provide an acceptable level of risk.

6.4.3.8 Center

This is helping the team to accept others' views and build confidence for all to respond and participate. Some team members might preface a remark with "This may be really off target" or "This may seem stupid" and then give their threat concern. Make certain that you reinforce the concept that during a brainstorming session no threat is incorrect. Each threat will be examined by the team during the risk level process. Whatever the team establishes as the probability of occurrence and the impact to the business objectives will determine the relative value of the comment.

6.4.3.9 Solve Problems

This means gathering relevant information about the issues at hand and helping the team establish an effective control objective. By ensuring that all deliverables from the pre-FRAAP are complete, the team will have the tools needed to complete the risk assessment process. Although it is important to keep the FRAAP session moving, do not sacrifice thoroughness for speed. Take the time to get the information correct.

6.4.3.10 Change Behavior

Look for those that appear not to be part of the process and bring them into active participation. I was conducting a FRAAP on Long Island a while back and there were 35 team members. Toward the front on my right-hand side sat a gentleman named Clevon. As the process went through its first round, when we got to Clevon, he passed. On the second round, he again passed. When we got halfway through the third round, I went over to Clevon and said, "Clevon, get ready. We're coming toward you." When we got to him, he was ready and had a threat. He just needed time to see how the process worked and that no one was ridiculed because of his response.

I make sure that I am in the room for the FRAAP as the team members come in. I watch to see if the members know each other. As the first matter of business, I have the members introduce themselves to the others. I request that they tell the other team members their name, department, location, and reason for being there. If I feel the group needs to become a team, I have a number of icebreaker quizzes and personality tests that I can administer.

Basic facilitation rules must be observed by all facilitators if the FRAAP is to be successful. FRAAP leaders must observe carefully and listen to all that the team says and does.

6.4.3.11 Recognize All Input and Encourage Participation

There are two basic personality types: introverts and extraverts. I consider myself to be an outspoken introvert. It is easy to identify the extraverts; they will appear to be self-confident and unafraid to put forth their ideas. The introvert, however, may require nurturing before he or she participates. Be aware of this need and make sure you bring introverts into the process.

6.4.3.12 Be Observant for Nonverbal Responses

If someone flashes you half of a peace sign, then you might examine how well things are going. Look for body language. If a male team member folds his arms across his chest, it usually means he has had enough. If a woman does that, it normally means she is cold. If she crosses her leg and her foot starts to bob, then she has had enough. Watch for people that back away from the table. These are signs that the team is reaching the end of its concentration limit.

6.4.3.13 Do Not Lecture; Listen and Get the Team Involved

Remember that you are the facilitator. The team is the subject matter experts. It is their expert opinion that the risk assessment process needs.

6.4.3.14 Never Lose Sight of the Objective

Keep the project scope statement posted in the room during the session. If the team lurches away from the objective, pull it back and direct its focus to the mission at hand.

6.4.3.15 Stay Neutral (or Always Appear to Remain Neutral)

As a security, audit, or risk management professional, you have ideas on how things should be done. When you are the facilitator, you must keep those opinions to yourself.

6.4.3.16 Learn to Expect Hostility, but Do Not Become Hostile

Remember that this is not personal. You are there to assist the owner in performing his due diligence. Sometimes rude or disparaging remarks are made in the heat of the discussion process. Frustration can boil over and cause the team members to act in ways or say things that are inflammatory. For instance, many employees know that the quickest way to get at the network administration group is to say something like "The network is running a little slow today." Here they are just baiting the network administrators, sometimes as a "joke" and other times to be mean. Watch out for these kinds of comments and help defuse the situation.

I once did six FRAAPs in a week. By the time I got to number 4, I was not as sweet and nice as I was in earlier sessions. The FRAAP is a physically and mentally demanding process. Try and schedule them so that you can have at least one off day between each FRAAP.

6.4.3.17 Avoid Being the Expert Authority

The facilitator's role is to listen, question, enforce the process, and offer alternatives. As stated above, the team contains the SMEs; the facilitator's job is to ensure that he stays on focus and completes the FRAAP in a timely and efficient manner.

6.4.3.18 Adhere to Time Frames and Be Punctual

Welcome to my pet peeve. The best way to show respect is to start and finish on time. The FRAAP is not a one-time activity. The members of the team may be called on by other owners to participate in other FRAAPs. By starting on time, resuming on time after the break, and stopping no later than the scheduled finish time, the SMEs are more likely to participate in other FRAAPs.

Be on the lookout for the "mercy" page or phone call. This activity is a variation on the old blind date technique where a half hour into the date, you have scheduled someone to call you. If the date is going badly, you say it is the baby-sitter and you have to go home. During many meetings employees will get a page or phone call within 20 minutes of starting the meeting and announce that there is an emergency and then leave. I have commented at the beginning of a session that those expecting mercy pages should take them now so as not to disrupt the FRAAP.

6.4.3.19 Use Breaks to Free a Discussion

If a discussion veers off point and gets some team members bogged down, try to move the discussion item to the deferred issues list. If that fails to break the discussion, call for a short break (10 minutes maximum). Meet with the discussion group and try to reach resolution. It may be necessary for them to take the discussion offline at a later time.

6.4.3.20 The Facilitator Is There to Serve the FRAAP Team

The goal of the facilitator is to be a part of a process that focuses on the team and its contributions to the risk assessment process. I have had two facilitators work for me that saw this as their chance to do stand-up comedy. This is not the true role of the facilitator. The process comes first; the opinions of the facilitator should never come up.

6.4.3.21 Stop the FRAAP if the Group Is Sluggish and Difficult to Control

Later on in the book, we will examine the prescreening process. This is conducted as the first deliverable of the pre-FRAAP meeting and can identify if the asset in question needs a complete risk assessment or business impact analysis (BIA). This process will save time by not conducting risk assessments on those applications, systems, business processes, or platforms that have no urgent need for this thorough of an examination.

Beware of external sources that might impact the results of the FRAAP. One time I was hired to go to Richmond, VA, to conduct a FRAAP training session and then conduct a FRAAP on a specific business application. I was scheduled to be there Monday through Thursday. On Wednesday and Thursday I would be working with the team to conduct a FRAAP and then help them prepare the documentation.

On Tuesday at lunchtime I was sitting in the cafeteria trying to figure out what was wrong with the training session. The attendees were nice enough to me, but they did not offer any comments and had no questions. As I was sitting there, one of the attendees came over and asked to sit down. He then told me that the previous Thursday all of the members of the team being trained had been told that they were not needed and would be discharged in two weeks.

I went to my contact and verified the facts and then was told that these people would be there on Wednesday to participate in the FRAAP. Well, it was one of those times when I hosted a FRAAP and no one attended.

Another time I was in San Francisco conducting a FRAAP and every 20 minutes or so one of the team members would leave. Some would come back and others did not. At the break I asked the contact what was happening. I was told that the day of the FRAAP was also the day the company scheduled reduction-in-force meetings. Those that came back were still employed; the others were not.

When conducting a FRAAP, be aware of outside influences. For some departments it could be a critical time in their calendar, such as end of month or quarter end. Make sure that the FRAAP is scheduled to best meet the needs of the owner and the team.

As the FRAAP facilitator, it will be necessary to develop your own FRAAP tool kit. This tool kit should include the items listed in Table 6.2.

Table 6.2   FRAAP Tool Kit

Flip charts
Masking tape and push pins
Color pens (e.g., Mr. Sketch Scented Markers (12))
Tent cards
Session agreements

Table 6.3   Session Agreements

Everyone participates.
Stay within identified roles.
Stick to the agenda/current focus.
All ideas have equal value.
Listen to other points of view.
No "plops" — all issues are recorded.
Deferred issues will be recorded.
Post the idea before discussing it.
Help scribe ensure all issues are recorded.
Allow only one conversation at a time.
Allow only one angry person at a time.
Apply the three-minute rule.
Be prompt, fair, nice, creative, and have fun.

6.4.4 Session Agreements

The session agreements (Table 6.3) will be reviewed at the beginning of each FRAAP session and the team will abide by them. This is another way to put the team at ease and to let them know what is expected of them. I have two facilitators that have printed out the session agreements on flip chart-size paper and glued them to poster board. At the beginning of each session they put them up on an easel and discuss them.

The agreements require that:

- *Everyone participates* — When we discuss the actual FRAAP threat-gathering process, it will become clear how this will be easier to accomplish.
- *Stay with identified roles* — The facilitator will facilitate and the scribe will scribe; everyone else will be on the team and participate.
- *Stick to the agenda/current focus* — The scope statement and visual model will be posted or given to all attendees. If there is a deviation from these, the facilitator will bring the team back to the current agenda.
- *All ideas have equal value* —George Orwell said that "all were equal, but some where more equal than others"; here we try for equality. When entering the threats into the FRAAP documentation, there is no reference made as to who proposed that topic. This allows the team to be more free with their discussions.
- *Listen to other points of view* — Get the team to actually listen to their fellow team members and not just wait for their turn with the token.

■ *No "plops" — all issues are recorded* — Jack Durner of the Mendon Group gave us this term; nothing "plops" onto the floor.

■ *Deferred issues will be recorded* — If an item is outside the scope of what is under review, it is recorded on the deferred issues list and someone will be assigned to resolve the issue.

■ *Post the idea before discussing it* — Get it on the flip chart first. This will ensure that everyone is discussing the same item.

■ *Help the scribe ensure that all issues are recorded* — I bring a scribe along with me to record what is posted on the flip charts. It is very difficult to transcribe the FRAAP materials after the session is completed. Have someone scribe the events as they occur; it will speed up the completion time.

■ *Allow only one conversation at a time* — Here is where your facilitation skills will be tested. Many times subdiscussions will break out. Try to nip them in the bud and regain the focus of the team.

■ *Allow only one angry person at a time* — I usually volunteer for this job.

■ *Apply the three- to five-minute rule* — All discussions must be concluded within the agreed upon time frame.

■ *Be prompt, fair, nice, creative, and have fun.*

6.4.5 The FRAAP Team

During the pre-FRAAP meeting, the business manager and project leader will need to identify who should be part of the FRAAP session. The ideal number of participants is between 7 and 15. It is recommended that representatives from the areas listed in Table 6.4 be included in the FRAAP.

There are no hard and fast rules as to who should attend, but to be successful, it will be necessary for the functional business owner and system users to be part of the FRAAP. It is their business process that will be reviewed, and thus it is important that they are part of the process.

■ The systems analysis group is made up of those bilingual individuals that speak fluent business and information systems. That can be vital in ensuring that what is spoken at a FRAAP is understood by all parties.

■ Applications programming consists of the individuals that will either create the new application or customize the existing application or third-party software to meet the functional owner's needs.

■ The database administrators are the technical individuals that understand how the mechanics of the database works and are often responsible for ensuring that database security mechanisms are working properly.

Table 6.4   FRAAP Team Members

Possible FRAAP Team Member	Crucial	Support
Functional owners	Yes	
System users	Yes	
Systems analysis	Yes	
Applications programming	Yes	
Database administration	Yes	
Auditing (if appropriate)		Yes
Physical security		Yes
Facilities management	Yes	
Telecommunication	Yes	
Network administration	Yes	
Legal (if necessary)		Yes
Regulatory affairs		Yes
Corporate communications		Yes
Human resources		Yes
Labor relations		Yes
Processing operations management	Yes	
System administrator	Yes	
Systems programming	Yes	
Information security	Yes	

■ The audit staff is a group that can offer some good ideas, but its presence often impacts the free flow of information. Unless you have a very good working relationship with the audit staff, it is recommended that the staff not take part in the FRAAP session. The audit team will see the results of the FRAAP later and will probably use the output when it conducts an audit of the resource.

■ Physical security and someone from facility engineering should be part of the team. They will bring a perspective of viewing concerns from the physical operations of the environment. In many organizations, facilities management is charged with maintaining the business continuity plans.

- If the resource under review is going to access the network or other telecommunication devices, then representatives from those areas must be part of the process.
- Any Web-based applications will require representatives from the Internet support organization, including the Web master and the firewall administrator.
- The legal staff is normally too busy for every FRAAP. However, if there is a resource under review that has a major impact on the enterprise, it will probably be appropriate to extend an invitation to the legal staff. I recommend that you meet with the staff to discuss what the FRAAP is, as we discussed above, and attempt to establish a guideline of when it needs to be part of the process or see specific risk concerns.
- Another group that can provide invaluable insight into a number of issues is regulatory affairs. This group is charged with keeping current on the various regulations that government agencies and industry groups require.
- Corporate communications is responsible for communicating with the public and other entities. If the asset under review impacts customers or business partners, then this group needs to be part of the team.
- Any issues that impact the employees will require the attendance of human resources. If union-represented employees are impacted by the risk assessment, then labor relations should be invited.
- The operations group is responsible for maintaining the production environment on the various platforms. Its input into how the data center disaster recovery plan works and how it will support the asset under review will be vital in discussing service level agreements (SLAs).
- The system(s) group is also an important part of the FRAAP team. The system administrator is normally found in the user department and has had some training in the new application or system and is the initial point of contact for users when they have problems.
- The systems programming group consists of those individuals that support the platforms and ensure that the current operating environment is working and properly configured.
- Information security should have a representative on the FRAAP team. Many FRAAPs are facilitated by someone from information security, but this is often a conflict of interest. The facilitator should have an aura of neutrality about him.

This list is not all-inclusive, nor does it represent the correct mix of players if the FRAAP moves away from the traditional information security risk assessment. The key here is to understand that to be successful, the FRAAP team must be made up of representation from a wide spectrum of employee groups.

6.4.6 Prescreening

Not every application, business process, or system needs to have a formal risk assessment process or business impact analysis conducted. What is needed is an enterprisewide formal methodology that allows for prescreening of applications and systems to determine needs. By using the processes learned in qualitative risk assessment, your organization will be able to develop a quick prescreening methodology that could save time and money.

In addition to the methodology, it will be necessary to create a standard set of *baseline controls* that will be used as part of the prescreening process. These baseline controls can be used with the prescreening methodology or when there is a problem with an owner stepping up to take responsibility for protecting information resources.

Table 6.5 is a baseline set of controls using the Health Insurance Portability and Accountability Act (HIPAA) as its basis.

When developing a prescreening methodology, it is best to start with a clear understanding of what the business objective or mission of the enterprise is. Using this information as a base, you can then develop a set of questions that can be completed by the project leader and the business manager during the pre-FRAAP meeting. These questions will allow the facilitator and owner to determine if a formal risk assessment or business impact analysis must be completed.

We will examine two different approaches to the prescreening process. The first one is an impact analysis process that is used by a financial institution; then we will review a process used by a major information systems service provider.

6.4.6.1 Prescreening Example 1

The first prescreening example examines the impact of new applications or systems on two selected elements of a financial institution: the sensitivity of the data involved and the resource impact. Resource impact includes financial (internal and external) and customer impact.

The project leader and the business manager are required to complete this questionnaire online to assess the application's level of impact to the enterprise and the type of technology to be used by the application. If the application is considered low sensitivity and low impact, then an

Table 6.5   Baseline Set of Controls Using HIPAA

Control	Classification	HIPAA Control Description
		Implement policies and procedures to prevent and detect.
Risk analysis	Required	Conduct an accurate and thorough assessment of the potential risks and vulnerabilities to the confidentiality, integrity, and availability of electronically protected health information (EPHI).
Risk management	Required	Implement security measures sufficient to reduce risks and vulnerabilities to a reasonable and appropriate level.
Sanction policy	Required	Apply appropriate sanctions against workforce members who fail to comply with the security policies and procedures of the covered entity.
Information system activity review	Required	Implement procedures to regularly review records of information systems activity.
		Identify the security official who is responsible for the development and implementation of the policies and procedures.
Privacy officer	Required	Identify a single person responsible for the development and implementation of the policies and procedures supporting HIPAA compliance.
		Implement policies and procedures to ensure that all members of the workforce have appropriate access to EPHI, and to prevent those workforce members who are not authorized to have access under the information access management standard from obtaining access to electronic health information.
Isolate healthcare clearinghouse functions	Required	If a covered entity (CE) operates a healthcare clearinghouse, it must implement policies and procedures to protect the EPHI maintained by the clearinghouse from unauthorized access by the larger organization.

Table 6.5   Baseline Set of Controls Using HIPAA (continued)

Control	Classification	HIPAA Control Description
		Implement policies and procedures to address security incidents.
Response and reporting	Required	Identify and respond to suspected or known security incidents; mitigate to the extent practicable harmful effects of the security incidents that are known to the CE; and document security incidents and their outcomes.
		Establish (and implement as needed) policies and procedures for responding to an emergency or other occurrence that damages systems that contain EPHI.
Data backup	Required	Establish and implement procedures to create and maintain retrievable exact copies of EPHI.
Disaster recovery plan	Required	Establish (and implement as needed) procedures to restore any loss of data.
Emergency mode operations plan	Required	Establish (and implement as needed) procedures to enable continuation of critical business processes to ensure access to EPHI and to provide for adequate protection of EPHI while operating in emergency mode.
		Implement policies and procedures that specify the proper functions to be performed, the manner in which those functions are to be performed, and the physical attributes of the surroundings of a specific workstation or class of workstation than can access EPHI.
Workstation security	Standard	Implement physical safeguards for all workstations that access EPHI to restrict access to authorized users.
Device and media control	Standard	Implement policies and procedures that govern the receipt and removal of hardware and electronic media that contain EPHI into and out of a facility, and the movement of these items within a facility.

Table 6.5 Baseline Set of Controls Using HIPAA (continued)

Control	Classification	HIPAA Control Description
Disposal	Required	Implement policies and procedures to address the final disposition of EPHI and the hardware or electronic media on which it is stored.
Media reuse	Required	Implement procedures for removal of EPHI from electronic media prior to reuse.
Accountability	Addressable	Maintain a record of the movement of hardware and software and any person responsible for movement.
Data backup and storage	Addressable	Create a retrievable, exact copy of EPHI, when needed, prior to moving equipment.
Unique user identification	Required	Assign a unique name and number for identifying and tracking user identity.
Emergency access procedure	Required	Establish (and implement as needed) procedures for obtaining necessary EPHI during an emergency.
Audit controls	Standard	Implement hardware, software, and procedural mechanisms that record and examine activity in information systems that contain or use EPHI.
Integrity	Standard	Implement policies and procedures to protect EPHI from improper alteration or destruction.
Authentication	Standard	Implement procedures to verify that a person or entity seeking access to EPHI is the one claimed.
Transmission security	Standard	Implement technical security measures to guard against unauthorized access to EPHI that is being transmitted over an electronic communications network.
Business associate contracts	Standard	The contract between the CE and its BA must meet the following requirements, as applicable:
		A CE is not in compliance if it knew of a pattern of activity or practice of the BA that constituted a material breach or

Table 6.5   Baseline Set of Controls Using HIPAA (continued)

Control	Classification	HIPAA Control Description
		violation of the BA's obligation under the contract, unless the CE took reasonable steps to cure the breach or end the violation, and if such steps were unsuccessful to: (A) Terminate the contract, if feasible; or (B) Report the problem to the secretary of HHS, if not.
		Implement reasonable and appropriate policies and procedures to comply with the standards, implementation specifications, and other requirements.
Documentation	Standard	Maintain the policies and procedures required by the security rule in writing, which may be electronic, and if an action, activity, or assessment is required to be documented, maintain a written record, which may be electronic.
Time limit	Required	Retain the documentation required by the security rule for six years from the date of its creation or the date when it was last in effect, whichever is later.
Availability	Required	Make documentation available to those persons responsible for implementing the procedures to which the documentation pertains.
Updates	Required	Review documentation periodically, and update as needed, in response to environmental and operational changes affecting the security of the EPHI.

implementation of baseline set controls is all that is required. If the application comes back as low, but the business manager does not want the baseline controls, then a formal risk analysis must be conducted.

For those applications identified as high impact or sensitivity, a formal risk analysis and business impact analysis must be scheduled. It is the responsibility of the business unit to complete the prescreening questionnaire and to schedule any additional follow-up risk assessments or business impact analysis as required.

Table 6.6   Prescreening Example 1 Table 1

Sensitivity Value	Sensitivity of Data
High	*Extreme sensitivity* — Restricted to specific individual need-to-know; its loss or compromise may cause severe financial, legal, regulatory, or reputation damage to the company
Medium	Used only by specific authorized groups with legitimate business need; may have significant adverse impact; possible negative financial impact
Low	Information for internal business use within the company; may have adverse impact; negligible financial impact

Table 6.7   Prescreening Example 1 Table 2

Impact Value	Project Cost: Total Approved Budget	Financial Impact: Daily Dollar Amount of Transactions Processed	Customer Impact: Number of Customers Impacted	Regulatory/ Compliance Impact
High	$1.5 million or more	$50 million or more	10,000 or more	Substantial financial penalties
Medium	$500,001 to $1.5 million	$1 to $49 million	1000 to 9999	Limited financial penalties
Low	$500,000 or less	$1 million or less	Less than 1000	No regulatory or compliance issues

The project leader and owner are asked two sets of questions. The first set of questions relates to the sensitivity of the data. Table 6.6 gives you an example of how the questions might look. The questions are based on the information classification policy for the company and provide the project leader and business manager with three levels of impact: high, medium, and low. Once the sensitivity of the data has been determined, the questionnaire requests the project leader and owner to answer four additional questions that address the impact to the organization.

These next four questions all have a financial twist to them. The first is looking for a project cost in the total budget approved. When developing your prescreening questions, the values plugged into these questions will need to reflect your enterprise (Table 6.7).

The first question on this table attempts to establish the budget for this project. Question 2 relates to the total dollar transaction value for a single day. This question will lead directly to a business impact analysis review and ultimately a level of requirement for contingency planning.

The third question is similar to question 2, but looks for a response in a little different manner. Here the number of customers impacted by the new transaction, application, or system is addressed. The threshold of pain for customers impacted will have to be determined by the business unit that is responsible for customer satisfaction.

The final question in this example attempts to determine the level of penalty imposed by regulatory agencies if the application or system is unavailable. The thresholds here would have to be established by the regulatory affairs unit of a financial institution.

If any of the responses come out high, then a formal risk assessment and business impact analysis must be scheduled. If two responses were medium, then a meeting between the information security team and the business unit must be called. If all of the answers are low, then the business unit must implement the standard set of baseline controls.

6.4.6.2 Prescreening Example 2

Another example of application or system prescreening was developed for a major service provider. This one examines two key elements: sensitivity of the information being handled and the mission criticality of the system.

Whereas the impact analysis process used low, medium, and high, this prescreening methodology has five values (Table 6.8). This specific number was selected because the company has five levels of information classification in its policy and the contingency planning team happened to have five categories of recovery windows.

If the owner selects 1 or 2 as the correct answer to either or both questions, then a formal risk assessment and business impact analysis must be conducted. If the answer to both questions is 3, 4, or 5, then the owner is asked to select the appropriate answer from two more sets of questions (Table 6.9).

If the owner selects 1 or 2 as the correct answer to either or both of these questions, then a formal risk assessment and business impact analysis must be conducted. If the answer to both questions is 3, 4, or 5, then the requirement is to implement the baseline set of controls.

The key to the prescreening process is to get input from the department that understands the threshold levels and impacts to the enterprise. This process, if properly established, will allow the business units to bypass unneeded control mechanisms while still providing an appropriate level of security.

Table 6.8   Prescreening Example 2 Table 1

Impact Value	Information Classification Level	Description	Longest Tolerable Outage
1	Top secret	Information that, if disclosed, could cause severe impact to the company's competitive advantage or business strategies	24 hours or less
2	Confidential	Information that, if disclosed, could violate the privacy of individuals, reduce competitive advantage, or damage the company	25–72 hours
3	Restricted	Information that is available to a specific subset of the employee population when conducting company business	73 hours–5 days
4	Internal use	Information that is intended for use by all employees when conducting company business	6–9 days
5	Public	Information that has been made available to the public through authorized company channels	10 days or more

Table 6.9   Prescreening Example 2 Table 2

Impact Value	Disclosure	Contractual Obligation
1	National or international press coverage	Unable to meet external obligations
2	State or local press coverage	Delay in meeting external obligations
3	Incident known throughout the company	Unable to meet internal obligations
4	Incident known only at the division or department level	Delay in meeting internal obligations
5	Little or no impact	Little or no impact

Being able to build on the information that has gone before will allow you to create a risk management program that will be cost-effective and acceptable to the user community. Nothing will cause you to succeed faster than implementing easy-to-conduct processes that cut down on the number of controls.

6.4.6.3 Prescreening Example 3

As I was working with these two examples of prescreening, I continued to get the feeling that there was something missing. Example 2 requires the owner to select for a sensitivity category (the classification of data levels) and a criticality or availability category (longest tolerable outage). Selecting a 1 or 2 in either category will require the owner to schedule both a risk assessment and a business impact analysis.

I felt that a more efficient prescreening methodology could be developed that would identify if a risk assessment or a business impact analysis, or both, was required. By using the model established in the various qualitative risk assessment methodologies we have discussed, I came up with the following example for a prescreening methodology.

At the Pre-FRAAP meeting, the owner, project leader, and facilitator will examine two sets of questions to determine what needs to be completed for this particular asset. The questions address sensitivity of data or information and the criticality of the system or business process.

The owner will select the category that most closely matches the asset's qualities (Table 6.10). This first set of categories relates to the information sensitivity level.

Table 6.10   Prescreening Example 3 Table 1

Disclosure Impact Level	Definition
High	Information is of such a nature that its unauthorized disclosure would cause media attention and negative customer response.
Medium	Information is of such a nature that its unauthorized disclosure might cause media attention and negative customer response.
Low	Information is of such a nature that its unauthorized disclosure would have little or no impact on the organization.

Table 6.11   Prescreening Example 3 Worksheet 1

Category	Impact Level	Matrix Score	Requirement
Disclosure	High		
Criticality			
Total			

Table 6.12   Prescreening Example 3 Table 2

Criticality Impact Level	Definition
High	Information is of such a nature that its unauthorized modification or destruction would cause media attention and negative customer response.
Medium	Information is of such a nature that its unauthorized modification or destruction might cause media attention and negative customer response.
Low	Information is of such a nature that its unauthorized modification or destruction would have little or no impact on the organization.

The owner selects the most appropriate category that describes the data or information that is handled, processed, or retained by the asset scheduled to undergo the risk assessment review. The impact level would be entered on the prescreening worksheet. We will select the category "Information is of such a nature that its unauthorized modification or destruction would cause media attention and negative customer response," or high (Table 6.11).

The owner will select the category that most closely matches the asset's qualities. This first set of categories relates to the information criticality level (Table 6.12).

The owner would then select the most appropriate category that describes the mission criticality of the asset scheduled to undergo the risk assessment. The impact level would be entered on the prescreening worksheet. We will select the category "Information is of such a nature that its unauthorized modification or destruction would have little or no impact on the organization," or low (Table 6.13).

The owner would then look to the prescreening matrix and find the intersection of the two levels and enter the number in the matrix score box of the worksheet (Figure 6.1).

Table 6.13   Prescreening Example 3 Worksheet 2

Category	Impact Level	Matrix Score	Requirement
Disclosure	High		
Criticality	Low		
Total			

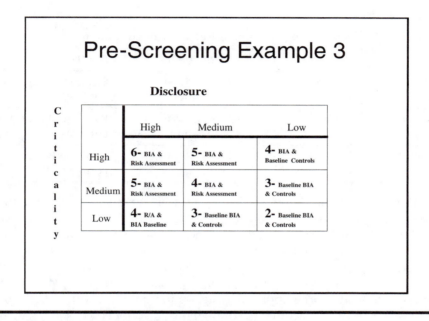

Figure 6.1   Prescreening example 2 matrix.

Table 6.14   Prescreening Example 3 Worksheet 3

Category	Impact Level	Matrix Score	Requirement
Disclosure	High	3	
Criticality	Low	1	
Impact Value		4	

The matrix scores are then entered onto the worksheet with the recommended course of action (Table 6.14).

Using the scoring table (Table 6.15), we can get a better picture of what is recommended by the prescreening process.

Table 6.15   Prescreening Example 3 Scoring

	High (3)	*Medium (2)*	*Low (1)*
High (3)	3 + 3 = 6	3 + 2 = 5	3 + 1 = 4
Medium (2)	2 + 3 = 5	2 + 2 = 4	2 + 1 = 3
Low (1)	1 + 3 = 4	1 + 2 = 3	1 + 1 = 2

Table 6.16   Prescreening Example 3 Recommended Action

	High (3)	*Medium (2)*	*Low(1)*
High (3)	BIA and risk assessment	BIA and risk assessment	BIA and baseline controls
Medium (2)	BIA and risk assessment	BIA and risk assessment	Baseline BIA and controls
Low (1)	Risk assessment and BIA baseline	Baseline BIA and controls	Baseline BIA and controls

Any category that is selected as high will get a value of 3 for that specific category. In our example the disclosure level was high; therefore, on the matrix we would select a 3. The criticality value was determine to be low, so we would select the intersection of high disclosure (3) and low criticality (1) for a total of 4, or a medium prescreening score.

The disclosure category addresses the issue of the sensitivity of the data or information. The appropriate action for any asset with a disclosure or sensitivity score of medium (2) or higher is to conduct a risk assessment.

The criticality category addresses the issue of required availability of the system and data. The appropriate action for any asset with a criticality factor of medium (2) or higher is to conduct a business impact analysis.

In our example, the disclosure level was high, so we know we have to conduct a risk assessment. However, the criticality level is low. The requirement here is to implement the baseline set of controls for continuity and disaster recovery planning; a BIA is not required. The owner should review these baseline standards, and if the owner determines that the baseline does not meet his needs, then he can request a BIA (Table 6.16). In Chapter 9, we will discuss how to conduct a business impact analysis using qualitative risk assessment skills and tools.

If the scoring results were high disclosure and low criticality, as the example was, then the recommended action is to conduct a risk assessment to examine threats, establish risk levels, and select possible mitigating controls. The business impact analysis recommendation is to classify the system criticality at a low priority and have it restored with the non-mission-critical systems, applications, and business processes. One additional point here, it will be necessary to identify any systems, applications, or business processes that are dependent on the one under review. If any mission-critical resource is dependent on the asset under review, then a BIA must be scheduled.

If the impact values selected were low in disclosure, then only the baseline set of information protection standards needs to be implemented. If the criticality was high, therefore giving an impact value of 4, then a BIA must be scheduled.

With a basic understanding of qualitative risk assessment, it will be possible to create a process that will improve the work flow of your organization. As part of a misunderstood group, security, audit, and risk management professionals are often viewed by the rest of the organization as overhead to the enterprise. One way to overcome this misconception is to implement processes such as prescreening that streamline control review requirements and possibly eliminate the need to perform some functions.

6.4.7 The Pre-FRAAP Meeting

6.4.7.1 Pre-FRAAP Meeting Process

The pre-FRAAP meeting is the key to the success of the project. The meeting is normally scheduled for an hour and a half and is usually conducted at the client office. The meeting should have the business manager (or representative), the project development leader, the facilitator, and the scribe. There will be six key deliverables to come out of this one-hour session.

1. *Prescreening results* — As we have just discussed, the results of the prescreening may alter the need to conduct a risk assessment.
2. *Scope statement* — The project leader and business manager will have to create a statement of opportunity for review. They are to develop in words what exactly is going to be reviewed. The scope statement was discussed in Chapter 2 and should be reviewed for content.
3. *Visual diagram* — There will need to be a visual model. This is a one-page or foil diagram depicting the process to be reviewed. The visual model will be used during the FRAAP session to acquaint the team with where the process begins and ends. There is good reason to require that a visual diagram or an information flow model be part of the FRAAP. The neural-linguistic programming is

a study of how people learn. This process has identified three basic ways in which people learn:

- *Auditory* — These people have to hear something to grasp it. During the FRAAP the owner will present the project scope statement to the team, and those that learn in this manner will be fulfilled.
- *Mechanical* — This learning type must write down the element to be learned. Those taking notes during meetings are typically mechanical learners.
- *Visual* — This type of learner, of which I am one, needs to see a picture or diagram to understand what is being discussed. People that learn via this method normally have white boards in their office and use them often. So the visual diagram or model will help these people understand what is being reviewed.

4. *Establish the FRAAP team* — A typical FRAAP has between 15 and 30 members. The team is made up of representatives from a number of business and infrastructure and business support areas. We discussed FRAAP team makeup earlier in this chapter.

5. *Meeting mechanics* — This is the business unit manager's meeting, and he or she is responsible for scheduling the room, setting the risk assessment time, and having the appropriate materials (overhead, flip charts, coffee and doughnuts) on hand. This risk assessment meeting is the responsibility of the owner. As the facilitator, you are assisting the owner in completing this task. It is not an information security, project management, audit, or risk management meeting. It is the owner's meeting, and that person is responsible for scheduling the place and inviting the team.

6. *Agreement on definitions* — The pre-FRAAP session is where the agreement on FRAAP definitions is completed. You will want to agree on the definitions of the review elements (integrity, confidentiality, availability). In addition to the review elements, it will be necessary to agree on the items in Table 6.17.

During the pre-FRAAP session, it will be important to discuss the process for prioritizing the threats. When examining the probability and impact of threats, it will be necessary to determine before the meeting if the threats are to be examined as if no controls were in place. This is typically the case when doing a risk assessment on an infrastructure resource. These resources include the information processing network, the operating system platform, and even the information security program.

For other applications, systems, and business processes, the examination of threats takes into account existing controls. When we discuss the

Table 6.17   Pre-FRAAP Meeting Definitions

Term	Definition
Threat	Potential events that have a negative impact on the business objectives or mission statement of the enterprise
Control	Measures taken to prevent, detect, reduce, or eliminate risk to the business objectives or mission statement of the enterprise
Integrity	Information is as intended, without unauthorized or undesirable modification or corruption
Confidentiality	Information has not undergone unauthorized or undesirable disclosure
Availability	Protection from unauthorized attempts to withhold information or computer resources
Probability	Chance that an event will occur or that a specific loss value may be attained should the event occur
High	Very likely that the threat will occur within the next year
Medium	Possible that the threat may occur within the next year
Low	Highly unlikely that the threat will occur within the next year
Impact	A measure of the magnitude of loss or harm on the value of an asset
High	Entire mission or business impacted
Medium	Loss is limited to single business unit or objective
Low	Business as usual

FRAAP session, we will examine each of these methods and how they work. This decision should be made during the pre-FRAAP meeting. Once the risk assessment process has been established, this discussion will not be necessary, as the organization will standardize the risk level protocol.

Table 6.18 is an example of a checklist that can be used during the pre-FRAAP meeting. By completing this checklist, the elements for the project scope statement will be nearly complete. Two of the key elements contained in the checklist that must be part of the project scope statement are the categories of *assumptions* and *constraints*. It is important that we understand what these are and how they impact the risk assessment process.

Table 6.18   Pre-FRAAP Meeting Checklist

Issue	Remarks
Prior to the Meeting	
Date of pre-FRAAP meeting Record when and where the meeting is scheduled.	
Project leader Identify the individual who is the primary point of contact for the project or asset under review.	
Project executive sponsor or owner Identify the owner or sponsor who has executive responsibility for the project.	
Pre-FRAAP meeting objective Identify what you hope to gain from the meeting.	
Assumptions Identify assumptions used in developing the approach to performing the FRAAP project.	
Project overview Prepare a project overview for presentation to the pre-FRAAP members during the meeting.	
Your understanding of the project scope	
The FRAAP methodology	
Milestones	
Prescreening methodology	
During the Meeting	
Business strategy, goals, and objectives Identify what the owner's objectives are and how they relate to larger company objectives.	

Table 6.18   Pre-FRAAP Meeting Checklist (continued)

Issue	Remarks
Project scope Define specifically the scope of the project and document it during the meeting so that all participating will know and agree.	
Applications/systems	
Business processes	
Business functions	
People and organizations	
Locations/facilities	
Time dependencies Identify time limitations and considerations the client may have.	
Risks/constraints Identify risks and constraints that could affect the successful conclusion of the project.	
Budget Identify any open budget/funding issues.	
FRAAP participants Identify by name and position the individuals whose participation in the FRAAP session is required.	
Administrative requirements Identify facility and/or equipment needs to perform the FRAAP session.	
Documentation Identify what documentation is required to prepare for the FRAAP session (provide the client with the FRAAP document checklist).	

I have a client that brings me in from time to time to conduct FRAAP refresher training for employees. This allows the employees who have taken the training before to be exposed to new ideas and concepts and other employees to be exposed to the process for the first time. Typically, this process is done over three or four days. It consists of a day and a half of training, and then the afternoon of day 2 the pre-FRAAP meeting is conducted. The following day the FRAAP session is conducted, and then that afternoon and the following day I work with the project leader and the facilitator to complete the risk assessment documentation.

On the afternoon of day 1, the project leader and his backup informed me that they had a meeting to attend and would be back the following day. Not only did they miss the afternoon training of day 1, but they also did not return for any of the day 2 training. On the afternoon of day 2 the attendees that were there decided to try and put together a project scope statement. The audience was almost exclusively information security and audit professionals. The scope statement lacked the business side, but at least we were able to be ready for the following day. Because of the team makeup, we did not address assumptions or constraints.

On the day of the FRAAP session the project leaders returned with the owner. This was the first time the owner had ever been exposed to a risk assessment process. We presented them with the scope statement that we had created, and the owner said that it looked OK to her. So after a brief introduction and an overview of the methodology, we began the process of identifying threats. After two hours or so the team had identified nearly 150 threats. As we were working through the FRAAP session I noticed that the owner's face had initially turned red and at the break was now white. I approached her to see if there was a problem. She informed me that the system was going to production on the following Monday and there was no way she could tell her bosses that 150 threats were uncovered.

During the break I thought about what had transpired, and when she came back I sat down with her to review the scope statement and to fill in the assumption area. A number of the threats identified were directly related to elements within the information security program, threats such as:

■ Passwords being posted on workstations
■ Employees leaving workstations logged on and unattended
■ Employees leaving work materials out after hours
■ Shoulder surfing passwords or other access codes
■ Unauthorized access to restricted areas

Although these were important threats, they were already addressed in the risk assessment conducted on the information security infrastructure previously and were not unique to the specific application under review. By modifying the assumptions section of the scope statement to include a reference to the fact that it was assumed that a risk assessment had been conducted on the information security infrastructure and that compensating controls were in place or were being implemented. We also addressed the processing infrastructure and applications development methodology in the same manner. By making sure the assumptions were properly identified, we reduced the number of threats from 150 to about 30.

The FRAAP was not diminished in any way. The 120 or so threats that were exorcized from the risk assessment report had already been identified in the infrastructure risk assessments and were being acted upon. If other risk assessments have been conducted, then enter that information into the assumptions area.

If the infrastructure risk assessments have not been conducted, then enter that information into the constraints area. This will allow the risk assessment to concentrate on the specific asset at hand, but puts the organization on notice that other risk assessments must be scheduled.

Other constraints might include concerns about the use of an obsolete operating system — those that are no longer supported by the manufacturer. The back level of patch application might also be a constraint to identify.

Assumptions and constraints allow the risk assessment team to focus on the asset at hand. The organization must conduct the other risk assessments to make certain that the infrastructure is as secure as possible.

6.4.7.2 Pre-FRAAP Summary

The pre-FRAAP meeting sets the stage for the FRAAP session and all of the work that is to follow. It is vital that all six of the deliverables be as complete as possible. As we have seen above, if they are not complete, then the risk assessment process will be flawed.

The six pre-FRAAP meeting deliverables are listed in Table 6.19.

Table 6.19 Pre-FRAAP Deliverables

1. Prescreening results
2. Project scope statement
3. Visual model
4. Definitions
5. Team members
6. Meeting mechanics

6.4.8 The FRAAP Session

6.4.8.1 The FRAAP Session Stage 1

6.4.8.1.1 Overview

The FRAAP session is divided into two stages; the first generally is scheduled for four hours and normally has between 15 and 25 team members. Some government agencies have expanded the session to last as long as three days, but typically in the business sector and most government agencies, four hours is about all that any group of people can devote to such a process. The deliverables from the first stage are:

- Threats identified
- Risk level established
- Possible controls documented

When the deliverables are complete, the system users and some business area infrastructure personal can be excused. The remaining team members will complete the FRAAP session stage 2 by rendering three deliverables:

- Wherever they are present, existing controls are to be identified.
- Where a high-level threat has no existing control, the owner will select a control.
- For each new control selected, the team will identify the group or individual responsible for implementation of that control.

6.4.8.1.2 The FRAAP Session Introduction

Once the FRAAP session is called together, the executive responsible for the asset under review will address the team with opening remarks. This overview will help the team members understand why they were asked to be part of the FRAAP and how important senior management considers the risk assessment process to be. When the overview is complete, the facilitator will present the agenda to the team. A typical agenda might include those items listed in Table 6.20.

The facilitator will explain the FRAAP to the team. This will include a discussion on the deliverables expected from each stage of the process. With the assistance of the facilitator, the team will identify threats to the asset under review. Using a formula of probability and impact, the team will then affix a risk level to each threat, and finally, the team will select possible controls to reduce the risk intensity to an acceptable level.

Table 6.20   FRAAP Session Agenda

FRAAP Session Agenda	Responsibility
Explain the FRAAP	Facilitator
Review scope statement	Owner
Review visual diagram	Technical support
Discuss definitions	Facilitator
Review objectives Identify threats Establish risk levels Identify possible safeguards	Facilitator
Identify roles and introduction	Team
Review session agreements	Facilitator

The business manager owner will then present the project scope statement. It will be important to discuss the assumptions and constraints identified in the statement. The team should have a copy of the scope statement so that it can refer to it as needed during the FRAAP session. The assumptions and constraints will be helpful in ensuring that the deliverables are as accurate as possible.

The technical support will then give a five-minute overview of the process using an information flow model or diagram. This will allow the team to visualize the process under review.

The facilitator will then review the term definitions to be used for this FRAAP session. Once the risk assessment process becomes part of the organization's culture, these definitions will become standard and the need for review will diminish. To expedite the process, the FRAAP session definitions should be included in the meeting notice.

The facilitator will then reiterate the objectives and deliverables of this initial stage. At this point stage 2 of this process should be briefly discussed. Notice that in the meeting it will be necessary to notify those individuals whose presence is required for stage 2 that they will be staying for an additional hour.

At this point the FRAAP team should introduce itself. Have each member introduce himself and provide the following information for the scribe to capture:

■ Team member name (first and last)
■ Department
■ Location
■ Phone number

Table 6.21   FRAAP Session Agreements

Everyone participates.
Stay within identified roles.
Stick to the agenda/current focus.
All ideas have equal value.
Listen to other points of view.
No "plops" — all issues are recorded.
Deferred issues will be recorded.
Post the idea before discussing it.
Help scribe ensure all issues are recorded.
Allow only one conversation at a time.
Allow only one angry person at a time.
Apply the three-minute rule.
Be prompt, fair, nice, creative, and have fun.

After the introductions, the facilitator will review the session agreements with the team members (Table 6.21).

When all of the preliminaries have been completed, the team is now ready to work the risk assessment process.

6.4.8.1.3 The FRAAP Threat Identification

When I conduct a FRAAP I like to have the room set up in a U shape. This allows me to work more closely with the team members and it allows the process to flow around a conference room table. By being set up in this manner, everyone is in the front row. If the room is set up classroom style, it is harder to get the people in the back to feel that they are part of the team.

In the room setup it is important to include pads of paper and pens or pencils for the team to use. The team will be writing down its ideas and it is always best to have the implements readily available, rather than taking time to try and find them.

During the FRAAP session I normally discourage the use of laptops or PDAs. The team has been called by the owner to assist him or her in meeting the owner's due diligence obligation. If the team members are busy answering e-mail or distracted by other activities, the risk assessment will suffer. I also request that all cell phones and pagers be placed on "stun," or vibrate, so as not to disturb the other team members.

To begin the brainstorming process, the facilitator will put the first review element up for the team to see. This will include the definition of the review element and some examples of threats that the team can use as thought starters. I normally use a PowerPoint slide (Figure 6.2) for this

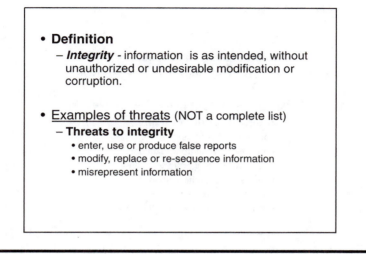

- **Definition**
  - *Integrity* - information is as intended, without unauthorized or undesirable modification or corruption.

- <u>Examples of threats</u> (NOT a complete list)
  - **Threats to integrity**
    - enter, use or produce false reports
    - modify, replace or re-sequence information
    - misrepresent information

Figure 6.2   FRAAP brainstorming definition 1.

process so that the entire team can see what it is that the FRAAP is trying to identify.

The team is given three to five minutes to write down threats that are of a concern. The facilitator will then go around the room getting one threat from each team member. Many will have more than one threat, but the process is to get one threat and then move to the next person. This way everyone gets a turn at participating. The process continues until everyone passes (that is, there are no more threats that the team can think of).

During the first two rounds most of the team members will participate. As the rounds progress, the number of team members with new threats will diminish. When it gets down to just a few still responding, you can just ask for a new threat from anyone rather than going around the table and calling on each person again.

If a person passes, it does not mean that he is then locked out of the round. If something new comes into his mind, then he can join back in when it is his turn to do so. This person may hear a threat from someone else that will jog his thought process. This is why I recommend that there be paper and pens available for the team members to write down these quick-hitting ideas. Most all of us suffer from terminal CRS (can't remember stuff). By providing paper and pens, the team members can capture these fleeting thoughts.

Unfortunately, to some people everything is a contest. Too often the brainstorming round will dwindle down to two team members. When this occurs, the battle to be "king of the threats" begins. They will continue

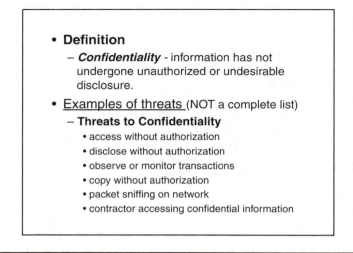

- **Definition**
  - *Confidentiality* - information has not undergone unauthorized or undesirable disclosure.
- <u>Examples of threats</u> (NOT a complete list)
  - **Threats to Confidentiality**
    - access without authorization
    - disclose without authorization
    - observe or monitor transactions
    - copy without authorization
    - packet sniffing on network
    - contractor accessing confidential information

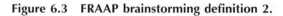

Figure 6.3   FRAAP brainstorming definition 2.

to throw out ever more absurd threats until one will finally yield. I share this with you only so that you can be on the alert for such behavior.

Once all of the integrity threats have been recorded, it is time for the facilitator to display the second review element with threat examples and give the team three to five minutes to write down threats (Figure 6.3).

During this phase I like to start the threat identification on the opposite side of the room from where I started last time. This allows those who were last to be first and get the best threats. The collecting of threats will continue until everyone has passed and there are no more confidentiality threats. After the scribe has indicated that everything has been captured, it will be time to go to the third element (Figure 6.4).

Once the threats have been recorded, the FRAAP documentation will look like Table 6.22.

When I am conducting a FRAAP session, I use different color pens for each element. Integrity might be blue, confidentiality green, and availability black. This will allow me to keep track of the threats by color coding them. As a flip chart page is filled up, I post it around the conference room. I record each threat sequentially within an element. For example, I will record all integrity threats in blue and number each threat in the order it was received, starting with threat one. When I move to confidentiality threats, I will switch to a green marker and start the numbering over again. I will do the same when I get to the availability threats.

When all the threats have been posted, I recommend that the team be given a 15-minute coffee break to do three important activities:

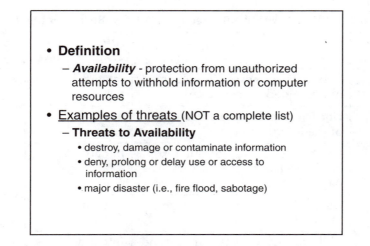

Figure 6.4   FRAAP brainstorming definition 3.

- Check messages
- Get rid of old coffee and get new
- Clean up the raw threats

As the team is having its break, have it review the threats and within the specific element delete duplicate threats and combine like threats. If a threat is repeated in the integrity and confidentiality elements, it is not considered to be a duplicate. It is only a duplicate if it appears more than once within a specific element. Only allow 15 minutes for this cleanup process.

6.4.8.1.4 FRAAP Session Risk Level Established

The establishment of the threat risk level is probably the most important and most difficult task to complete in the risk assessment process. All of the other activities that follow will be dependent on what the team does during this phase. To be successful, the team will have to understand what is being done and what caveats are being applied. In this example, the team will examine each threat as if there are no controls in place.

This caveat is normally applied to risk assessments that are conducted against infrastructure assets. That is a risk assessment of the network, operations processing environment, applications development methodology, information security controls, or platforms.

Table 6.22   FRAAP Worksheet after Threats Have Been Identified

Threat Number	Threat	Review Element	Risk Level	Possible Control
1	Information accessed by personnel not intended to have access	Integrity		
2	Unclear or nonexistent versioning of the information	Integrity		
3	Database could be corrupted by hardware failure or incorrect or bad software	Integrity		
4	Data could be corrupted by an incomplete transaction	Integrity		
5	Ability to change data in transit and then change it back to cover the activity	Integrity		
6	A failure to report integrity issues	Integrity		
7	Incompletely run process or failure to run a process that could corrupt the data	Integrity		
8	Lack of internal processes to create and control, and manage data across functions	Integrity		
9	No notification of integrity problems	Integrity		
10	Information being used in the wrong context	Integrity		

The team will consider each threat in turn and will examine the threat based first on the likelihood that it will occur using definitions like those in Table 6.23.

The team will discuss how likely the threat is to occur during the specified time frame. The groups that are going to have the most problem with discussing threats occurring with no controls in place will be those groups that have in-depth knowledge of the existing controls. Typically, these will be network administration, database administration, change control, or information security.

Examining threats in this manner allows the organization to establish a baseline of risk. Once this is calculated, the team can examine existing controls to determine how effective those controls are in reducing risk. When you are facilitating this process, it will be necessary to remind the

Table 6.23   FRAAP Probability Definitions

Term	Definition
Probability	Chance that an event will occur or that a specific loss value may be attained should the event occur
High	Very likely that the threat will occur within the next year
Medium	Possible that the threat may occur within the next year
Low	Highly unlikely that the threat will occur within the next year

Table 6.24   FRAAP Impact Definitions

Term	Definition
Impact	A measure of the magnitude of loss or harm on the value of an asset
High	Entire mission or business impacted
Medium	Loss is limited to single business unit or objective
Low	Business as usual

IT people of the caveat and be watchful for those who push back and appear to stop participating.

In this example, after the probability has been established, the team will determine the impact if the threat were it to occur with no controls in place. The team would use impact definitions such as the ones in Table 6.24.

Having established the probability and impact level, the team will look at the risk level matrix (Figure 6.5) and establish the risk level for that threat.

As in the matrices we have examined in the past, the team will look to see where the probability level and impact level intersect and enter this information onto the FRAAP worksheet (Table 6.25).

In the next chapter we will examine variations on the FRAAP theme and will look at how the FRAAP can be used with existing controls in place. For now, we have established the risk levels based on the concept that no controls are in place.

6.4.8.1.5 FRAAP Control Selection

The final process in the FRAAP session is to identify controls for those threats identified as having a high risk level. In our example, those would

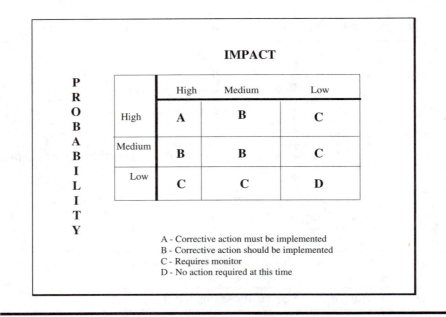

Figure 6.5 FRAAP risk level matrix.

be anything identified as having a risk level of A or B. A sample controls list should be sent out to all team members with the meeting notice and copies should be available for the team during the FRAAP session.

During this step, the risk assessment team will determine which security controls could generally best reduce the threat risk level to a more acceptable level. There are a number of sources for standards that can assist the risk assessment team in establishing an effective set of controls. These sources might include some of the following:

- "Information Technology: Code of Practice for Information Security Management" (ISO 17799)
- "Security Technologies for Manufacturing and Control Systems" (ISA-TR99.00.01-2004)
- "Integrating Electronic Security into Manufacturing and Control Systems Environment" (ISA-TR99.00.02-2004)
- Federal Information Processing Standards Publications (FIPS Pubs)
- National Institute of Standards and Technology
- CobiT® Security Baseline
- Health Insurance Portability and Accountability Act (HIPAA)
- The Basel Accords
- Privacy Act of 1974
- Gramm–Leach–Bliley Act (GLBA)

Table 6.25   FRAAP Worksheet after Risk Level Has Been Established

Threat Number	Threat	Review Element	Risk Level	Possible Control
1	Information accessed by personnel not intended to have access	Integrity	B	
2	Unclear or nonexistent versioning of the information	Integrity	B	
3	Database could be corrupted by hardware failure or incorrect or bad software	Integrity	D	
4	Data could be corrupted by an incomplete transaction	Integrity	C	
5	Ability to change data in transit and then change it back to cover the activity	Integrity	C	
6	A failure to report integrity issues	Integrity	A	
7	Incompletely run process or failure to run a process that could corrupt the data	Integrity	B	
8	Lack of internal processes to create and control, and manage data across functions	Integrity	A	
9	No notification of integrity problems	Integrity	A	
10	Information being used in the wrong context	Integrity	B	

- Sarbanes–Oxley Act (SOX)
- "Information Security for Banking and Finance" (ISO/TR 13569)
- FFEIC examination guidelines

For this example, we will be using a set of controls based on the IT organizations and groups that support the business processes. There are 34 controls that the team can select from (Table 6.26). It is not necessary to try to select the one perfect control at this time. Remember, one of the goals of risk assessment is to record all of the alternatives that were considered.

Table 6.26 IT Organizations and Groups That Support the Business Processes

Control Number	IT Group	Descriptor	Definition
1	Operations controls	Backup	Backup requirements will be determined and communicated to operations, including a request that an electronic notification that backups were completed be sent to the application system administrator. Operations will be requested to test the backup procedures.
2	Operations controls	Recovery plan	Develop, document, and test recovery procedures designed to ensure that the application and information can be recovered, using the backups created, in the event of loss.
3	Operations controls	Risk analysis	Conduct a risk analysis to determine the level of exposure to identified threats, and identify possible safeguards or controls.
4	Operations controls	Antivirus	(1) Ensure that the local area network (LAN) administrator installs the corporate standard antiviral software on all computers. (2) Training and awareness of virus prevention techniques will be incorporated into the organization's information protection (IP) program.
5	Operations controls	Interface dependencies	Systems that feed information will be identified and communicated to operations to stress the impact to the functionality if these feeder applications are unavailable.

Table 6.26   IT Organizations and Groups That Support the Business Processes (continued)

Control Number	IT Group	Descriptor	Definition
6	Operations controls	Maintenance	Time requirements for technical maintenance will be tracked and a request for adjustment will be communicated to management if experience warrants.
7	Operations controls	Service level agreement	Acquire service level agreements to establish level of customer expectations and assurances from supporting operations.
8	Operations controls	Maintenance	Acquire maintenance and supplier agreements to facilitate the continued operational status of the application.
9	Operations controls	Change management	Production migration controls, such as search and remove processes, to ensure data stores are clean.
10	Operations controls	Business impact analysis	A formal business impact analysis will be conducted to determine the asset's relative criticality with other enterprise assets.
11	Operations controls	Backup	Training for a backup to the system administrator will be provided and duties rotated between them to ensure the adequacy of the training program.
12	Operations controls	Backup	A formal employee security awareness program has been implemented and is updated and presented to the employees at least on an annual basis.
13	Operations controls	Recovery plan	Implement a mechanism to limit access to confidential information to specific network paths or physical locations.

Table 6.26 IT Organizations and Groups That Support the Business Processes (continued)

Control Number	IT Group	Descriptor	Definition
14	Operations controls	Risk analysis	Implement user authentication mechanisms (such as firewalls, dial-in controls, secure ID) to limit access to authorized personnel.
15	Application controls	Application control	Design and implement application controls (data entry edit checking, fields requiring validation, alarm indicators, password expiration capabilities, checksums) to ensure the integrity, confidentiality, and availability of application information.
16	Application controls	Acceptance testing	Develop testing procedures to be followed during applications development and during modifications to the existing application that include user participation and acceptance.
17	Application controls	Training	Implement user programs (user performance evaluations) designed to encourage compliance with policies and procedures in place to ensure the appropriate utilization of the application.
18	Application controls	Training	Application developers will provide documentation, guidance, and support to the operations staff (operations) in implementing mechanisms to ensure that the transfer of information between applications is secure.
19	Application controls	Corrective strategies	The development team will develop corrective strategies such as reworked processes, revised application logic, etc.

Table 6.26   IT Organizations and Groups That Support the Business Processes (continued)

Control Number	IT Group	Descriptor	Definition
20	Security controls	Policy	Develop policies and procedures to limit access and operating privileges to those with business need.
21	Security controls	Training	User training will include instruction and documentation on the proper use of the application. The importance of maintaining the confidentiality of user accounts, passwords, and the confidential and competitive nature of information will be stressed.
22	Security controls	Review	Implement mechanisms to monitor, report, and audit activities identified as requiring independent reviews, including periodic reviews of user IDs to ascertain and verify business need.
23	Security controls	Asset classification	The asset under review will be classified using enterprise policies, standards, and procedures on asset classification.
24	Security controls	Access control	Mechanisms to protect the database against unauthorized access, and modifications made from outside the application, will be determined and implemented.
25	Security controls	Management support	Request management support to ensure the cooperation and coordination of various business units.
26	Security controls	Proprietary	Processes are in place to ensure that company proprietary assets are protected and that the company is in compliance with all third-party license agreements.

Table 6.26 IT Organizations and Groups That Support the Business Processes (continued)

Control Number	IT Group	Descriptor	Definition
27	Security controls	Security awareness	Implement an access control mechanism to prevent unauthorized access to information. This mechanism will include the capability of detecting, logging, and reporting attempts to breach the security of this information.
28	Security controls	Access control	Implement encryption mechanisms (data, end to end) to prevent unauthorized access to protect the integrity and confidentiality of information.
29	Security controls	Access control	Adhere to a change management process designed to facilitate a structured approach to modifications of the application, to ensure appropriate steps and precautions are followed. Emergency modifications should be included in this process.
30	Security controls	Access control	Control procedures are in place to ensure that appropriate system logs are reviewed by independent third parties to review system update activities.
31	Security controls	Access control	In consultation with facilities management, facilitate the implementation of physical security controls designed to protect the information, software, and hardware required of the system.

Table 6.26   IT Organizations and Groups That Support the Business Processes (continued)

Control Number	IT Group	Descriptor	Definition
32	Systems controls	Change management	Backup requirements will be determined and communicated to operations, including a request that an electronic notification that backups were completed be sent to the application system administrator. Operations will be requested to test the backup procedures.
33	Systems controls	Monitor system logs	Develop, document, and test recovery procedures designed to ensure that the application and information can be recovered, using the backups created, in the event of loss.
34	Physical security	Physical security	Conduct a risk analysis to determine the level of exposure to identified threats and identify possible safeguards or controls.

The team will be selecting controls for only those threats that registered as high risks (those with A or B levels). Those threats with a risk level of C will be monitored for change, and those with a D level require no action at this time (Table 6.27). All possible controls are to be entered into the FRAAP worksheet.

The FRAAP team must understand that a trade-off must be made between business objectives and controls. Every control or safeguard will impact the business process in some manner as resources are expended to implement the control. Accidents, errors, and omissions generally account for more losses than deliberate acts. No control can or should be 100% effective. The ultimate goal is to achieve an acceptable level of security.

The FRAAP will not eliminate every threat. Management has the duty to determine which threats it will implement controls on and which ones to accept. The FRAAP team is to assist management in making that informed business decision.

The FRAAP session stage 1 is complete when the three deliverables are finished. Those three steps are:

Table 6.27   FRAAP Worksheet with Controls Identified

Threat Number	Threat	Review Element	Risk Level	Possible Control
1	Information accessed by personnel not intended to have access	Integrity	B	3, 5, 6, 11, 12, 16
2	Unclear or nonexistent versioning of the information	Integrity	B	9, 13, 26
3	Database could be corrupted by hardware failure or incorrect or bad software	Integrity	D	
4	Data could be corrupted by an incomplete transaction	Integrity	C	
5	Ability to change data in transit and then change it back to cover the activity	Integrity	C	
6	A failure to report integrity issues	Integrity	A	7, 11–13, 20, 21
7	Incompletely run process or failure to run a process that could corrupt the data	Integrity	B	1, 2, 12–15, 18, 20, 21, 25
8	Lack of internal processes to create and control, and manage data across functions	Integrity	A	7, 13, 17, 20, 23, 25
9	No notification of integrity problems	Integrity	A	7, 13, 26
10	Information being used in the wrong context	Integrity	B	11, 12, 19

- Threats identified
- Risk level established
- Possible controls identified

6.4.8.2 The FRAAP Session Stage 2

The stage 2 process will require a subset of the risk assessment team. The stage 2 members are the owner, the project leader, and the infrastructure support personnel. This stage will take one to two hours and will have three deliverables. For any threats with a risk level of A or B, the stage 2 the team will:

- Identify existing controls
- Identify a control for any high-level threat with no existing control
- Identify the department, group, or individual who will be responsible for implementing the new control

In the column where the responsible person is identified, if the control is already in place, use the term *complete* to denote this (Table 6.28).

This process will take one to two hours but will save three to five days in the post-FRAAP. By taking the time to identify what controls are already in place, the number of open items will typically be reduced by nearly 75 percent. The one to two hours will then be reduced once this process has been practiced a few times.

6.4.8.3 FRAAP Session Summary

At this point, the FRAAP session is complete. The team was given an overview of the risk assessment process and what will be expected of its members. The owner then discussed the scope of the risk assessment, and a technical support person reviewed the information flow model. The facilitator then walked the team through the review elements (integrity, confidentiality, and availability). Once all threats were identified and recorded, the team took a few minutes to edit and consolidate the threats. Once the consolidation was complete, the team examined each threat for probability of occurrence and then impact to the business process. The team examined each threat as if there were no controls in place. One the risk levels were established, the team used a list of possible controls and identified all those that could reduce the threat risk to an acceptable level.

At this point, the stage 1 phase of the FRAAP session was complete, and the infrastructure team with the owner stayed on to complete stage 2 of the FRAAP session. This group identified existing controls for all high-level threats. Once this was complete, the owner with the help of the infrastructure team selected a compensating control for all open high-level threats. For each of these controls the team also identified the entity that would be responsible for implementation of the control.

When this process is complete, the FRAAP session is complete and the meeting is adjourned. A total of six deliverables come out of the FRAAP sessions.

- Stage 1
  - Threats identified
  - Risk levels established
  - Possible controls noted

Table 6.28   FRAAP Session Stage 2 Worksheet 4

Threat Number	Threat	Possible Control	Risk Level	Existing Controls or Selected Control	Responsible Person
1	Information accessed by personnel not intended to have access	3, 5, 6, 11, 12, 16	B	Access controls lists to be reviewed quarterly	Owner
2	Unclear or nonexistent versioning of the information	9, 13, 26	B	Production migration controls, such as search and remove processes, to ensure data stores are clean	Production control
3	Database could be corrupted by hardware failure or incorrect or bad software		D		
4	Data could be corrupted by an incomplete transaction		C		
5	Ability to change data in transit and then change it back to cover the activity		C		
6	A failure to report integrity issues	7, 11–13, 20, 21	A	A formal employee security awareness program has been implemented and is updated and presented to the employees at least on an annual basis	Complete

7	Incompletely run process or failure to run a process that could corrupt the data	1, 2, 12–15, 18, 20, 21, 25	B	Design and implement application controls (data entry edit checking, fields requiring validation, alarm indicators, password expiration capabilities, checksums) to ensure the integrity, confidentiality, and availability of application information	Applications development
8	Lack of internal processes to create and control, and manage data across functions	7, 13, 17, 20, 23, 25	A	Acquire service level agreements to establish level of customer expectations and assurances from supporting operations	IT operations
9	No notification of integrity problems	7, 13, 26	A	A formal employee security awareness program has been implemented and is updated and presented to the employees at least on an annual basis	Complete
10	Information being used in the wrong context	11, 12, 19	B	A formal employee security awareness program has been implemented and is updated and presented to the employees at least on an annual basis	Complete

■ Stage 2
  – Existing controls identified
  – Controls for open high-level risks selected
  – Responsible person or entity identified

6.4.9 The Post-FRAAP

Just as the 30-minute risk analysis is a misnomer, so is the concept that the FRAAP can be completed in four hours. As we have seen, the pre-FRAAP meeting takes an hour and the FRAAP session will take around four hours. These two together are only the information-gathering portion of the risk analysis process. The standard rule of thumb is that for every hour of information gathering, allow four to five hours for analysis and reporting writing.

This phase of the FRAAP generates the reports that will establish what the risk assessment accomplished and how management performed its required due diligence. During this phase the facilitator and the owner will work to assemble the risk assessment action plan. This plan will include all of the deliverables from the FRAAP session stages 1 and 2:

■ Threats identified
■ Risk levels established
■ Possible controls noted
■ Existing controls identified
■ Controls for open threats selected
■ Responsible persons or departments documented

This information will be combined with the examination of the control costs, and a final report will emerge. The post-FRAAP has three deliverables:

■ Time frames to implement controls established
■ Management summary report
■ Controls cross-reference sheet

We will examine each of the deliverables from this phase of the FRAAP.

6.4.9.1 Complete Action Plan

When the FRAAP session stage 2 was finished the worksheet contained the information in Table 6.29.

Table 6.29   FRAAP Session Worksheet 4

Threat Number	Threat	Possible Control	Risk Level	Existing Controls or Selected Control	Responsible Person
1	Information accessed by personnel not intended to have access	3, 5, 6, 11, 12, 16	B	Access controls lists to be reviewed quarterly	Owner
2	Unclear or nonexistent versioning of the information	9, 13, 26	B	Production migration controls, such as search and remove processes, to ensure data stores are clean	Production control
3	Database could be corrupted by hardware failure or incorrect or bad software		D		
4	Data could be corrupted by an incomplete transaction		C		
5	Ability to change data in transit and then change it back to cover the activity		C		
6	A failure to report integrity issues	7, 11–13, 20, 21	A	A formal employee security awareness program has been implemented and is updated and presented to the employees at least on an annual basis	Complete

Table 6.29 FRAAP Session Worksheet 4

Threat Number	Threat	Possible Control	Risk Level	Existing Controls or Selected Control	Responsible Person
7	Incompletely run process or failure to run a process that could corrupt the data	1, 2, 12–15, 18, 20, 21, 25	B	Design and implement application controls (data entry edit checking, fields requiring validation, alarm indicators, password expiration capabilities, checksums) to ensure the integrity, confidentiality, and availability of application information	Applications development
8	Lack of internal processes to create and control, and manage data across functions	7, 13, 17, 20, 23, 25	A	Acquire service level agreements to establish level of customer expectations and assurances from supporting operations	IT operations
9	No notification of integrity problems	7, 13, 26	A	A formal employee security awareness program has been implemented and is updated and presented to the employees at least on an annual basis	Complete
10	Information being used in the wrong context	11, 12, 19	B	A formal employee security awareness program has been implemented and is updated and presented to the employees at least on an annual basis	Complete

Table 6.30 FRAAP Action Plan

Threat Number	Risk Level	Owner Selected Action	Responsible Group	Due Date	Additional Comments
1	B	ACF2 has been implemented and the access controls list will be reviewed to identify authorized users	Owner and information protection (IP)	7/15/2004	
2	B	Change management procedures already in place	Operations	Complete	
3	D				
4	C				
5	C				
6	A	Employee training sessions scheduled	HR	8/15/2004	
7	B	Backup SLA to be reviewed with operations	Owner and operations	7/31/2004	
8	A	SLA with service provider to be implemented	Owner	8/20/2004	
9	A	SLA with service provider to be implemented	Owner	8/20/2004	
10	B	Train users on proper use of data	Owner/information security	9/28/2004	

This information contained in the worksheets will be used to complete the action plan (Table 6.30). This will include either the agreed upon implementation date of the control or that management has decided to accept the risk. This last item is one of the hardest things for information security, audit, and risk management professionals to accept. Our goals are to provide the highest level of security as possible. Management, however, must examine all of the elements and at times must select the option of going with the threat. This decision could be made because the compensating controls are too costly, or there is not a workable solution, or the impact to the business process would be too great a burden. Whatever the reason, the risk assessment process has been established to provide management with the information needed to make an informed business decision. If, after going through the risk assessment process, management decides to accept the threat risk level, then that meets the elements of performing due diligence.

If management decides to accept a threat that has been identified with a high risk level, I note that in the comments section of the action plan. I like to highlight the specific threat in a specific color, such as red, or shaded, as in Table 6.31.

During the risk assessment process it may become clear that an existing control is not working the way the organization expected it to. If this comes to light, it is important to make note of the deficiencies in the action plan (Table 6.32). This is typically done by using the comments section and identifying the need to have a vulnerability assessment performed on the existing control.

6.4.9.2 FRAAP Management Summary Report

As with any process, a management summary report must be generated that will encapsulate the findings of the process in a brief document. The management summary report will provide an overview of the risk assessment findings and is used to supplement the full findings documentation. This report is sectioned off into six key areas:

- Assessment team members
- Management summary
- Assessment methodology used
- Assessment findings and action plan
- Full findings documentation
- Conclusion

I like to begin any report to management with a listing of all of those who participated in the process. Over my almost 40 years in the business of information processing, management always seems to want to know

Table 6.31   FRAAP Action Plan Example 1 (Management Accepts Risks)

Threat Number	Risk Level	Owner Selected Action	Responsible Group	Due Date	Additional Comments
1	B	ACF2 has been implemented and access controls list will be reviewed to identify authorized users.	Owner and IP	Accept risk	Management has determined that accepting the risk is in the best interest of the organization.

Table 6.32   FRAAP Action Plan Example 2 (Control Requires Vulnerability Assessments)

Threat Number	Risk Level	Owner Selected Action	Responsible Group	Due Date	Additional Comments
2	B	Change management procedures already in place.	Operations	Complete	Change management process needs to be reviewed to determine if it is meeting the needs of the organization. A vulnerability assessment is suggested.

Table 6.33 Assessment Team Attendance

Assessment Team	Gilbert Godfried	Nicole Kidmann
	Katherine Turner	Lloyd Nolan
	Bill Aikman	Liane Bronco
	Leonard Elmore	Gerry Lee
	Myra Osmond	Melvinia Nattia
	Mike Illich	Ryan Harris
	Wayne Fontes	MaryJane Ashman
	Linda Wright	
Facilitator	U.R. Name	
Scribe	Lisa Bryson	

who was part of the team. So in most of my reports the first item I include is a list of who attended (Table 6.33).

Depending on the culture of an organization, the attendance list can include those that were invited but did not attend. This is something that can help make a point, but it can also help to make an enemy. If you are going to use this option, it might be better to use the phrase "unable to attend."

After who was part of the team has been established, it is important to verify what was done. In a paragraph or two, identify what the topic of the risk assessment was. Be as detailed as necessary to establish how it was determined what was to be reviewed. This would include references to any reports, audits, or other documents that were used to establish a clear project scope statement for the risk assessment.

Table 6.34 is a sample of what the scope summary would look like.

The third section of the management summary report is a brief discussion on the methodology used to perform the risk assessment. Remember that the reports are historical documents and anything that can help someone later on will be beneficial to establishing how the risk assessment was conducted. Typically, this section would be only one or two paragraphs explaining the methodology used during the risk assessment. Although it is important to be brief and to the point, it is also important to state precisely what was used and how it was completed. This might look like Table 6.35.

The meat of the report comes next — the findings. It will be necessary to keep this information as high level as possible, but enough detail must be included to allow management to grasp what the major issues are and what course of action must be taken.

Table 6.34 Management Summary Scope Statement

Scope Summary
On October 23, 2004, the GLBA Bank (GLBA) risk assessment team and Peltier and Associates met to review the scope of a risk assessment to be conducted on nonpublic personal customer information held and processed at GLBA. The team discussed the most recent Office of the Comptroller of the Currency (OCC) examination of GLBA. The team also reviewed the December 21, 2003, Visioneering, Inc. (VI) information system audit; the Gross Technology Partners (GTP) November 18, 2003, penetration test and network vulnerability assessment report; and the GLBA internal audit report of November 30, 2003. The findings of these reviews, assessments, and audits were used to develop a risk assessment scope statement.
On October 24, 2004, GLBA staff at 45 North Main Avenue, Buzzover, UT, conducted the risk assessment. The intent of this process was to identify threats that could signify risk to the integrity, confidentiality, and availability of nonpublic personal customer information held and processed by GLBA.
Fifteen GLBA employees participated in the process. These employees represented a variety of users with a broad range of expertise and knowledge of GLBA operations and business processes. The various bank areas represented helped support a multidisciplinary and knowledge-based approach to the risk assessment process. These employees were asked to participate within a candid, reflective atmosphere so that a thorough and clear representation of GLBA's potential business risks to customer information could be developed.

I usually start this section off with a statistical breakdown of the risk assessment findings: total number of threats identified and then the percentage of those threats that were categorized as moderate to low. Of the remaining percentage, identify those that were categorized as moderately high and high.

By combining similar threats, you will be able to present your findings in an easy-to-read table (Table 6.36).

From this table identify the highest number of similar threats and what the course of action is going to be. That might look like Table 6.37.

Once the findings have been established, the next section should reference where the reader can obtain a copy of the full findings of the risk assessment.

Finally, the management summary report wraps up with the conclusion section. State your conclusions as to the quality of the risk assessment process. In this section, make certain to identify any threats or concerns that need special attention. Include any controls that might require a vulnerability assessment.

Table 6.35   Management Summary Report Methodology

Assessment Methodology
The Facilitated Risk Analysis and Assessment Process (FRAAP) was created by Peltier and Associates in 1993. The FRAAP was received within the information security industry through its inclusion as a course in the 1995 Computer Security Institute's calendar of classes. The FRAAP was further promoted in the industry upon publication of the book *Information Security Risk Analysis* by Auerbach Publications/CRC Press. The General Accounting Office (GAO) reviewed the FRAAP in 1998 and issued in May 1998 the "Executive Guide for Information Security Management" (GAO/AIMD 98-68). This executive guide supplemented the Office of Management and Budget revision of Circular A-130, Appendix III, recommending qualitative risk analysis for government agencies.
FRAAP is consistent with the National Institute of Standards and Technology October 2001 Special Publication "Risk Management Guide of Information Technology Systems" and the FFIEC December 2002 "Information Security Risk Assessment."
A senior facilitator led the process, assisted by GLBA information security personnel. Participants were asked to identify risks to the availability, confidentiality, and integrity of customer information held and processed by GLBA bank.
All risks were reviewed and consolidated to eliminate redundancy. All risks were then examined to determine if an existing control or safeguard was in place at GLBA. Typically, the examination of existing controls is conducted after the risk level has been established. Due to time constraints, these steps were transposed to effect a more streamlined, accelerated risk assessment process.
Participants were asked to rate each risk in terms of probability of occurrence (high, medium, and low), and then business impact (high, medium, low). The GLBA risk assessment team, with assistance from Peltier and Associates, examined the controls identified to determine whether existing controls were adequate. Low-criticality items are not included in final counts summarized in the assessment findings, as they are normally deferred to a "monitor" status in final recommendations.

A sample management summary report is included in the appendices of this book.

6.4.9.3 Cross-Reference Report

To assist in the cost–benefit analysis, a way must be developed to show which controls can have the biggest effect on the identified threats. The

Table 6.36 Management Summary Risk Levels

Risk Level	Number of Similar Threats	Description of Threat Scenario
A	4	Physical intrusion
A	2	Power failure
B	10	Information handling and classification
B	4	Password weakness or sharing
B	4	People masquerading as customers
B	3	Firewall concerns
B	2	Computer viruses
B	2	Workstations left unattended
B	2	Employee training
B	27	Individual threats identified

cross-reference sheet is one of those ways. Initially, the cross-reference sheet took each control and then cut and pasted each of the threats that selected that specific control. Table 6.38 is an example of what one control and the threats that selected it might look like.

When we first began using the FRAAP methodology we were using an Excel spreadsheet, and so the cross-reference document had to be done via cut and paste. Two of my facilitators came to me one day and said the FRAAP was not working. So I called a team meeting to discuss what went wrong. I asked them to present their latest risk assessment reports. We reviewed the scope statement, the action plan, the definitions list, and the controls sheet, and there was nothing. I asked them about the cross-reference sheet and they looked at me and asked, "What cross-reference sheet?"

It turned out that they did not like to cut and paste, so they eliminated that portion of the report. I had them complete the cross-reference sheets and provide them to their clients along with the other documentation, and then ask the clients what was the most beneficial portion of the risk assessment documentation. Both clients identified the cross-reference sheets as most important. It allowed clients to see which control would give them the biggest return on their investment.

My two facilitators then created an Access database that automatically creates the cross-reference documentation. Being a low-tech kind of guy, I came up with an alternative. I took the controls list and added a number in parenthesis that indicated how many threats selected that control. The report was included in the management summary report and looked like Table 6.39.

Table 6.37 Management Summary Report Action Plan

Threat	Action Plan
1. Restricted physical access areas should be considered throughout GLBA.	A physical security risk assessment will be conducted to determine if there is a need to create restricted access areas or increase physical access controls.
2. Power failure could cause corruption of information or prevent access to the system.	Network uninterruptible power supply (UPS) may not be adequate for a power outage outside of regular business hours. Install a backup domain controller at Ualena Street and connect it to the Ualena Street UPS.
3. Information classification scheme is incomplete.	GLBA has created a draft information classification policy that addresses five categories: public, internal use, restricted, confidential, and classified. The new policy requirements are to be disseminated to the GLBA staff and will become part of the new employee orientation and the annual employee awareness program.
4. There is concern that the weakness of passwords for some information systems user accounts could allow compromise of the password and permit unauthorized access to GLBA systems and information.	The GLBA Passwords Policy is to be modified to require strong passwords. GLBA Information Security Department (ISD) will investigate software solutions to enforce a strong password requirement.
5. Someone could impersonate a customer to corrupt or access bank records or accounts.	This concern is to be addressed at the GLBA employee awareness program and new employee orientation.

Copies of the risk assessment scope statement, action plan, and cross-reference documentation are included in the case study found in the appendices.

Table 6.38 Cross-Reference Sheet Example 1

Control Number	Control Description	Threats Number	Threat	Review Element	Risk Level
19	User controls — Implement user programs (user performance evaluations) designed to encourage compliance with policies and procedures in place to ensure the appropriate utilization of the application.				
		10	Information being used in the wrong context	Integrity	B
		13	Data updated internally but not being made externally	Integrity	B
		17	Security and authorization procedures are so bureaucratic as to hamper the business process	Integrity	A
		19	Personnel making changes are not adequately trained	Integrity	B
		20	Information could be published without proper authorization	Integrity	B
		21	Corporate embarrassment due to unauthorized changing of information	Integrity	B

Table 6.38 Cross-Reference Sheet Example 1 (continued)

Control Number	Control Description	Threats Number	Threat	Review Element	Risk Level
		24	Wrong use of the security administration procedures in applications with sensitive information	Confidentiality	B
		32	Confusion over where to store sensitive information	Confidentiality	B
		33	Unclear/unknown process for classifying data	Confidentiality	B

Table 6.39 Cross-Reference Example 2

Control Number	(Number of Times Selected, Rank)	Class	Definition
1	(6, 20)	Backup	Backup requirements will be determined and communicated to the service provider, including a request that an electronic notification that backups were completed be sent to the application system administrator. The service provider will be requested to test the backup procedures.
2	(7, 18)	Recovery plan	Develop, document, and test recovery procedures designed to ensure that the application and information can be recovered, using the backups created, in the event of loss.
3	(21, 4)	Access control	Implement an access control mechanism to prevent unauthorized access to information. This mechanism will include the capability of detecting, logging, and reporting attempts to breach the security of this information.
4	(9, 13)	Access control	Implement a mechanism to limit access to confidential information to specific network paths or physical locations.
5	(12, 8)	Access control	Implement user authentication mechanisms (such as firewalls, dial-in controls, secure ID) to limit access to authorized personnel.
6	(12, 8)	Access control	Implement encryption mechanisms (data, end to end) to prevent unauthorized access to protect the integrity and confidentiality of information.

Table 6.39 Cross-Reference Example 2 (continued)

Control Number	(Number of Times Selected, Rank)	Class	Definition
7	(20, 5)	Application control	Design and implement application controls (data entry edit checking, fields requiring validation, alarm indicators, password expiration capabilities, checksums) to ensure the integrity, confidentiality, and availability of application information.
8	(8, 6)	Acceptance testing	Develop testing procedures to be followed during applications development and during modifications to the existing application that include user participation and acceptance.
9	(11, 11)	Change management	Adhere to a change management process designed to facilitate a structured approach to modifications, to ensure that appropriate steps and precautions are followed. Emergency modifications should be included in this process.
10	(5, 22)	Antivirus	(1) Ensure that the local area network (LAN) administrator installs the corporate standard antiviral software on all computers.
			(2) Training and awareness of virus prevention techniques will be incorporated in the organization's information protection (IP) program.

Table 6.39   Cross-Reference Example 2 (continued)

Control Number	(Number of Times Selected, Rank)	Class	Definition
11	(27, 3)	Policy	Develop policies and procedures to limit access and operating privileges to those with business need.
12	(36, 2)	Training	User training will include instruction and documentation on the proper use of the application. The importance of maintaining the confidentiality of user accounts, passwords, and the confidential and competitive nature of information will be stressed.
13	(49, 1)	Audit/monitor	Implement mechanisms to monitor, report, and audit activities identified as requiring independent reviews, including periodic reviews of user IDs to ascertain and verify business need.
14	(3, 24)	Backup	Operations controls — Training for a backup to the system administrator will be provided and duties rotated between them to ensure the adequacy of the training program.
15	(7, 18)	Training	Operations controls — Application developers will provide documentation, guidance, and support to the operations staff (service provider) in implementing mechanisms to ensure that the transfer of information between applications is secure.

Table 6.39 Cross-Reference Example 2 (continued)

Control Number	(Number of Times Selected, Rank)	Class	Definition
16	(11, 11)	Access control	Operations controls — Mechanisms to protect the database against unauthorized access, and modifications made from outside the application, will be determined and implemented.
17	(3, 25)	Interface dependencies	Operations controls — Systems that feed information will be identified and communicated to the service provider to stress the impact to the functionality if these feeder applications are unavailable.
18	(5, 22)	Maintenance	Operations controls — Time requirements for technical maintenance will be tracked and a request for adjustment will be communicated to management if experience warrants.
19	(9, 13)	Training	User controls — Implement user programs (user performance evaluations) designed to encourage compliance with policies and procedures in place to ensure the appropriate utilization of the application.
20	(18, 6)	Service level agreement	Acquire service level agreements to establish level of customer expectations and assurances from supporting operations.
21	(6, 20)	Maintenance	Acquire maintenance and supplier agreements to facilitate the continued operational status of the application.

Table 6.39 Cross-Reference Example 2 (continued)

Control Number	(Number of Times Selected, Rank)	Class	Definition
22	(9, 13)	Physical security	In consultation with facilities management, facilitate the implementation of physical security controls designed to protect the information, software, and hardware required of the system.
23	(13, 7)	Management support	Request management support to ensure the cooperation and coordination of various business units, to facilitate a smooth transition to the application.
24	(3, 25)	Proprietary	Proprietary controls
25	(11, 11)	Corrective strategies	The development team will develop corrective strategies such as reworked processes, revised application logic, etc.
26	(8, 17)	Change management	Production migration controls, such as search and remove processes, to ensure data stores are clean

6.4.9.4 Summary

The risk assessment is not complete until the paperwork is done. The action plan must have the threats identified, the risk levels established, and the controls selected. Once the controls have seen selected, the action plan must identify who will implement the control and by what date. If the management owner decides to accept the risk, then this action must be identified in the action plan and the management summary report.

The final element of the risk assessment documentation is the cross-reference report. In the material above we presented three different variations on the cross-reference work. If you can generate an Access database, that will save you time and effort. The second approach is less time-consuming and may offer documentation as good as the full report.

Like all important tasks, the proof in how well it went lies in the documentation that supports the process. Remember, the results of a risk assessment will be used twice: once when a decision must be made and again when something goes wrong. By having complete documentation, management will be able to show when the decision was made, who was involved in the process, what was discussed, and what alternatives were considered.

6.5 Conclusion

Capturing the threats and selecting controls are important, but the most important element in an effective risk assessment process is establishing the risk levels. Before any organization can decide what to do, it must have a clear picture of where the problems are. As you will see in the next chapter, there are numbers of ways to modify the risk assessment process to meet the organization's needs. The process requires that the facilitator be flexible and work with the owner to establish needs before the risk assessment process begins.

When the risk level is to be determined, it will be vital for the team to understand how each of the threats is to be judged. Is the team going to factor in existing controls, or will the team be establishing a baseline for the implementation of a standard set of controls? In the next chapter there are a number of different matrices used to determine risk level. Select the model that works best for your organization.

Chapter 7

Variations on the FRAAP

7.1 Overview

Over the years it has become apparent that nearly every organization has its own special requirements for the risk assessment process. This could be the mapping of specific control requirements based on regulatory requirements or performing risk assessments on different elements of the organization business processes. In this chapter we will examine some of the current modifications to the standard Facilitated Risk Analysis and Assessment Process (FRAAP).

7.2 Infrastructure FRAAP

Perhaps the FRAAP that remains the closest to the original FRAAP is the one that is used today when a risk assessment of the business or information technology infrastructure must be performed. Two of the key components of the project scope statement are the assumptions and the constraints. The infrastructure FRAAP is conducted to address the issues around basic processing and business capabilities.

An organization must create a safe and secure working environment for its employees and the services they provide. The infrastructure FRAAP will examine the platforms, networks, operating systems, business processes, programs (such as the information security program), and other basic business functions.

Table 7.1   Standard Risk Assessment Elements

Standard Risk Assessment Elements
1. Identify the asset owner or risk assessment champion.
2. Create a project scope statement.
3. Conduct a prescreening to ensure risk assessment is required.
4. Select a quality team.
5. Agree on all definitions.
6. Create a controls sheet reflecting the organization's specific needs.

The result of an infrastructure FRAAP is the establishment of a baseline risk level from which reasonable and prudent controls, safeguards, and countermeasures can be implemented. Before conducting a risk assessment on a new application, the organization should conduct an infrastructure FRAAP to examine the change management or promotion to production procedures.

Implementing reasonable and prudent safeguards and controls must be mapped back to a process that identifies the requirements for those countermeasures. Implementation of controls without establishing a need is counterproductive and cost-inefficient. The infrastructure FRAAP will establish the business need for any controls and will provide the organization with two important deliverables: a baseline set of control standards and the ability to show clients, customers, and employees how the organization protects its assets.

7.2.1 The Infrastructure FRAAP

All of the FRAAP variations begin with the standard risk assessment elements (Table 7.1). Once these are completed, the team can then work the risk assessment process.

In the infrastructure FRAAP the team will identify threats just as before. Once all threats have been recorded and the team has edited the duplicates and combined similar threats, the team will proceed to establish the risk level of each of the threats as if there were no controls in place. This will be done using the agreed upon definitions for probability and impact. The team would use the matrix shown in Figure 7.1 to establish the baseline risk level for each threat.

As the team moves through the identified threats and establishes the appropriate risk level, that information is recorded on the Risk Assessment Threat Worksheet (Table 7.2).

Once the team has established the baseline risk levels, it will be asked to identify existing controls or to select from a pre-agreed upon controls list. The team is asked to first identify the controls that are currently

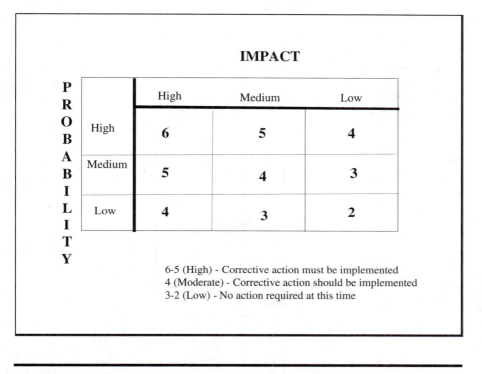

Figure 7.1   Threat impact table.

implemented to address the specific threat. The quality of the control will be examined in the next step; for this process, the facilitator needs to ensure that all existing controls are identified. Once the existing controls have been entered, the team can select controls from the controls list for open threats or it can reassess the risk level with the existing controls in place. The recording of the control process might look like Table 7.3.

The infrastructure FRAAP allows an organization to determine its current level of secure processing or operation. The results from these sessions will be recorded in a management summary report similar to the one discussed in the previous chapter. The action plan created from the FRAAP can be used as a blueprint to create an architecture from which standards, procedures, and practices are implemented.

7.2.1.1 Infrastructure FRAAP Summary

By conducting the infrastructure FRAAP, the organization will have established a secure processing level that will allow the future risk assessments to understand that a baseline set of controls is in place. This will allow

Table 7.2 Infrastructure FRAAP Threat Table 1

Threat	Applicable Yes/No	Probability 1 = Low 2 = Medium 3 = High	Impact 1 = Low 2 = Medium 3 = High	Risk Level	Control Selected	New Risk Level
Confidentiality						
Insecure e-mail could contain confidential information		3	3	High		
Internal theft of information		1	3	Medium		
Employee is not able to verify the identity of a client (e.g., phone masquerading)		1	1	Low		
Confidential information is left in plain view on a desk		3	3	High		
Social discussions outside the office could result in disclosure of sensitive information		1	1	Low		

Information could be salvaged by unauthorized persons from dumpsters or other waste receptacles		3	3	High
Information sent to third parties may be misused		1	3	Medium
Unattended computer could give unauthorized access to files		1	2	Low
Passwords may not be required for all workstations		3	3	High
Mailing two or more different customer statements/documents in one envelope	No			

Table 7.3 Infrastructure FRAAP Threat Table 2

Threat	Applicable Yes/No	Probability 1 = Low 2 = Medium 3 = High	Impact 1 = Low 2 = Medium 3 = High	Risk Level	Control Selected	New Risk Level
Confidentiality						
Insecure e-mail could contain confidential information		3	3	High	Information classification policy and handling standards are being implemented	Medium
Internal theft of information		1	3	Medium	Employee code of conduct and conflicts of interest addresses proprietary rights of the company and sanctions to be taken for breeches	Low
Employee is not able to verify the identity of a client (e.g., phone masquerading)		1	1	Low		

Confidential information is left in plain view on a desk	3	3	High	Information classification policy and handling standards are being implemented	Medium
Social discussions outside the office could result in disclosure of sensitive information	1	1	Low		
Information could be salvaged by unauthorized persons from dumpsters or other waste receptacles	3	3	High	Information classification policy and handling standards are being implemented	Low
Information sent to third parties may be misused	1	3	Medium	Nondisclosure and service level agreements address proper use and disclosure	Low
Unattended computer could give unauthorized access to files	1	2	Low		

the risk assessments to focus on the asset at hand and will not require the team to address extraneous threats and concerns.

7.2.2 Application FRAAP

7.2.2.1 Overview

For most applications, systems, business processes, or other activities, the application FRAAP will be the process that will be used. Because the infrastructure FRAAPs have been completed, the team can streamline the risk assessment process, and as we all know, anything that can save time is great.

As we discussed, the six standard risk assessment elements must be completed before the application FRAAP can begin. With a scope statement in hand, the team will brainstorm threats based on the review elements. Because this is a book on information security risk analysis, we will use the review elements of integrity, confidentiality, and availability.

As before, the team will identify threats, and when the team has exhausted itself and the threats, it will consolidate duplicate and similar threats. Once this is complete, the risk assessment process would normally attempt to determine the risk level. However, in the applications FRAAP the team is to identify existing controls (Table 7.4).

After the existing controls have been identified, the team will begin the process of assessing the probability and impact and assign a risk level. By identifying existing controls, the team should be able to concentrate its efforts on those threats with no controls or those with ineffective controls. With the risk level established, the team will then select controls for high-level open threats. Additionally, the team can select controls to complement those that have been identified as inadequate (Table 7.5).

By identifying existing controls prior to determining the risk level, the team is performing a form of vulnerability assessment. Any existing control that does not reduce the risk level or increases the risk level needs to have further examination conducted on it. In the management summary report the facilitator would identify these worrisome controls.

7.2.2.2 Summary

This process works best when an active risk assessment program has been implemented. Combining this with the infrastructure FRAAP will provide each client with the process it needs to ensure that adequate controls are in place.

7.2.3 Other Variations

Recently I have had a number of requests by clients to modify the risk assessment process to meet specific audit or regulatory requirements. When a risk assessment process can be altered to meet specific needs, then I know the client will be happy.

Here are some examples of what can be done when using the basic qualitative FRAAP.

7.2.3.1 Variation Example 1

This first example was from a bank that had just recently had the Office of the Comptroller of the Currency (OCC) in to conduct an audit of the bank's information processing environment in general and the information security program specifically. Because the risk assessment is addressing a specific audit report, the scope statement has already been created. To expedite the risk assessment process, when the meeting notice was sent out to the team, a copy of the audit findings that were specific to each member was included. The team member was to do his or her homework and be ready to report the status of his or her assigned tasks (Table 7.6).

As you can see by this example, the bank selected each audit item where we would typically enter the threat scenario. The severity level was assigned by the audit team and was entered into the report similar to the way in which a typical risk assessment would identify the risk level. The bank's response is similar to the selection of controls or identification of existing controls. The observation field allows the reviewer to record the current status of the implementation of the identified corrective action. If the process is complete, the team would enter that date. If incomplete, then the team would enter the proposed completion date.

7.2.3.2 Variation Example 2

Borrowing from the concepts in the first variation example, we recently conducted a risk assessment using a very similar worksheet. The process began with the implementation of the six standard elements of a risk assessment process. Using the FRAAP brainstorming process, threats to the integrity, confidentiality, and availability of nonpublic personal customer data held and processed at this institution were reviewed. Once the threats were edited and recorded, the team established the risk level using processes similar to ones we have already discussed. Their selection criteria were high, moderate, and low risks.

Table 7.4 Application Threat Table 1

Threat	Existing Control	Probability 1 = Low 2 = Medium 3 = High	Impact 1 = Low 2 = Medium 3 = High	Risk Level	New or Enhanced Selected Control	New Risk Level
Confidentiality						
Insecure e-mail could contain confidential information						
Internal theft of information	Employee code of conduct and conflicts of interest addresses proprietary rights of the company and sanctions to be taken for breeches					
Employee is not able to verify the identity of a client (e.g., phone masquerading)						
Confidential information is left in plain view on a desk						

Social discussions outside the office could result in disclosure of sensitive information					
Information could be salvaged by unauthorized persons from dumpsters or other waste receptacles					
Information sent to third parties may be misused	Nondisclosure and service level agreements address proper use and disclosure				
Unattended computer could give unauthorized access to files					
Passwords may not be required for all workstations					
Mailing two or more different customer statements/documents in one envelope					

Table 7.5 Application FRAAP Threat Table 2

Threat	Existing Control	Probability 1 = Low 2 = Medium 3 = High	Impact 1 = Low 2 = Medium 3 = High	Risk Level	New or Enhanced Selected Control	New Risk Level
Confidentiality						
Insecure e-mail could contain confidential information		3	3	High	Information classification policy and handling standards are being implemented	
Internal theft of information	Employee code of conduct and conflicts of interest addresses proprietary rights of the company and sanctions to be taken for breeches	1	2	Low		
Employee is not able to verify the identity of a client (e.g., phone masquerading)		1	1	Low		

Confidential information is left in plain view on a desk	3	3	High	Information classification policy and handling standards are being implemented	Medium
Social discussions outside the office could result in disclosure of sensitive information	1	1	Low		
Information could be salvaged by unauthorized persons from dumpsters or other waste receptacles	3	3	High	Information classification policy and handling standards are being implemented	Medium
Information sent to third parties may be misused	1	2	Low	Nondisclosure and service level agreements address proper use and disclosure	
Unattended computer could give unauthorized access to files	1	2	Low		

Table 7.6   Variation Example 1

Audit Item	Severity Level	Bank's Response	Observations	Completion Date
Data stream could be intercepted	Moderate	Vacant ports are to be disconnected	Network administration has documented the process to identify vacant ports; a quarterly review of ports has been established	10/27/2004

For all high or moderate risks, the team identified any existing controls. At that point, the FRAAP session was concluded. Over the next few days the facilitator reviewed the risk controls and determined whether the identified controls were adequate. If they were determined to be inadequate, then an action item was entered into the worksheet (Table 7.7).

The second half of the worksheet included the categories listed in Table 7.8.

Once the corrective action was selected, the bank wanted to include in its risk assessment the identification of how frequently the control item was to be checked for compliance and what entity would be responsible for the compliance review or audit.

7.2.3.3 Variation Example 3

Anytime there is a discussion on risk assessment, the concept of vulnerability always comes up. How does a risk assessment process measure the vulnerability of existing safeguards and controls? First, we must define what this vulnerability analysis is and what we hope to find out about it.

A vulnerability is defined as a flaw in security procedures, software, internal system controls, or implementation of system that may affect the integrity, confidentiality, accountability, or availability of data or services. Vulnerabilities include flaws that may be deliberately exploited and those that may cause failure due to inadvertent human actions or natural disasters.

A vulnerability assessment, then, is the systematic examination of a critical infrastructure, the interconnected systems on which it relies, its information, or a product to determine the adequacy of security measures, identify security deficiencies, evaluate security alternatives, and verify the adequacy of such measures after implementation.

Table 7.7 Variation Example 2

Threat Scenarios	Risk Level	Risk Controls	Observations	Action Item
Integrity				
Data stream could be intercepted	Medium	Vacant ports are disconnected		Information classification policy and handling standards are being implemented
Faulty programming could (inadvertently) modify data	Low	Programs are tested before going into production, and change management procedures are in place; bank's *Information Technology Policies and Procedures Manual 7-11*, ISD documentation, and the test plan and test analysis report standard have established the testing criteria	Controls appear adequate	Employee code of conduct and conflicts of interest addresses proprietary rights of the company and sanctions to be taken for breeches

For the information security professional there needs to be a way of doing that as quickly as possible. One example of how to do that might be the variation on the standard FRAAP shown in Table 7.9.

In this risk assessment process the team identifies threats as in any other process. The risk level is established by using a matrix (Figure 7.2) similar to the ones we have used before, but with one modification.

In one of my recent training classes I had an attendee that wanted to know if it would be all right to change *probability* to *vulnerability*. I did not see why that would not work, so he made the change and was happy. The establishment of the risk level is the important process here. What you call the x and y axes means little as long as the definitions are correct.

Table 7.8   Variation Example 2 Second Half of Table

Threat Scenarios	Risk Level	Action Item	Test Frequency	By Whom	Additional Comments
Integrity					
Data stream could be intercepted	Medium	Information classification policy and handling standards are being implemented	Review classification reports annually	Information System Security Officer (ISSO)	
Faulty programming could (inadvertently) modify data	Low	Employee code of conduct and conflicts of interest addresses proprietary rights of the company and sanctions to be taken for breeches	Spot-check for compliance, not to exceed annual review	Audit	

Table 7.9   Vulnerability Assessment Example

Threat	Risk Level	Possible Controls	Selected Controls	Residual Risk	Acceptable Risk Level Yes/No	If No, Identify Action Plan
Confidentiality						

In this risk assessment process, once the risk level was established, the team would identify all possible controls. In the next step, the team would select the best control and perform the risk level process on the threat with the selected control in place. The results from this process are entered into the column headed "Residual Risk." The residual risk is the

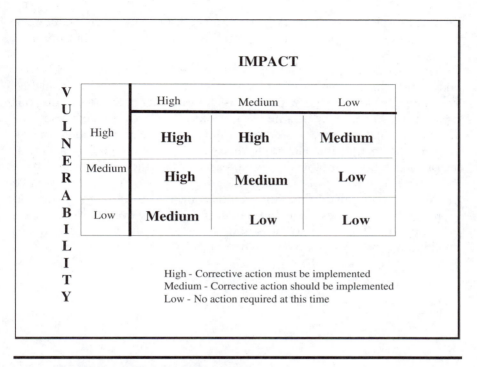

Figure 7.2   Vulnerability assessment matrix.

potential for the occurrence of an adverse event after adjusting for the impact of all in-place safeguards. If the team determines that the residual risk is adequate, then no other action is required. If the residual risk is higher than acceptable, then either another control is to be selected and the risk level process repeated or the management owner can choose to accept the risk.

7.3 Conclusion

The Facilitated Risk Analysis and Assessment Process has been designed to be flexible. Because it requires no additional hardware or expensive software, it can be shaped and molded to meet the changing needs of any organization. Because it is so flexible, facilitators sometimes forget to make certain that the documentation is always current.

Listen to the needs of your customers. If you work for a corporation or a government agency, you have customers just like consultants and independent contractors do. Work with the customer to design a risk assessment process that meets his needs. Risk assessment has three standard deliverables: it identifies threats, establishes the risk level of the threat, and selects possible safeguards and controls. Within this framework the risk assessment process is open to the needs of the organization and the customer.

The variations of the FRAAP theme were presented to provide you with a stimulus to open your mind and explore what avenues are available. The correct risk assessment process is the one that works best for your organization. There may be a need to modify the process to meet a specific audit or regulatory need. Use the examples and create additional ones.

The reason that the FRAAP is this way is because time is a critical factor. Our fellow employees have their own tasks to perform and have little spare time to devote to such things as risk assessment. If you have the luxury of unlimited time, then there is no end to how complete and thorough the risk assessment can be. Most of us, however, have little time to spare, so as the facilitator, it is your job to meet the basic deliverables quickly and modify the process when appropriate.

Chapter 8

Mapping Controls

8.1 Controls Overview

Once the risk assessment process has established the need for security, the team must select controls to ensure the risks are reduced to an acceptable level. Controls can be selected from any number of sources, or new controls can be designed to meet specific needs wherever necessary. There are many ways of managing risk, and the control sheets that we will examine can provide the reader with examples of common approaches. It is, however, necessary to recognize that some of the controls are not applicable to every information system or environment. As such, they may not be practicable for all organizations.

As an example, one of the key tenets of the information security profession is the requirement for the segregation of duties to prevent fraud and errors. However, it may not be possible for smaller organizations to segregate all tasks, and therefore, they must explore other ways of achieving the same control objective. Some organizations have opted for having a third party review the audit logs of activity relating to sensitive work activities.

Controls must be selected based on the cost of implementation (which includes cost of procurement, implementation, awareness, training, and maintenance) in relation to the threat risk level being reduced and the potential impacts if a breach were to occur. When considering impact, remember to include intangible factors such as loss of reputation as well as tangible monetary losses.

8.2 Creating Your Controls List

Creating a controls list to work from will ensure that the risk assessment process moves along more quickly than if the team had to brainstorm controls, and it helps ensure that regulatory requirements are met. The first two control sheets that we will examine are fairly generic in nature. They address standard information security architecture issues, but leave the more detailed controls to either the team or the infrastructure support personnel to identify.

The later controls sheets will examine the emerging legislative and regulatory standards that have become part of the information security landscape over the past five years or so. Because there has been so much activity in this area, I found it helpful to establish a base set of controls using the Information Technology: Code of Practice for Information Security Management (ISO 17799). Although this document is not the complete answer to all of the possible security solutions, it offers a strong baseline from which to build such a set of controls.

What I liked most about ISO 17799 is that it brought back to mind issues that I had addressed previously and had pushed to the back of my mind. So by having an internationally approved set of controls addressing the far-ranging issues of the information security field, I was more comfortable putting together a baseline set of controls that could be used as a starting point for risk level resolution.

8.2.1 Information Security Baseline Controls

When creating your organization's controls list, remember that a number of controls should be considered as the baseline principles for your organization's information security management program. These should be based on appropriate legislation, regulatory requirements, or industry best practices. Over the years I have been able to identify ten key elements to use as a foundation when implementing an information security program (Table 8.1).

Table 8.1 Information Security Baseline Principles

Baseline Control	Description
Information security policy	Senior management should set a clear direction and demonstrate its support for and commitment to information security through the issuance of an information security policy across the organization.

Table 8.1   Information Security Baseline Principles (continued)

Baseline Control	Description
Establish an information security steering committee	A standing committee made up of representatives from each of the business units needs to be created. Its task will be to champion the information security program and approve security policy and direction.
Establish employees' responsibilities	Responsibilities for the protection of information assets and for carrying out specific security processes should be explicitly defined. The policy definitions should be established to identify such entities as *owner, custodian,* and *user.*
Information classification policy	To identify sensitivity levels and maintain appropriate protection of organizational assets. All major information assets should be classified and the owner identified.
Information security education and training	Users should be given adequate security education and technical training.
Report and respond to security incidents	Procedures and employee awareness sessions must be implemented to provide employees with the knowledge of what to do when confronted by a security incident.
Business continuity planning (BCP) policy	There should be a managed process in place for developing and maintaining business continuity plans across the organization. The enterprise should establish a BCP position headed up by a non-IT person.
Copyright compliance program	Attention must be drawn to the legal restrictions on the use of copyright material. A copyright compliance policy and awareness program must be implemented.
Records management policy and program	A formal records management policy and supporting procedures must be implemented. The policy must address all applicable legal requirements for retention.
Information security compliance program	Audit will conduct regular audits to assess the compliance level with security policies and standards.

This list is not a complete set of standards that an organization would implement, but it is a starting point to be used when examining the contents of your organization's information security program. These controls should apply to most organizations, but it should be understood that all controls should be examined based on your organization's specific needs and requirements.

When creating controls lists, remember that a control is only appropriate if it is based on a sound risk assessment discovered need. In other words, just because it appears on a list does not mean it must be implemented. Look upon controls lists as suggestions and not requirements.

8.2.2 Control Requirements Considerations

To implement a risk management controls list, it will be important to consider the following questions:

- Has the information security policy successfully addressed the business objectives or mission of the organization?
- Is the information security program in sync with the prevailing culture of the organization?
- Does the program have visible support and commitment from senior management?
- Does the organization have a good awareness of the need for due diligence?
- Is there an active program to sell information security to management and employees?
- Are the security policies, standards, and procedures readily available to all employees?
- Are employees regularly trained on how to use information security tools?
- Is there an effective way to measure the effectiveness of the security and risk management programs?

8.2.3 A Final Cautionary Note

The controls list tables that we will be examining — the legislation and regulatory requirements that impact your organization — should be regarded as a starting point for your organization's specific needs. No organization should attempt to simply implement controls, safeguards, or countermeasures just because they are there or because it can. This could cause serious impact to the organization's need to meet business objectives and could cause employees to lose confidence in the information security and risk management programs. On the other hand, there may be a need to add controls to your list.

When new legislation or regulatory requirements appear, map the new controls to an existing list. This will allow the organization to see how compliant it already is to the new requirements. As you will see, the new documents, such as the following, are fairly well covered in the ISO 17799 controls:

- "Security Technologies for Manufacturing and Control Systems" (ISA-TR99.00.01-2004)
- "Integrating Electronic Security into Manufacturing and Control Systems Environment" (ISA-TR99.00.02-2004)
- Federal Information Processing Standards Publications (FIPS Pubs)
- National Institute of Standards and Technology
- CobiT® Security Baseline
- Health Insurance Portability and Accountability Act (HIPAA)
- The Basel Accords
- Privacy Act of 1974
- Gramm–Leach–Bliley Act (GLBA)
- Sarbanes–Oxley Act (SOX)
- "Information Security for Banking and Finance" (ISO/TR 13569)
- FFEIC examination guidelines

It is important for an effective risk management program to have generally acceptable controls that can be mapped back to industry guidelines, regulatory requirements, applicable laws, and best practices.

8.3 Controls List Examples

The next several pages are devoted to controls lists that address particular industry concepts or best practices. After we examine those, we will review the controls list created through the use of ISO 17799. Once this base has been established, we will examine a controls list for emerging laws and regulations and map them back to ISO 17799. We will briefly look at CobiT and examine how its information security and ISO 17799 map together very well.

8.3.1 Controls by Security Categories

In Chapter 2 we briefly looked at the first two controls list examples. The first one uses basic security control categories such as management, operational, and technical. It is not uncommon to see categories that include logical and administration controls (Table 8.2).

Table 8.2   Controls List by Security Categories

Security Category	Control
Management	Risk assessment
	Security planning
	System and service acquisition procedures
	Control vulnerability assessment
	Processing authorization
Operational	Personnel security
	Physical and environmental controls
	Continuity planning
	Configuration management
	Hardware and software maintenance
	System integrity
	Media protection
	Incident response
	Security awareness program
Technical	Identification and authentication
	Logical access control
	Audit trails and logs
	Communication protection
	System protection

8.3.2 Controls List by Information Security Layer

When I first began working in the information security field, the security layer in use discussed controls that were categorized as prevention, detection, containment, and recovery layers. In the first line of defense, organizations needed to implement controls that could prevent security incidents from happening. Because 100 percent security means 0 percent productivity, no set of controls could or should prevent all threats. So, the second layer of controls must detect when an incident occurs and notify the appropriate personnel to respond. To ensure that conditions do not move to an out-of-control situation, the organization will want to implement controls that will contain the incident until the team can respond and implement the recovery controls.

In 1999, Dr. Peter Stephenson presented a different perspective on the security layers. The layers are similar to the older model, but work well in the rapidly expanding connectivity environment of the modern information processing environment. These new category layers are avoidance, assurance, detection, and recovery. The newer security model is represented in the controls list in Table 8.3.

8.3.3 Controls List by Information Technology Organization

This controls list uses typical areas within information technology as the category headings. In addition to the three areas that are used in this example, it would be appropriate to establish control requirements for areas such as:

- Production control
- System programming
- Applications development
- Database administration
- Telecommunications
- Network management
- Web administration
- Desktop computing

Each area should have several controls that can be selected to reduce threat levels. When performing a risk assessment, the infrastructure team can actively add and modify the controls list (Table 8.4). Below we will examine a variation on this theme.

8.3.4 Controls List Using ISO 17799

The Information Technology: Code of Practice for Information Security Management (ISO 17799) is an internationally developed standard that adopted much of its direction and focus from the British Standard 7799. This standard gives recommendations for information security management tools to initiate, implement, and maintain an information security program. It has been specifically created to form a common platform for the development of organizational security standards. The implementation of effective standards will provide management with the tools to ensure

Table 8.3   Controls List by Security Architecture Layer

Control Category	
Avoidance	Encryption and authentication
	System security architecture
	Facilitated risk analysis process
	Information awareness program
	Information security program
	Interruption prevention
	Policies and standards
	Public key infrastructure
	Secure application architecture
	Secure communications plans
Assurance	Application security review
	Standards testing
	Penetration testing
	Periodic perimeter scans
	Vulnerability assessment
Detection	Intrusion detection
	Remote intrusion monitoring
Recovery	Business continuity planning
	Business impact analysis
	Crisis management planning
	Disaster recovery planning
	Incident response procedures
	Investigation tools

employees, customers, clients, stakeholders, and other interested bodies that management is meeting its fiduciary responsibility to protect the assets of the organization. The controls within the ISO 17799 should be selected after performing a formal risk assessment to assess need and should be used in accordance with all applicable laws and regulations (Table 8.5).

Table 8.4 Controls List by IT Organization

Control Number	IT Group	Descriptor	Definition
1	Operations controls	Backup	Backup requirements will be determined and communicated to operations, including a request that an electronic notification that backups were completed be sent to the application system administrator. Operations will be requested to test the backup procedures.
2	Operations controls	Recovery plan	Develop, document, and test recovery procedures designed to ensure that the application and information can be recovered, using the backups created, in the event of loss.
3	Operations controls	Risk analysis	Conduct a risk analysis to determine the level of exposure to identified threats and identify possible safeguards or controls.
4	Operations controls	Antivirus	(1) Ensure that the local area network (LAN) administrator installs the corporate standard antiviral software on all computers. (2) Training and awareness of virus prevention techniques will be incorporated in the organization's information protection (IP) program.
5	Operations controls	Interface dependencies	Systems that feed information will be identified and communicated to operations to stress the impact to the functionality if these feeder applications are unavailable.
6	Operations controls	Maintenance	Time requirements for technical maintenance will be tracked and a request for adjustment will be communicated to management if experience warrants.

Table 8.4 Controls List by IT Organization (continued)

Control Number	IT Group	Descriptor	Definition
7	Operations controls	Service level agreement	Acquire service level agreements to establish level of customer expectations and assurances from supporting operations.
8	Operations controls	Maintenance	Acquire maintenance and supplier agreements to facilitate the continued operational status of the application.
9	Operations controls	Change management	Production migration controls, such as search and remove processes, to ensure data stores are clean.
10	Operations controls	Business impact analysis	A formal business impact analysis will be conducted to determine the asset's relative criticality with other enterprise assets.
11	Operations controls	Backup	Training for a backup to the system administrator will be provided and duties rotated between them to ensure the adequacy of the training program.
12	Operations controls	Backup	A formal employee security awareness program has been implemented and is updated and presented to the employees at least on an annual basis.
13	Operations controls	Recovery plan	Implement a mechanism to limit access to confidential information to specific network paths or physical locations.
14	Operations controls	Risk analysis	Implement user authentication mechanisms (such as firewalls, dial-in controls, secure ID) to limit access to authorized personnel.

Table 8.4   Controls List by IT Organization (continued)

Control Number	IT Group	Descriptor	Definition
15	Application controls	Application control	Design and implement application controls (data entry edit checking, fields requiring validation, alarm indicators, password expiration capabilities, checksums) to ensure the integrity, confidentiality, and availability of application information.
16	Application controls	Acceptance testing	Develop testing procedures to be followed during applications development and during modifications to the existing application that include user participation and acceptance.
17	Application controls	Training	Implement user programs (user performance evaluations) designed to encourage compliance with policies and procedures in place to ensure the appropriate utilization of the application.
18	Application controls	Training	Application developers will provide documentation, guidance, and support to the operations staff (operations) in implementing mechanisms to ensure that the transfer of information between applications is secure.
19	Application controls	Corrective strategies	The development team will develop corrective strategies such as reworked processes, revised application logic, etc.
20	Security controls	Policy	Develop policies and procedures to limit access and operating privileges to those with business need.

Table 8.4   Controls List by IT Organization (continued)

Control Number	IT Group	Descriptor	Definition
21	Security controls	Training	User training will include instruction and documentation on the proper use of the application. The importance of maintaining the confidentiality of user accounts, passwords, and the confidential and competitive nature of information will be stressed.
22	Security controls	Review	Implement mechanisms to monitor, report, and audit activities identified as requiring independent reviews, including periodic reviews of user IDs to ascertain and verify business need.
23	Security controls	Asset classification	The asset under review will be classified using enterprise policies, standards, and procedures on asset classification.
24	Security controls	Access control	Mechanisms to protect the database against unauthorized access, and modifications made from outside the application, will be determined and implemented.
25	Security controls	Management support	Request management support to ensure the cooperation and coordination of various business units.
26	Security controls	Proprietary	Processes are in place to ensure that company proprietary assets are protected and that the company is in compliance with all third-party license agreements.
27	Security controls	Security awareness	Implement an access control mechanism to prevent unauthorized access to information. This mechanism will include the capability of detecting, logging, and reporting attempts to breach the security of this information.

Table 8.4   Controls List by IT Organization (continued)

Control Number	IT Group	Descriptor	Definition
28	Security controls	Access control	Implement encryption mechanisms (data, end to end) to prevent unauthorized access to protect the integrity and confidentiality of information.
29	Security controls	Access control	Adhere to a change management process designed to facilitate a structured approach to modifications of the application, to ensure appropriate steps and precautions are followed. Emergency modifications should be included in this process.
30	Security controls	Access control	Control procedures are in place to ensure that appropriate system logs are reviewed by independent third parties to review system update activities.
31	Security controls	Access control	In consultation with facilities management, facilitate the implementation of physical security controls designed to protect the information, software, and hardware required of the system.
32	Systems controls	Change management	Backup requirements will be determined and communicated to operations, including a request that an electronic notification that backups were completed be sent to the application system administrator. Operations will be requested to test the backup procedures.
33	Systems controls	Monitor system logs	Develop, document, and test recovery procedures designed to ensure that the application and information can be recovered, using the backups created, in the event of loss.

Table 8.4 Controls List by IT Organization (continued)

Control Number	IT Group	Descriptor	Definition
34	Physical security	Physical security	Conduct a risk analysis to determine the level of exposure to identified threats and identify possible safeguards or controls.

8.3.5 Mapping ISO 17799 and HIPAA

The Health Insurance Portability and Accountability Act (HIPAA), also known as Kassebaum–Kennedy, after the two senators who spearheaded the bill, was passed in 1996 to help people buy and keep health insurance (portability), even when they have serious health conditions; the law sets basic requirements that health plans must meet. Because states can and have modified and expanded upon these provisions, consumers' protections vary from state to state.

The law expanded to include strict rules for privacy and security of health information, giving individuals more control over how their health information is used. The privacy and security rules within HIPAA govern the use, disclosure, and handling of any identifiable patient information by covered healthcare providers. The law covers the information in whatever form it is seen or heard and applies to the information in whatever manner it is to be used.

Many healthcare-related organizations have been working to ensure that the required and standard elements of the act are incorporated into the information security program. As I began working with clients to help them meet these requirements, I began to notice similarities between HIPAA and ISO 17799. Because we did not want to duplicate efforts and needed to know what else would be required under HIPAA, we mapped HIPAA to ISO 17799 using a table similar to Table 8.6.

8.3.6 Controls List Mapping ISO 17799 and GLBA

The Gramm–Leach–Bliley Act (GLBA) was signed into law in 1999. Its primary purpose is to provide privacy of customer information by financial service organizations, and comprehensive data protection measures are required. Depending on the financial institution's supervisory authority, GLBA compliance audits are conducted by either the Office of the Comptroller of the Currency (OCC), the Federal Reserve Systems (Fed), the Federal Deposit Insurance Corporation (FDIC), or the Office of Thrift

Table 8.5   Controls List Using ISO 17799

Control Number	ISO 17799 Section	Class[a]	Control Description
1		Risk assessment (2)	Conduct an accurate and thorough assessment of the potential risks and vulnerabilities to the confidentiality, integrity, and availability of information resources.
2	Security policy	Policy (3.1)	Develop and implement an information security policy.
3	Organizational security	Management information security forum (4.1)	Establish a corporate committee to oversee information security. Develop and implement an information security organization mission statement.
4	Organizational security	Security of third-party access (4.2)	Implement a process to analyze third-party connection risks and implement specific security standards to combat third-party connection risks.
5	Organizational security	Security requirements in outsourcing contracts (4.3)	Ensure that the security requirements of the information owners have been addressed in a contract between the owners and the outsource organization.
6	Asset classification and control	Accounting of assets (5.1)	Establish an inventory of major assets associated with each information system.
7	Asset classification and control	Information classification (5.2)	Implement standards for security classification and the level of protection required for information assets.
8	Asset classification and control	Information labeling and handling (5.2)	Implement standards to ensure the proper handling of information assets.
9	Personnel security	Security in job descriptions (6.1)	Ensure that security responsibilities are included in employee job descriptions.

Table 8.5 Controls List Using ISO 17799 (continued)

Control Number	ISO 17799 Section	Class[a]	Control Description
10	Personnel security	User training (6.2)	Implement training standards to ensure that users are trained in information security policies and procedures, security requirements, business controls, and correct use of IT facilities.
11	Personnel security	Responding to security incidents and malfunctions (6.3)	Implement procedures and standards for formal reporting and incident response action to be taken on receipt of an incident report.
12	Physical and environmental security	Secure areas (7.1)	Implement standards to ensure that physical security protections exist, based on defined perimeters through strategically located barriers throughout the organization.
13	Physical and environmental security	Equipment security (7.2)	Implement standards to ensure that equipment is located properly to reduce risks of environmental hazards and unauthorized access.
14	Physical and environmental security	General controls (7.3)	Implement a clear desk/clear screen policy for sensitive material to reduce risks of unauthorized access, loss, or damage outside normal working hours.
15	Communications and operations management	Documented operating procedures (8.1)	Implement operating procedures to clearly document that all operational computer systems are operated in a correct, secure manner.
16	Communications and operations management	System planning and acceptance (8.2)	Implement standards to ensure that capacity requirements are monitored, and future requirements projected, to reduce the risk of system overload.

17	Communications and operations management	Protection from malicious software (8.3)	Implement standards and user training to ensure that virus detection and prevention measures are adequate.
18	Communications and operations management	Housekeeping (8.4)	Establish procedures for making regular backup copies of essential business data and software to ensure that it can be recovered following a computer disaster or media failure.
19	Communications and operations management	Network management (8.5)	Implement appropriate standards to ensure the security of data in networks and the protection of connected services from unauthorized access.
20	Communications and operations management	Media handling and security (8.6)	Implement procedures for the management of removable computer media such as tapes, disks, cassettes, and printed reports.
21	Communications and operations management	Exchanges of information and software (8.7)	Implement procedures to establish formal agreements, including software escrow agreements when appropriate, for exchanging data and software (whether electronically or manually) between organizations.
22	Access control	Business requirement for system access (9.1)	Implement a risk analysis process to gather business requirements to document access control levels.
23	Access control	User access management (9.2)	Implement procedures for user registration and deregistration access to all multiuse IT services.
24	Access control	User responsibility (9.3)	Implement user training to ensure users have been taught good security practices in the selection and use of passwords.

Table 8.5   Controls List Using ISO 17799 (continued)

Control Number	ISO 17799 Section	Class[a]	Control Description
25	Access control	Network access control (9.4)	Implement procedures to ensure that network and computer services that can be accessed by an individual user or from a particular terminal are consistent with business access control policy.
26	Access control	Operating system access control (9.5)	Implement standards for automatic terminal identification to authenticate connections to specific locations.
27	Access control	Application access control (9.6)	Implement procedures to restrict access to applications system data and functions in accordance with defined access policy and based on individual requirements.
28	Access control	Monitoring system access and use (9.7)	Implement audit trails that record exceptions and other security-relevant events that produce and maintain to assist in future investigations and in access control.
29	Access control	Remote access and telecommuting (9.8)	Implement a formal policy and supporting standards that address the risks of working with mobile computing facilities, including requirements for physical protection, access controls, cryptographic techniques, backup, and virus protection.
30	Systems development and maintenance	Security requirements of systems (10.1)	Implement standards to ensure that analysis of security requirements is part of the requirement analysis stage of each development project.

31	Systems development and maintenance	Security in application systems (10.2)	Implement standards to ensure that data that is input into applications systems is validated to ensure that it is correct and appropriate.
32	Systems development and maintenance	Cryptography (10.3)	Implement policies and standards on the use of cryptographic controls, including management of encryption keys, and effective implementation.
33	Systems development and maintenance	Security of system files (10.4)	Implement standards to exercise strict control over the implementation of software on operational systems.
34	Systems development and maintenance	Security in development and support environments (10.5)	Implement standards and procedures for formal change management process.
35	Business continuity management	Aspects of business continuity planning (11.1)	Implement procedures for the development and maintenance of business continuity plans across the organization.
36	Compliance	Compliance with legal requirements (12.1)	Implement standards to ensure that all relevant statutory, regulatory, and contractual requirements are specifically defined and documented for each information system.
37	Compliance	Reviews of security policy and technical compliances (12.2)	Implement standards to ensure that all areas within the organization are considered for regular review to ensure compliance with security policies and standards.

a The numbers in parentheses are the matching section numbers found in ISO 17799.

Table 8.6   Controls List Mapping ISO 17799 and HIPAA

ISO 17799 Section	Control[a]	HIPAA
Risk assessment	Risk assessment (2)	Risk analysis (required)
Security policy	Policy (3.1)	Isolate healthcare clearinghouse functions (required)
		Integrity (standard)
Organizational security	Management information security forum (4.1)	Risk management (required)
		Sanction policy (required)
		Privacy officer (required)
Organizational security	Security of third-party access (4.2)	Business associate contracts (standard)
Organizational security	Security requirements in outsourcing contracts (4.3)	Audit controls (required)
Asset classification and control	Accounting of assets (5.1)	Inventory all assets
Asset classification and control	Information classification (5.2)	Information is an asset and the property of the enterprise
Asset classification and control	Information labeling and handling (5.2)	
Personnel security	Security in job descriptions (6.1)	
Personnel security	User training (6.2)	
Personnel security	Responding to security incidents and malfunctions (6.3)	
Physical and environmental security	Secure areas (7.1)	Workstation security (standard)
Physical and environmental security	Equipment security (7.2)	
Physical and environmental security	General controls (7.3)	

Table 8.6   Controls List Mapping ISO 17799 and HIPAA (continued)

ISO 17799 Section	Control[a]	HIPAA
Communications and operations management	Documented operating procedures (8.1)	Response and reporting (required) Emergency mode operations plan (required) Transmission security (standard)
Communications and operations management	System planning and acceptance (8.2)	
Communications and operations management	Protection from malicious software (8.3)	
Communications and operations management	Housekeeping (8.4)	Data backup (required)
Communications and operations management	Network management (8.5)	
Communications and operations management	Media handling and security (8.6)	Device and media control (standard) Media reuse (required)
Communications and operations management	Exchanges of information and software (8.7)	
Access control	Business requirement for system access (9.1)	Risk analysis (required)
Access control	User access management (9.2)	Authentication (standard)
Access control	User responsibility (9.3)	
Access control	Network access control (9.4)	
Access control	Operating system access control (9.5)	Emergency access procedure (required)

Table 8.6   Controls List Mapping ISO 17799 and HIPAA (continued)

ISO 17799 Section	Control[a]	HIPAA
Access control	Application access control (9.6)	Unique user identification (required)
Access control	Monitoring system access and use (9.7)	
Access control	Remote access and telecommuting (9.8)	
Systems development and maintenance	Security requirements of systems (10.1)	Risk analysis
Systems development and maintenance	Security in application systems (10.2)	
Systems development and maintenance	Cryptography (10.3)	
Systems development and maintenance	Security of system files (10.4)	
Systems development and maintenance	Security in development and support environments (10.5)	
Business continuity management	Aspects of business continuity planning (11.1)	Data backup (required) Disaster recovery plan (required) Emergency mode operations plan (required)
Compliance	Compliance with legal requirements (12.1)	
Compliance	Reviews of security policy and technical compliances (12.2)	Information system activity review (required) Audit controls (required)

[a] The numbers in parentheses are the matching section numbers found in ISO 17799.

Supervision (OTS). All financial service organizations must comply with GLBA data protection requirements. These requirements do not pertain only to providers receiving federal funds (Table 8.7).

GLBA requires financial institutions to:

■ Insure the security and confidentiality of customer records and information
■ Protect against any anticipated threats or hazards to the security or integrity of such records
■ Protect against unauthorized access

8.3.7 Controls List Mapping ISO 17799, GLBA, and Sarbanes–Oxley

Sarbanes–Oxley (SOX) was signed into law on July 30, 2002, and the provisions of the act have a meaningful impact on both public companies and auditors (Table 8.8). Two important sections of the act are:

■ Section 302 ("Disclosure Controls and Procedures," or DC&P), which requires quarterly certification of financial statements by the CEO and CFO. The CEO and CFO must certify completeness and accuracy of the filings and attest to the effectiveness of internal control.
■ Section 404 ("Internal Control Attest"), which requires annual affirmation of management's responsibility for internal controls over financial reporting. Management must attest to effectiveness based on an evaluation, and the auditor must attest and report on management's evaluation.

8.3.8 Controls List Mapping ISO 17799 and Federal Sentencing Guidelines

The Federal Sentencing Guidelines for Criminal Activity (FSGCA) define executive responsibility for fraud, theft, and antitrust violations, and establish a mandatory point system for federal judges to determine appropriate punishment. Because much fraud and falsifying corporate data involves access to computer-held data, liability established under the guidelines extends to computer-related crime as well. What has caused many executives concern is that the mandatory punishment could apply even when intruders enter a computer system and perpetrate a crime.

Table 8.7 Controls List Mapping ISO 17799 and GLBA

ISO 17799 Section	Control[a]	GLBA
Risk assessment	Risk assessment (2)	Assess risk
Security policy	Policy (3.1)	Board approves written policy and program
Organizational security	Management information security forum (4.1)	Involve the board of directors Assign specific responsibilities
Organizational security	Security of third-party access (4.2)	Contract clauses meet guidance objectives
Organizational security	Security requirements in outsourcing contracts (4.3)	Report program effectiveness to board
Asset classification and control	Accounting of assets (5.1)	Implement policies to evaluate sensitivity of customer information
Asset classification and control	Information classification (5.2)	Implement standards and procedures to protect customer information
Asset classification and control	Information labeling and handling (5.2)	Implement standards
Personnel security	Security in job descriptions (6.1)	Background check on certain positions
Personnel security	User training (6.2)	Train staff to implement program
Personnel security	Responding to security incidents and malfunctions (6.3)	Incident response program
Physical and environmental security	Secure areas (7.1)	Implement physical access restrictions
Communications and operations management	Documented operating procedures (8.1)	Implement measures to protect against information destruction or damage
Communications and operations management	Housekeeping (8.4)	Protect information destruction or loss

Table 8.7   Controls List Mapping ISO 17799 and GLBA (continued)

ISO 17799 Section	*Control[a]*	*GLBA*
Access control	Business requirement for system access (9.1)	Risk assessment required
Access control	User access management (9.2)	Authorized access only
Access control	User responsibility (9.3)	Train users
Access control	Operating system access control (9.5)	Implement incident response program
Access control	Monitoring system access and use (9.7)	Monitor systems and intrusion detection
Systems development and maintenance	Security requirements of systems (10.1)	Risk assessment
Systems development and maintenance	Cryptography (10.3)	Assess encryption requirements
Business continuity management	Aspects of business continuity planning (11.1)	Implement measures to protect against loss, destruction, or damage of information
Compliance	Reviews of security policy and technical compliances (12.2)	Report findings to board annually

[a] The numbers in parentheses are the matching section numbers found in ISO 17799.

While the guidelines have a mandatory scoring system for punishment, they also have an incentive for proactive crime prevention. The requirement here is for management to show *due diligence* in establishing an effective compliance program. There are seven elements that capture the basic functions inherent in most compliance programs:

1. Establish policies, standards, and procedures to guide the workforce.
2. Appoint a high-level manager to oversee compliance with the policy, standards, and procedures.
3. Exercise due care when granting discretionary authority to employees.
4. Ensure compliance policies are being carried out.

Table 8.8 Controls List Mapping ISO 17799, GLBA, and SOX

ISO 17799 Section	Control[a]	GLBA	Sarbanes–Oxley
Security policy	Risk assessment (2)	Assess risk	Assess current internal controls
Security policy	Policy (3.1)	Board approves written policy and program	Policies and procedures must support effective internal control of assets
Organizational security	Management information security forum (4.1)	Involve the board of directors Assign specific responsibilities	Corporation management is responsible for ensuring that internal controls are adequate
Organizational security	Security requirements in outsourcing contracts (4.3)	Report program effectiveness to board	Management must report on internal controls' effectiveness
Asset classification and control	Accounting of assets (5.1)	Implement policies to evaluate sensitivity of customer information	Identify all assets of the corporation
Asset classification and control	Information classification (5.2)	Implement standards and procedures to protect customer information	Information is an asset and the property of the enterprise
Systems development and maintenance	Security requirements of systems (10.1)	Risk assessment	Assess effectiveness of internal controls
Systems development and maintenance	Cryptography (10.3)	Assess encryption requirements	
Compliance	Reviews of security policy and technical compliances (12.2)	Report findings annually to board	Management must report on internal controls' effectiveness

a The numbers in parentheses are the matching section numbers found in ISO 17799.

5. Communicate the standards and procedures to all employees and others.
6. Enforce the policies, standards, and procedures consistently through appropriate disciplinary measures.
7. Implement procedures for corrections and modifications in case of violations.

These guidelines reward those organizations that make a good-faith effort to prevent unethical activity; this is done by lowering potential fines if, despite the organization's best efforts, unethical or illegal activities are still committed by the organization or its employees. To be judged effective, a compliance program need not prevent all misconduct; however, it must show due diligence in seeking to prevent and detect inappropriate behavior (Table 8.9).

8.3.9 Controls List Mapping ISO 17799, HIPAA, GLBA, SOX, and FSGCA

If your organization happens to be a multinational corporation that handles financial information of healthcare providers and clients, a set of controls for you might look like Table 8.10.

8.3.10 National Institute of Standards and Technology Controls List

The National Institute of Standards and Technology (NIST) has been publishing its 800 series of special publications for years. "An Introduction to Computer Security: The NIST Handbook" (800-12) has been the go-to document for information security professionals since it was first published in 1992.

The NIST documents listed in Table 8.11 can be obtained by accessing their Web site at csrc.nist.gov/publications/nistpubs/. For draft documents, access the following Web site: csrc.nist.gov/publications/drafts.html.

In November 2001 NIST published a self-assessment guide for information technology systems. This document provides a checklist assessment of tasks and functions to run a secure IT organization. With a few hours of editing, an effective controls list can be put together (Table 8.12). This controls list is too long to be effective in a risk assessment process. A subset should be created, similar to that in Table 8.13.

Use the NIST documents to help you find control ideas. Check the NIST Web site regularly to keep abreast of updates and changes.

Table 8.9   Controls List Mapping ISO 17799 and FSGCA

ISO 17799 Section	Control[a]	Federal Sentencing Guidelines
Security policy	Policy (3.1)	Establish policies, procedures, and standards to guide the workforce
Organizational security	Management information security forum (4.1)	Appoint high-level management to oversee compliance with program
Personnel security	Security in job descriptions (6.1)	Enforce the policies, standards, and procedures consistently through appropriate disciplinary measures
Personnel security	User training (6.2)	Communicate the standards and procedures to all employees and others
Access control	Business requirement for system access (9.1)	Exercise due care when granting discretionary authority to employees
Access control	User responsibility (9.3)	Communicate the standards and procedures to all employees and others
Compliance	Reviews of security policy and technical compliances (12.2)	Enforce the policies, standards, and procedures consistently through appropriate disciplinary measures

[a] The numbers in parentheses are the matching section numbers found in ISO 17799.

8.3.11 Controls List Mapping ISO 17799 and CobiT

CobiT (Controls Objectives for Information and Related Technology) was introduced in 1996 to provide a framework of generally applicable and accepted IT control practices. The work to create this set of practices was sponsored by the Information Systems Audit and Control Foundation. This suite of documents and processes can provide the information security and audit professional with a solid framework of controls and practices from which to form a solid risk assessment program. CobiT is copyrighted; for additional information on how to obtain a copy of the CobiT process,

Table 8.10 Controls List Mapping ISO 17799, HIPAA, GLBA, SOX, and FSGCA

ISO 17799 Section	Control[a]	HIPAA	GLBA	Sarbanes–Oxley	Federal Sentencing Guidelines
Risk assessment	Risk assessment (2)	Risk analysis (required)	Assess risk	Assess current internal controls	
Security policy	Policy (3.1)	Isolate healthcare clearinghouse functions (required) Integrity (standard)	Board approves written policy and program	Policies and procedures must support effective internal control of assets	Establish policies, procedures, and standards to guide the workforce
Organizational security	Management information security forum (4.1)	Risk management (required) Sanction policy (required) Privacy officer (required)	Involve the board of directors Assign specific responsibilities	Corporation management is responsible for ensuring that internal controls are adequate	Appoint high-level management to oversee compliance with program
Organizational security	Security of third-party access (4.2)	Business associate contracts (standard)	Contract clauses meet guidance objectives		
Organizational security	Security requirements in outsourcing contracts (4.3)	Audit controls (required)	Report program effectiveness to board	Management must report on internal controls' effectiveness	

Table 8.10 Controls List Mapping ISO 17799, HIPAA, GLBA, SOX, and FSGCA (continued)

ISO 17799 Section	Control[a]	HIPAA	GLBA	Sarbanes–Oxley	Federal Sentencing Guidelines
Asset classification and control	Accounting of assets (5.1)	Inventory all assets	Implement policies to evaluate sensitivity of customer information	Identify all assets of the corporation	
Asset classification and control	Information classification (5.2)	Information is an asset and the property of the enterprise	Implement standards and procedures to protect customer information	Information is an asset and the property of the enterprise	
Asset classification and control	Information labeling and handling (5.2)		Implement standards		
Personnel security	Security in job descriptions (6.1)		Background check on certain positions		Enforce the policies, standards, and procedures consistently through appropriate disciplinary measures

			Train staff to implement program	Communicate the standards and procedures to all employees and others
Personnel security	User training (6.2)		Train staff to implement program	
Personnel security	Responding to security incidents and malfunctions (6.3)		Incident response program	
Physical and environmental security	Secure areas (7.1)	Workstation security (standard)	Implement physical access restrictions	
Physical and environmental security	Equipment Security (7.2)			
Physical and environmental security	General controls (7.3)			
Communications and operations management	Documented operating procedures (8.1)	Response and reporting (required) Emergency mode operations plan (required) Transmission security (standard)	Implement measures to protect against information destruction or damage	

Table 8.10 Controls List Mapping ISO 17799, HIPAA, GLBA, SOX, and FSGCA (continued)

ISO 17799 Section	Control[a]	HIPAA	GLBA	Sarbanes–Oxley	Federal Sentencing Guidelines
Communications and operations management	System planning and acceptance (8.2)				
Communications and operations management	Protection from malicious software (8.3)				
Communications and operations management	Housekeeping (8.4)	Data backup (required)	Protect information destruction or loss		
Communications and operations management	Network management (8.5)				
Communications and operations management	Media handling and security (8.6)	Device and media control (standard) Media reuse (required)			
Communications and operations management	Exchanges of information and software (8.7)				

Access control	Business requirement for system access (9.1)	Risk analysis (required)	Risk assessment required	Exercise due care when granting discretionary authority to employees
Access control	User access management (9.2)	Authentication (standard)	Authorized access only	
Access control	User responsibility (9.3)		Train users	Communicate the standards and procedures to all employees and others
Access control	Network access control (9.4)			
Access control	Operating system access control (9.5)	Emergency access procedure (required)	Implement incident response program	
Access control	Application access control (9.6)	Unique user identification (required)		
Access control	Monitoring system access and use (9.7)		Monitoring systems and intrusion detection	

Table 8.10   Controls List Mapping ISO 17799, HIPAA, GLBA, SOX, and FSGCA (continued)

ISO 17799 Section	Control[a]	HIPAA	GLBA	Sarbanes–Oxley	Federal Sentencing Guidelines
Access control	Remote access and telecommuting (9.8)				
Systems development and maintenance	Security requirements of systems (10.1)	Risk analysis	Risk assessment	Assess effectiveness of internal control	
Systems development and maintenance	Security in application systems (10.2)				
Systems development and maintenance	Cryptography (10.3)		Assess encryption requirements		
Systems development and maintenance	Security of system files (10.4)				
Systems development and maintenance	Security in development and support environments (10.5)				

Business continuity management	Aspects of business continuity planning (11.1)	Data backup (required) Disaster recovery plan (required) Emergency mode operations plan (required)	Implement measures to protect against loss, destruction, or damage of information		
Compliance	Compliance with legal requirements (12.1)				
Compliance	Reviews of security policy and technical compliances (12.2)	Information system activity review (required) Audit controls (required)	Report findings annually to board	Management must report on internal controls' effectiveness	Enforce the policies, standards, and procedures consistently through appropriate disciplinary measures

[a] The numbers in parentheses are the matching section numbers found in ISO 17799.

Table 8.11   NIST 800 Series of Special Publications

NIST Special Publication Number	Title	Date
SP 800-2	Public-Key Cryptography	April 1991
SP 800-3	Establishing a Computer Security Incident Response Capability (CSIRC)	November 1991
SP 800-4	Computer Security Considerations in Federal Procurements: A Guide for Procurement Initiators, Contracting Officers, and Computer Security Officials	March 1992
SP 800-5	A Guide to the Selection of Anti-Virus Tools and Techniques	December 1992
SP 800-6	Automated Tools for Testing Computer System Vulnerability	December 1992
SP 800-7	Security in Open Systems	July 1994
SP 800-8	Security Issues in the Database Language SQL	August 1993
SP 800-9	Good Security Practices for Electronic Commerce, Including Electronic Data Interchange	December 1993
SP 800-10	Keeping Your Site Comfortably Secure: An Introduction to Internet Firewalls	December 1994
SP 800-11	The Impact of the FCC's Open Network Architecture on NS/EP Telecommunications Security	February 1995
SP 800-12	An Introduction to Computer Security: The NIST Handbook	October 1995
SP 800-13	Telecommunications Security Guidelines for Telecommunications Management Network	October 1995
SP 800-14	Generally Accepted Principles and Practices for Securing Information Technology Systems	September 1996
SP 800-15	Minimum Interoperability Specification for PKI Components (MISPC), Version 1	January 1998

Table 8.11   NIST 800 Series of Special Publications (continued)

NIST Special Publication Number	Title	Date
SP 800-16	Information Technology Security Training Requirements: A Role- and Performance-Based Model (supersedes NIST Special Publication 500-172)	April 1998
SP 800-17	Modes of Operation Validation System (MOVS): Requirements and Procedures	February 1998
SP 800-18	Guide for Developing Security Plans for Information Technology Systems	December 1998
SP 800-19	Mobile Agent Security	October 1999
SP 800-20	Modes of Operation Validation System for the Triple Data Encryption Algorithm (TMOVS): Requirements and Procedures	Revised April 2000
SP 800-21	Guideline for Implementing Cryptography in the Federal Government	November 1999
SP 800-22	A Statistical Test Suite for Random and Pseudo-Random Number Generators for Cryptographic Applications	October 2000 Revised May 15, 2001
SP 800-23	Guideline to Federal Organizations on Security Assurance and Acquisition/Use of Tested/Evaluated Products	August 2000
SP 800-24	PBX Vulnerability Analysis: Finding Holes in Your PBX before Someone Else Does	August 2000
SP 800-25	Federal Agency Use of Public Key Technology for Digital Signatures and Authentication	October 2000
SP 800-26	Security Self-Assessment Guide for Information Technology Systems	November 2001
SP 800-27	Engineering Principles for Information Technology Security (A Baseline for Achieving Security)	June 2001
SP 800-28	Guidelines on Active Content and Mobile Code	October 2001

Table 8.11   NIST 800 Series of Special Publications (continued)

NIST Special Publication Number	Title	Date
SP 800-29	A Comparison of the Security Requirements for Cryptographic Modules in FIPS 140-1 and FIPS 140-2	June 2001
SP 800-30	Risk Management Guide for Information Technology Systems	January 2002
SP 800-31	Intrusion Detection Systems (IDS)	November 2001
SP 800-32	Introduction to Public Key Technology and the Federal PKI Infrastructure	February 2001
SP 800-33	Underlying Technical Models for Information Technology Security	December 2001
SP 800-34	Contingency Planning Guide for Information Technology Systems	June 2002
SP 800-38A	Recommendation for Block Cipher Modes of Operation: Methods and Techniques	December 2001
SP 800-40	Procedures for Handling Security Patches	September 2002
SP 800-41	Guidelines on Firewalls and Firewall Policy	January 2002
SP 800-44	Guidelines on Securing Public Web Servers	September 2002
SP 800-45	Guidelines on Electronic Mail Security	September 2002
SP 800-46	Security for Telecommuting and Broadband Communications	September 2002
SP 800-47	Security Guide for Interconnecting Information Technology Systems	September 2002
SP 800-51	Use of the Common Vulnerabilities and Exposures (CVE) Vulnerability Naming Scheme	September 2002
SP 800-55	Security Metrics Guide for Information Technology Systems	July 2003
SP 800-59	Guideline for Identifying an Information System as a National Security System	August 2003
SP 800-61	Computer Security Incident Handling Guide	January 2004

Table 8.11   NIST 800 Series of Special Publications (continued)

NIST Special Publication Number	Title	Date
SP 800-63	Electronic Authentication Guideline: Recommendations of the National Institute of Standards and Technology	June 2004
SP 800-64	Security Considerations in the Information System Development Life Cycle	October 2003
SP 800-65	Integrating Security into the Capital Planning and Investment Control Process	Draft
SP 800-66	An Introductory Resource Guide for Implementing the Health Insurance Portability and Accountability Act (HIPAA) Security Rule	Draft
SP 800-67	Recommendation for the Triple Data Encryption Algorithm (TDEA) Block Cipher	May 2004
SP 800-68	Guidance for Securing Microsoft Windows XP Systems for IT Professionals: A NIST Security Configuration Checklist	Draft
SP 800-70	The NIST Security Configuration Checklist Program	Draft
SP 800-72	Guidance on PDA Forensics	Draft

contact the Information Systems Audit and Control Foundation at www.ITgovernance.org.

The CobiT process maps itself to ISO 17799. Table 8.14 shows a brief example of what you can get from CobiT.

8.3.12 Other Sources

The Instrumentation, Systems, and Automation Society (ISA) issued two technical reports in the spring of 2004. "Security Technologies for Manufacturing and Control Systems" (ISA-TR99.00.01) and "Integrating Electronic Security into the Manufacturing and Control Systems Environment" (ISA-TR99.00.02) address the controls that should be implemented to protect process control machines. In ISA-TR99.00.01, Section 6.4, "Program Tasks," item 1 identifies the need to define risks through a formal methodology.

Table 8.12 Controls List Using NIST SP 800-26

Category	Description	Reference
1. Risk management		Office of Management and Budget (OMB) Circular A-130, III
	1.1.1 Document current system configuration; include links to other systems.	NIST SP 800-18
	1.1.2 Perform and document risk assessments on a regular basis or whenever the system, facilities, or other conditions change.	Federal Information System Controls Audit Manual (FISCAM) SP-1
	1.1.3 Implement a process to identify data sensitivity and integrity.	FISCAM SP-1
	1.1.4 Identify threat sources, both natural and man-made.	FISCAM SP-1
	1.1.5 Maintain a list of known system vulnerabilities, system flaws, or weaknesses that could be exploited by the threat sources.	NIST SP 800-30
	1.1.6 Conduct an analysis to determine whether the security requirements in place adequately mitigate vulnerabilities.	NIST SP 800-30
	1.2.1 Document final risk determinations and related management approvals.	FISCAM SP-1
	1.2.2 Conduct a mission/business impact analysis.	NIST SP 800-30
	1.2.3 Identify additional controls to sufficiently mitigate identified risks.	NIST SP 800-30
2. Review of security controls		OMB Circular A-130, III FISCAM SP-5 NIST SP 800-18
	2.1 1 Conduct periodic reviews of the system and all network boundaries.	FISCAM SP-5.1

Table 8.12   Controls List Using NIST SP 800-26 (continued)

Category	Description	Reference
	2.1.2 Have an independent review performed when significant changes occur.	OMB Circular A-130, III FISCAM SP-5.1 NIST SP 800-18
	2.1.3 Conduct routine self-assessments.	NIST SP 800-18
	2.1.4 Conduct tests and examinations of key controls routinely, i.e., network scans, analyses of router and switch settings, penetration testing.	OMB Circular A-130, 8B3 NIST SP 800-18
	2.1.5 Review and analyze security alerts and security incidents and remedial actions.	FISCAM SP-3.4 NIST SP 800-18
	2.2.1 Implement an effective and timely process for reporting significant weakness and ensure effective remedial action.	FISCAM SP-5.1 and SP-5.2 NIST SP 800-18
3. Life cycle		OMB Circular A-130, III FISCAM CC-1.1
Initiation phase		
	3.1.1 Determine system sensitivity.	OMB Circular A-130, III FISCAM AC-1.1 and AC-1.2 NIST SP 800-18
	3.1.2 Document a business case to include the resources required for adequately securing the system.	Clinger–Cohen Act (CCA) Intended to reform acquisition laws and information technology of the federal government
	3.1.3 A process is in place to authorize and document software modifications.	FISCAM CC-1.2

Table 8.12 Controls List Using NIST SP 800-26 (continued)

Category	Description	Reference
	3.1.4 The budget request is to include required system security resources.	Government Information Security Reform Act (GISRA)
Development/ acquisition phase		
	3.1.5 During the system design, identify security requirements.	NIST SP 800-18
	3.1.6 Perform an initial risk assessment to determine security requirements.	NIST SP 800-30
	3.1.7 Obtain written agreement with management owner on the security controls employed and residual risk.	NIST SP 800-18
	3.1.8 Ensure security controls are consistent with and an integral part of the IT architecture.	OMB Circular A-130, 8B3
	3.1.9 Develop appropriate security controls with associated evaluation and test procedures before the procurement action.	NIST SP 800-18
	3.1.10 Include security requirements in all solicitation documents (e.g., request for proposals).	NIST SP 800-18
	3.1.11 Establish requirements in the solicitation documents regardless of whether it is permitted to update security controls as new threats/vulnerabilities are identified and as new technologies are implemented.	NIST SP 800-18
Implementation phase		
	3.2.1 Implement standards to ensure design reviews and system tests are done prior to placing the system in production.	FISCAM CC-2.1 NIST SP 800-18

Table 8.12   Controls List Using NIST SP 800-26 (continued)

Category	Description	Reference
	3.2.2 Document the test results.	FISCAM CC-2.1 NIST SP 800-18
	3.2.3 Document certification testing of security controls.	NIST SP 800-18
	3.2.4 Ensure documentation is updated when security controls are added after the development phase.	NIST SP 800-18
	3.2.5 Ensure added security controls are tested and documented.	FISCAM CC-2.1 NIST SP 800-18
	3.2.6 Conduct application technical evaluation to ensure that it meets applicable laws, regulations, policies, guidelines, and standards.	NIST SP 800-18
	3.2.7 Establish a process for written authorization to operate the system either on an interim basis with planned corrective action or full authorization.	NIST SP 800-18
Operation/ maintenance phase		
	3.2.8 Document the approval of the system security plan.	OMB Circular A-130, III FISCAM SP 2-1 NIST SP 800-18
	3.2.9 For systems connecting to other systems, ensure the controls have been established and disseminated to the owners of the interconnected systems.	NIST SP 800-18
	3.2.10 Implement procedures to ensure system security plans are kept current.	OMB Circular A-130, III FISCAM SP 2-1 NIST SP 800-18

Table 8.12   Controls List Using NIST SP 800-26 (continued)

Category	Description	Reference
Disposal phase		
	3.2.11 Implement procedures to ensure official electronic records are properly disposed of or archived.	NIST SP 800-18
	3.2.12 Institute procedures to ensure information or media is purged, overwritten, degaussed, or destroyed when disposed of or used elsewhere.	FISCAM AC-3.4 NIST SP 800-18
	3.2.13 Record who implemented the disposal actions and verify that the information or media was sanitized.	NIST SP 800-18
4. Authorize processing		OMB Circular A-130, III FIPS 102
	4.1.1 Implement procedure to ensure a technical or security evaluation has been completed or conducted when significant changes have occurred.	NIST SP 800-18
	4.1.2 Conduct a risk assessment when a significant change occurs.	NIST SP 800-18
	4.1.3 Implement an employee rights and responsibility statement and have it signed by all users.	NIST SP 800-18
	4.1.4 Develop and test a contingency plan.	NIST SP 800-18
	4.1.5 Implement procedures to have system security plans developed, updated, and reviewed.	NIST SP 800-18
	4.1.6 Implement procedures to ensure in-place controls are operating as intended.	NIST SP 800-18

Table 8.12 Controls List Using NIST SP 800-26 (continued)

Category	Description	Reference
	4.1.7 Ensure that planned and in-place controls are consistent with identified risks and the system and data sensitivity.	NIST SP 800-18
	4.1.8 Implement procedures to ensure that management authorizes interconnections to all systems (including systems owned and operated by another program, government agency, organization, or contractor).	NIST SP 800-18
	4.2.1 Implement procedures to ensure that management initiates prompt action to correct deficiencies.	NIST SP 800-18
5. System security plan		OMB Circular A-130, III NIST SP 800-18 FISCAM SP-2.1
	5.1.1 Have the system security plan approved by key affected parties and the information security steering committee.	FISCAM SP-2.1 NIST SP 800-18
	5.1.2 Ensure that the security plan addresses the topics prescribed by regulatory controls and directives.	NIST SP 800-18
	5.2.1 Implement procedures to ensure that the security plan is reviewed periodically and adjusted to reflect current conditions and risks.	NIST SP 800-18
6. Personnel security		OMB Circular A-130, III
	6.1.1 Ensure that all positions are reviewed for sensitivity level.	FISCAM SD-1.2 NIST SP 800-18
	6.1.2 Document job descriptions to accurately reflect assigned duties and responsibilities.	FISCAM SD-1.2

Table 8.12 Controls List Using NIST SP 800-26 (continued)

Category	Description	Reference
	6.1.3 Implement procedures to ensure that sensitive functions are divided among different individuals.	OMB Circular A-130, III FISCAM SD-1 NIST SP 800-18
	6.1.4 Implement procedures to ensure that distinct system support functions are performed by different individuals.	FISCAM SD-1.1
	6.1.5 Establish policies and awareness programs to notify users that they are responsible for their actions.	OMB Circular A-130, III FISCAM SD-2 and SD-3.2
	6.1.6 Require regularly scheduled vacations and periodic job/shift rotations.	FISCAM SD-1.1 FISCAM SP-4.1
	6.1.7 Establish procedures for the hiring, transferring, and termination of employees.	FISCAM SP-4.1 NIST SP 800-18
	6.1.8 Establish a process for requesting, establishing, issuing, and closing user accounts.	FISCAM SP-4.1 NIST 800-18
	6.2.1 Implement procedures to ensure that individuals who are authorized to bypass significant technical and operational controls are screened prior to access and periodically thereafter.	OMB Circular A-130, III FISCAM SP-4.1
	6.2.2 Implement nondisclosure agreements for employees and other personnel assigned to work with sensitive information.	FISCAM SP-4.1
	6.2.3 Implement procedures to screen individuals when controls cannot adequately protect the information.	OMB Circular A-130, III
7. Physical and environmental protection		FISCAM AC-3 NIST SP 800-18

Table 8.12   Controls List Using NIST SP 800-26 (continued)

Category	Description	Reference
Physical access control		
	7.1.1 Implement access control to facilities.	FISCAM AC-3 NIST SP 800-18
	7.1.2 Have management regularly review the list of persons with physical access to sensitive facilities.	FISCAM AC-3.1
	7.1.3 Implement procedures to authorize and log all deposits and withdrawals of tapes and other storage media from the library.	FISCAM AC-3.1
	7.1.4 Restrict access to the computer room and tape/media library.	FISCAM AC-3.1
	7.1.5 Implement procedures to secure unused keys or other entry devices.	FISCAM AC-3.1
	7.1.6 Implement controls to ensure that emergency exit and reentry procedures ensure that only authorized personnel are allowed to reenter after fire drills, etc.	FISCAM AC-3.1
	7.1.7 Require all visitors to sensitive areas to sign in and be escorted.	FISCAM AC-3.1
	7.1.8 Change entry codes periodically.	FISCAM AC-3.1
	7.1.9 Monitor physical accesses through audit trails and implement procedures to investigate apparent security violations and implement remedial action.	FISCAM AC-4
	7.1.10 Implement procedures to investigate suspicious access activity and document corrective action.	FISCAM AC-4.3

Table 8.12   Controls List Using NIST SP 800-26 (continued)

Category	Description	Reference
	7.1.11 Implement procedures to require that visitors, contractors, and maintenance personnel be authenticated through the use of preplanned appointments and identification checks.	FISCAM AC-3.1
Fire safety factors		
	7.1.12 Ensure that all appropriate fire suppression and prevention devices are installed and working.	FISCAM SC-2.2 NIST SP 800-18
	7.1.13 Implement procedures to periodically review all fire ignition sources, such as failures of electronic devices or wiring, improper storage materials, and the possibility of arson.	NIST SP 800-18
Supporting utilities		
	7.1.14 Implement controls to properly maintain heating and air-conditioning systems.	NIST SP 800-18
	7.1.15 Implement redundant air-cooling systems where appropriate.	FISCAM SC-2.2
	7.1.16 Review electric power distribution, heating plants, water, sewage, and other utilities periodically for risk of failure.	FISCAM SC-2.2 NIST SP 800-18
	7.1.17 Implement controls to ensure that building plumbing lines are identified and do not endanger the system.	FISCAM SC-2.2 NIST SP 800-18
	7.1.18 Has an uninterruptible power supply or backup generator been provided?	FISCAM SC-2.2

Table 8.12   Controls List Using NIST SP 800-26 (continued)

Category	Description	Reference
	7.1.19 Implement a business continuity plan to address the mitigation of other disasters, such as floods, earthquakes, etc.	FISCAM SC-2.2
Interception of data		
	7.2.1 Implement controls to ensure that computer monitors are located in such as way as to eliminate viewing by unauthorized persons.	NIST SP 800-18
	7.2.2 Restrict physical access to data transmission lines.	NIST SP 800-18
Mobile and portable systems		
	7.3.1 Encrypt sensitive data files on all portable systems.	NIST SP 800-14
	7.3.2 Store securely all portable systems.	NIST SP 800-14
8. Production input–output controls		NIST SP 800-18
	8.1.1 Establish a help desk or group to offer advice.	NIST SP 800-18
	8.2.1 Implement processes to ensure that unauthorized individuals cannot read, copy, alter, or steal printed or electronic information.	NIST SP 800-18
	8.2.2 Implement processes for ensuring that only authorized users pick up, receive, or deliver input and output information and media.	NIST SP 800-18

Table 8.12   Controls List Using NIST SP 800-26 (continued)

Category	Description	Reference
	8.2.3 Create audit trails to be used for receipt of sensitive inputs and outputs.	NIST SP 800-18
	8.2.4 Implement controls for transporting or mailing media or printed output.	NIST SP 800-18
	8.2.5 Require internal and external labeling for data sensitivity.	NIST SP 800-18
	8.2.6 Ensure that the external label contains special handling instructions.	NIST SP 800-18
	8.2.7 Implement audit trails for inventory management.	NIST SP 800-18
	8.2.8 Ensure that electronic media are sanitized prior to reuse.	FISCAM AC-3.4 NIST SP 800-18
	8.2.9 Implement procedures to destroy damaged media.	NIST SP 800-18
	8.2.10 Require hard-copy media to be shredded or destroyed when no longer needed.	NIST SP 800-18
9. Contingency planning		OMB Circular A-130, III
	9.1.1 Document critical data files and identify operations requirements for the frequency of file backup.	FISCAM SC-1.1 and SC-3.1 NIST SP 800-18
	9.1.2 Identify all resources supporting critical operations.	FISCAM SC-1.2
	9.1.3 Processing priorities established by a formal business impact analysis (BIA) must be approved by management.	FISCAM SC-1.3
	9.2.1 Implement the approval process for key affected parties.	FISCAM SC-3.1
	9.2.2 Assign all recovery responsibilities.	FISCAM SC-3.1

Table 8.12   Controls List Using NIST SP 800-26 (continued)

Category	Description	Reference
	9.2.3 Document detailed instructions for restoring operations.	FISCAM SC-3.1
	9.2.4 For any alternate processing site, ensure that the contract or reciprocal agreement is in place.	FISCAM SC-3.1 NIST SP 800-18
	9.2.5 Identify the location of stored backups.	NIST SP 800-18
	9.2.6 Implement procedures to back up files on a prescribed basis and rotate them off site often enough to avoid disruption if current files are damaged.	FISCAM SC-2.1
	9.2.7 Maintain system and application documentation at the off-site location.	FISCAM SC-2.1
	9.2.8 Implement procedures to ensure that all system defaults reset after being restored from a backup.	FISCAM SC-3.1
	9.2.9 Ensure that the backup storage site and alternate site are geographically removed from the primary site and physically protected.	FISCAM SC-2.1
	9.2.10 Ensure that the contingency plan has been distributed to all appropriate personnel.	FISCAM SC-3.1
	9.3.1 Store securely off site an up-to-date copy of the plan.	FISCAM SC-3.1
	9.3.2 Regularly train employees in their roles and responsibilities.	FISCAM SC-2.3 NIST SP 800-18
	9.3.3 Test and readjust the plan periodically.	FISCAM SC-2.3 NIST SP 800-18
10. Hardware and software maintenance		OMB Circular A-130, III

Table 8.12   Controls List Using NIST SP 800-26 (continued)

Category	Description	Reference
	10.1.1 Implement restrictions on all who perform maintenance and repair activities.	OMB Circular A-130, III FISCAM SS-3.1 NIST SP 800-18
	10.1.2 Restrict and monitor access to all program libraries.	FISCAM CC-3.2 and CC-3.3
	10.1.3 Implement on-site and off-site maintenance procedures (e.g., escort of maintenance personnel, sanitization of devices removed from the site).	NIST SP 800-18
	10.1.4 Configure operating systems to prevent circumvention of the security software and application controls.	FISCAM SS-1.2
	10.1.5 Implement procedures to monitor the use of system utilities.	FISCAM SS-2.1
	10.2.1 Conduct an impact analysis to determine the effect of proposed changes on existing security controls, including the required training needed to implement the control.	NIST SP 800-18
	10.2.2 Implement procedures to test, document, and approve system components (operating system, utility, applications) prior to promotion to production.	FISCAM SS-3.1, SS-3.2, and CC-2.1 NIST SP 800-18
	10.2.3 Require software change request forms to document requests and related approvals.	FISCAM CC-1.2 NIST SP 800-18
	10.2.4 Require that detailed system specifications be prepared and reviewed by management.	FISCAM CC-2.1
	10.2.5 Specify the type of test data to be used (i.e., production or made up).	NIST SP 800-18

Table 8.12   Controls List Using NIST SP 800-26 (continued)

Category	Description	Reference
	10.2.6 Set default settings of security features to the most restrictive mode.	PSN Security Assessment Guidelines
	10.2.7 Implement controls to ensure that all locations affected by software distribution implementation have the effective date.	FISCAM CC-2.3
	10.2.8 Implement version control.	NIST SP 800-18
	10.2.9 Label and inventory all programs.	FISCAM CC-3.1
	10.2.10 Implement procedures to document and review the distribution and implementation of new or revised software.	FISCAM SS-3.2
	10.2.11 Implement controls to document and approve emergency changes, either prior to the change or after the fact.	FISCAM CC-2.2
	10.2.12 Update contingency plans and other associated documentation to reflect system changes.	FISCAM SC-2.1 NIST SP 800-18
	10.2.13 Implement controls to identify and document the use of copyrighted software or shareware and personally owned software/equipment.	NIST SP 800-18
	10.3.1 Periodically review systems to identify and, when possible, eliminate unnecessary services (e.g., FTP, HTTP, mainframe supervisor calls).	NIST SP 800-18
	10.3.2 Periodically review systems for known vulnerabilities and install software patches promptly.	NIST SP 800-18
11. Data integrity		OMB Circular A-130, 8B3

Table 8.12   Controls List Using NIST SP 800-26 (continued)

Category	Description	Reference
	11.1.1 Update virus signature files routinely.	NIST SP 800-18
	11.1.2 Implement automatic virus scanning.	NIST SP 800-18
	11.2.1 Require use of reconciliation routines by applications, i.e., checksums, hash totals, record counts.	NIST SP 800-18
	11.2.2 Implement procedures to investigate and institute appropriate corrective actions when inappropriate or unusual activity is reported.	FISCAM SS-2.2
	11.2.3 Implement procedures to determine compliance with password standards.	NIST SP 800-18
	11.2.4 Ensure that integrity verification programs used by applications look for evidence of data tampering, errors, and omissions.	NIST SP 800-18
	11.2.5 Implement intrusion detection tools.	NIST SP 800-18
	11.2.6 Implement procedures to ensure that intrusion detection reports are routinely reviewed and suspected incidents are handled accordingly.	NIST SP 800-18
	11.2.7 Implement system performance monitoring to analyze system performance logs in real-time to look for availability problems, including active attacks.	NIST SP 800-18
	11.2.8 Perform penetration testing on systems where and when appropriate.	NIST SP 800-18
	11.2.9 Implement message authentication.	NIST SP 800-18

Table 8.12   Controls List Using NIST SP 800-26 (continued)

Category	Description	Reference
12. Documentation		OMB Circular A-130, 8B3
	12.1.1 Verify receipt of vendor-supplied documentation of purchased software.	NIST SP 800-18
	12.1.2 Verify receipt of vendor-supplied documentation of purchased hardware.	NIST SP 800-18
	12.1.3 Require application documentation for in-house applications.	NIST SP 800-18
	12.1.4 Require network diagrams and documentation on setups of routers and switches.	NIST SP 800-18
	12.1.5 Require documentation of software and hardware testing procedures and results.	NIST SP 800-18
	12.1.6 Implement standard operating procedures for all the topic areas covered in this document.	NIST SP 800-18
	12.1.7 Create user manuals.	NIST SP 800-18
	12.1.8 Document emergency procedures.	NIST SP 800-18
	12.1.9 Require backup procedures.	NIST SP 800-18
	12.2.1 Identify the system security plan.	OMB Circular A-130, III FISCAM SP-2.1 NIST SP 800-18
	12.2.2 Require a contingency plan.	NIST SP 800-18
	12.2.3 Implement written agreements regarding how data is shared between interconnected systems.	OMB Circular A-130, III NIST SP 800-18
	12.2.4 Maintain risk assessment reports for seven years.	NIST SP 800-18

Table 8.12   Controls List Using NIST SP 800-26 (continued)

Category	Description	Reference
	12.2.5 Retain certification and accreditation documents and a statement authorizing the system to process.	NIST SP 800-18
13. Security awareness, training, and education		OMB Circular A-130, III
	13.1.1 Ensure that all employees receive a copy of the employee's standard of conduct.	NIST SP 800-18
	13.1.2 Document employee training and professional development.	FISCAM SP-4.2
	13.1.3 Require mandatory annual refresher training and awareness.	OMB Circular A-130, III
	13.1.4 Implement methods to make employees aware of security, i.e., posters, booklets.	NIST SP 800-18
	13.1.5 Ensure that employees received a copy of or have easy access to security procedures and policies.	NIST SP 800-18
14. Incident response capability		OMB Circular A-130, III FISCAM SP-3.4 NIST 800-18
	14.1.1 Implement a formal incident response capability.	FISCAM SP-3.4 NIST SP 800-18
	14.1.2 Implement a process for reporting incidents.	FISCAM SP-3.4 NIST SP 800-18
	14.1.3 Monitor and track incidents until they are resolved.	NIST SP 800-18
	14.1.4 Train personnel to recognize and handle incidents.	FISCAM SP-3.4 NIST SP 800-18

Table 8.12   Controls List Using NIST SP 800-26 (continued)

Category	Description	Reference
	14.1.6 Implement a process to modify incident handling procedures and control techniques after an incident occurs.	NIST SP 800-18
	14.2.1 Implement a process to share incident information and common vulnerabilities or threats with stakeholders.	OMB Circular A-130, III NIST SP 800-18
	14.2.2 Implement procedures to report incident information with all appropriate controlling bodies.	OMB Circular A-130, III GISRA
	14.2.3 Implement procedures to report incident information with local law enforcement when necessary.	OMB Circular A-130, III GISRA
15. Technical controls		OMB Circular A-130, III FISCAM AC-2 NIST SP 800-18
	15.1.1 Maintain a current list of approved authorized users and their access.	FISCAM AC-2 NIST SP 800-18
	15.1.2 Require that digital signatures be used when appropriate.	NIST SP 800-18
	15.1.3 Prohibit access scripts with embedded passwords.	NIST SP 800-18
	15.1.4 Implement procedures to authorize emergency and temporary access.	FISCAM AC-2.2
	15.1.5 Match personnel files with user accounts to ensure that terminated or transferred individuals do not retain system access.	FISCAM AC-3.2

Table 8.12   Controls List Using NIST SP 800-26 (continued)

Category	Description	Reference
	15.1.6 Require password changes at least every 90 days, or earlier if needed.	FISCAM AC-3.2 NIST SP 800-18
	15.1.7 Require passwords to be unique and difficult to guess (e.g., do passwords require alphanumeric, upper- and lowercase, and special characters?).	FISCAM AC-3.2 NIST SP 800-18
	15.1.8 Disable inactive user identifications after a specified period.	FISCAM AC-3.2 NIST SP 800-18
	15.1.9 Require that passwords not be displayed when entered.	FISCAM AC-3.2 NIST SP 800-18
	15.1.10 Implement procedures for handling lost and compromised passwords.	FISCAM AC-3.2 NIST SP 800-18
	15.1.11 Distribute passwords securely and inform users not to reveal their passwords to anyone (social engineering).	NIST SP 800-18
	15.1.12 Transmit and store passwords using secure protocols/algorithms.	FISCAM AC-3.2 NIST SP 800-18
	15.1.13 Replace vendor-supplied passwords immediately.	FISCAM AC-3.2 NIST SP 800-18
	15.1.14 Establish a limit to the number of invalid access attempts that may occur for a given user.	FISCAM AC-3.2 NIST SP 800-18
	15.2.1 Require the system to correlate actions to users.	OMB Circular A-130, III FISCAM SD-2.1
	15.2.2 Implement procedures to ensure that data owners periodically review access authorizations to determine whether they remain appropriate.	FISCAM AC-2.1

Table 8.12   Controls List Using NIST SP 800-26 (continued)

Category	Description	Reference
16. Logical access controls		OMB Circular A-130, III FISCAM AC-3.2 NIST SP 800-18
	16.1.1 Ensure that the security controls detect unauthorized access attempts.	FISCAM AC-3.2 NIST SP 800-18
	16.1.2 Implement access control software that prevents an individual from having all the necessary authority or information access to allow fraudulent activity without collusion.	FISCAM AC-3.2 NIST SP 800-18
	16.1.3 Restrict access to security software to security administrators.	FISCAM AC-3.2
	16.1.4 Implement workstations' disconnect or screen savers' lock system after a specific period of inactivity.	FISCAM AC-3.2 NIST SP 800-18
	16.1.5 Implement procedures to monitor and remove inactive users' accounts when not needed.	FISCAM AC-3.2 NIST SP 800-18
	16.1.6 Use internal security labels (naming conventions) to control access to specific information types or files.	FISCAM AC-3.2 NIST SP 800-18
	16.1.7 Ensure that all uses of encryption meet all appropriate standards.	NIST SP 800-18
	16.1.8 Implement procedures for key generation, distribution, storage, use, destruction, and archiving.	NIST SP 800-18
	16.1.9 Restrict access to files at the logical view or field.	FISCAM AC-3.2

Table 8.12   Controls List Using NIST SP 800-26 (continued)

Category	Description	Reference
	16.1.10 Monitor access to identify apparent security violations and investigate such events.	FISCAM AC-4
	16.2.1 Implement communication software to restrict access via specific terminals.	FISCAM AC-3.2
	16.2.2 Disable insecure protocols (e.g., UDP, FTP).	PSN Security Assessment Guidelines
	16.2.3 Reinitialize all vendor-supplied default security parameters to more secure settings.	PSN Security Assessment Guidelines
	16.2.4 Restrict controls that allow remote access to the system.	NIST SP 800-18
	16.2.5 Maintain and review network activity logs.	FISCAM AC-3.2
	16.2.6 Automatically disconnect the network connection at the end of a session.	FISCAM AC-3.2
	16.2.7 Restrict trust relationships among hosts and external entities appropriately.	FISCAM AC-3.2
	16.2.8 Monitor dial-in access.	FISCAM AC-3.2
	16.2.9 Restrict and monitor access to telecommunications hardware or facilities.	FISCAM AC-3.2
	16.2.10 Install firewalls or secure gateways.	NIST SP 800-18
	16.2.11 Ensure that installed firewalls comply with firewall policies and rules.	FISCAM AC-3.2
	16.2.12 Implement controls over guest and anonymous accounts to ensure that they are authorized and monitored.	PSN Security Assessment Guidelines

Table 8.12   Controls List Using NIST SP 800-26 (continued)

Category	Description	Reference
	16.2.13 Ensure that an approved standardized log-on banner is displayed on the system warning unauthorized users that they have accessed a restricted system and can be punished.	FISCAM AC-3.2 NIST SP 800-18
	16.2.14 Encrypt sensitive data transmissions.	FISCAM AC-3.2
	16.2.15 Restrict access to tables defining network options, resources, and operator profiles.	FISCAM AC-3.2
	16.3.1 Post the organization's privacy policy on the Web site.	OMB-99-18
17. Audit trails		OMB Circular A-130, III FISCAM AC-4.1 NIST SP 800-18
	17.1.1 Ensure that the audit trail provides a trace of user actions.	NIST SP 800-18
	17.1.2 Ensure that the audit trail supports after-the-fact investigations of how, when, and why normal operations ceased.	NIST SP 800-18
	17.1.3 Strictly control access to online audit logs.	NIST SP 800-18
	17.1.4 Retain offline storage of audit logs for a period, and strictly control access to audit logs.	NIST SP 800-18
	17.1.5 Implement a separation of duties between security personnel who administer the access control function and those who administer the audit trail.	NIST SP 800-18
	17.1.6 Review audit trails frequently.	NIST SP 800-18

Table 8.12   Controls List Using NIST SP 800-26 (continued)

Category	Description	Reference
	17.1.7 Where possible, use automated tools to review audit records in real-time or near-real-time.	NIST SP 800-18
	17.1.8 Implement procedures to investigate suspicious activity and take appropriate action.	FISCAM AC-4.3
	17.1.9 Use keystroke monitoring and notify users of the control.	NIST SP 800-18

Table 8.13   NIST Controls List Subset

Control Category	Description
1. Risk management	Implement a formal risk assessment process.
	Management owners must be part of the risk assessment process and approve the findings.
2. Review security controls	Review the security controls of the system and interconnected systems on a regular basis.
	Ensure that management implements corrective actions.
3. Life cycle	Implement a system development life cycle methodology.
	Implement procedures to ensure that changes are controlled as programs progress through testing to final approval.
4. Authorize processing	Implement processes to ensure that the systems are reviewed and, where applicable, certified or recertified.
	For systems operating on an interim authority to process implemented procedures, ensure that they are in accordance with specified procedures.
5. System security plan	Document the system security plan and all interconnected systems if the boundary controls are ineffective.
	Implement controls to keep the plan current.

Table 8.13 NIST Controls List Subset (continued)

Control Category	Description
6. Personnel security	Implement controls to ensure that the tenets of separation of duty, least privilege, and individual accountability are ensured.
	Conduct background screening for sensitive positions prior to granting access.
7. Physical and environmental protection	Implement physical security controls that are commensurate with the risks of physical damage or access.
	Implement procedures to protect data from interception.
	Implement procedures to ensure that mobile and portable systems are protected.
8. Production input–output controls	Implement a process to ensure that the user community is properly supported.
	Implement controls to ensure that media are properly controlled.
9. Continuity planning	Implement a BIA to identify mission-critical and sensitive operations.
	Implement processes to identify supporting computer resources for all mission-critical activities.
	Implement and document a comprehensive continuity plan.
	Implement procedures to test business continuity and disaster recovery plans at least annually.
10. Hardware and software maintenance	Implement controls to limit access to all system software and hardware.
	Ensure that the change management process authorizes, tests, and approves all new and revised hardware and software before implementation.
	Implement procedures to ensure that systems are managed in a manner to reduce vulnerabilities.
11. Data integrity	Implement and maintain virus detection and elimination software.
	Implement controls to ensure the data's integrity and validity to provide assurance that the information has not been altered and the system functions as intended.

Table 8.13 NIST Controls List Subset (continued)

Control Category	Description
12. Documentation	Include in documentation an explanation of how software or hardware is to be used.
	Document all security and operational procedures.
13. Security awareness, training, and education	Ensure that all employees receive adequate training to fulfill their security responsibilities.
14. Incident response capability	Implement emergency response procedures to ensure that there is the capability to provide help to users when a security incident occurs in the system.
	Where appropriate, share incident-related information with appropriate business partners and stakeholders.
15. Identification and authentication	Implement controls to ensure that users are individually authenticated.
	Implement controls to enforce segregation of duties.
16. Logical access control	Implement controls to ensure that logical access restricts users to authorized transactions and functions only.
	Implement logical controls over network access.
	Implement controls to control public accesses to the system.
17. Audit trails	Log, monitor, and investigate all possible security violations.

In ISA-TR99.00.02 the controls listed include a notation to "Follow ISO 17799:2000."

Whatever industry you are working in, check the control requirements against ISO 17799 to see your level of compliance. ISO 17799 is not the answer; a controls list that maps to the needs of your organization is what will work best.

Table 8.14 Controls List Mapping ISO 17799 and CobiT

	CobiT Security Baseline		
Control Objectives	*Description*	*ISO 17799 Reference*	*CobiT Reference*
Identify mission-critical applications, systems, and business processes.	Conduct a formal business impact analysis (BIA).	11.1	PO1: 1.1, 1.8 PO2: 2.2, 2.3, 2.4
Define and communicate security responsibilities.	Define specific responsibilities for management, employees, and other personnel	4.1, 6.1, 8.1	PO4: 4.5, 4.6, 4.9, 4.10
Define and communicate management's objectives with regard to information security.	Communicate and discuss on a regular basis security incident reporting and response activities.	3.1, 4.1, 6.1, 7.2, 8.7, 9.3, 9.4, 12.1	PO6: 6.2, 6.3, 6.6, 6.8, 6.9, 6.11
Ensure that sensitive functions are staffed properly.	Establish job description requirements and conduct thorough background checks.	6.1	PO7: 7.1, 7.2, 7.6
Implement a program to ensure that the organization is in compliance with laws, regulations, and other requirements.	Implement procedures to review laws and regulations to ensure that intellectual property is properly protected.	8.7, 12.1	PO8: 8.2, 8.3, 8.4, 8.5, 8.6 DS12: 12.4
Implement a process to identify threats, prioritize the threats, and contain or accept the associated risks.	Implement an active risk management program.	4.1, 4.2, 5.2, 10.1	PO9: 9.1, 9.3 DS5: 5.8

Chapter 9

Business Impact Analysis (BIA)

9.1 Overview

The principal objective of the business impact analysis (BIA) is to determine the effect that mission-critical information system failures have on the viability and operations of enterprise core business processes. By using all of the techniques discussed in this book, you can create a facilitated process for BIA. Once the critical resources are scored, the organization can identify appropriate controls to ensure that the business continues to meet its business objectives or mission.

Just as scoring tables were developed with the assistance of other departments, so will the BIA work the same process. The enterprise will have to determine what elements are important to it and then develop a process to score those elements. The BIA will use those tables to examine the business processes, establish their priorities, and determine what other processes are dependent on them.

There are a number of tangible and intangible elements that should be considered in the BIA process. In the section on qualitative risk assessment, we examined tables that addressed corporate embarrassment, value to competitors, legal implications, cost of disruption, and financial loss. This BIA process has similar types of tables and modifies them to meet each business's requirements.

Part of the BIA process comes from the risk analysis process itself. When reviewing system and application availability, the business manager can use the results from this process to see the need for a BIA. The process will review the business areas for vulnerability — such items as cash flow, telecommunication systems, computer operations, or critical dependencies.

9.2 Creating a BIA Process

The results of the BIA process will be used by the organization to determine how critical a specific application, system, business process, or other asset is relative to all of the other assets in the organization. The BIA results are submitted to the senior management oversight committee, typically the information security steering committee, for review and approval.

The BIA process begins with the creation of a set of definitions of possible impacts to the business or mission of the organization. These might include the areas listed in Table 9.1.

From these definitions, a set of impact tables should be created that will identify the impact thresholds for the various categories. The BIA team will work with the specific departments to establish the criticality thresholds. We discussed the development of these types of tables in Chapter 4 on qualitative risk assessment.

The impact table might look like Table 9.2.

The financial staff is interviewed to determine how much is enough. To assist in this process, a financial impact worksheet is developed. There are some problems with the figures that this will generate. The worksheet takes into account the effects of outages during the most critical time of the business cycle for each business process. So, the value that is obtained from the review includes loss of sales in addition to other costs of doing business in an outage situation. The total business impacts from each of these sheets can add up to more than the revenue generated in annual sales by the enterprise. Although this figure may be correct, it will require some quick discussion on your part to make management understand that an outage of 10 days can lead to losses beyond the annual gross income. Be very careful how you use the figures generated from a worksheet like Table 9.3.

I recommend that the first value you present to management for one day's outage be something along the line of the total gross revenue divided by 264 (the typical number of working days in a year). So, if your enterprise has an annual gross income of $50 million, then the first day's losses would equal ($50,000,000/264 = $190,300.69). Once you have established that you understand the annual revenues, you can discuss the increasing costs of being out of business.

Table 9.1   BIA Definitions

Category	If the Asset Was Unavailable:
Competitive disadvantage	What would be the impact to our competitive standing?
Direct business loss	What would be the impact to our business revenues or profits?
Loss of public confidence or reputation	What would be the impact to our customer confidence, public image, or shareholder or supplier loyalty?
Poor morale	What would be the impact to our employee morale?
Fraud	What level of goods, services, or funds would be diverted?
Wrong management decisions	What would be the impact to management having access to information to make informed business decisions?
Business disruption	What other applications, programs, systems, or business processes would be impacted?
Legal liability	Could the organization be in breach of legal, regulatory, or contractual obligations?
Privacy loss	Could our customers, clients, or employees suffer loss of personal privacy information?
Safety risk	What would be the impact to our customers', clients', and employees' health and safety?

Once the values for each element are determined for each business process affected by the application or system, those figures are plugged into a table like Table 9.4.

A typical BIA process would look at a program, system, business process, or application and fill in the worksheet based on what the business unit believes is the longest tolerable outage. The purchasing department might have determined that five days is its impact level, and it would fill in a BIA that looks like Table 9.5.

The accounts payable department at year-end has determined that two days is its longest tolerable outage, and its worksheet might look like Table 9.6.

The purchasing business process is categorized as a tier 3 recovery level (three to five days), and accounts payable is a level 2.

Business impact analysis is an example of what can be done once the basics of qualitative risk analysis are mastered. The only limit that is imposed on you is what you can think of to use the process for.

Table 9.2 BIA Impacts

Impact Value	Health and Safety	Interruption of Production Impact	Public Image	Environmental Release	Financial
		Intangible Loss (Dollar Loss Difficult to Estimate)			Tangible Loss
1	Loss of life or limb	1 week	Total loss of public confidence and reputation	Permanent damage to environment	More than $10M
2	Requires hospitalization	3 days	Long-term blemish of company image	Long-term (1 year or more) damage to environment	$1,000,001–$10M
3	Cuts, bruises, requires first aid	1–2 days	Temporary blemish of company image	Temporary (6 months to 1 year) damage	$100,001–$1M
4	Major exposure to unsafe work environment	1 day	Company business unit image damaged	Department noncompliant	$50,001–$100,000
5	Little or no negative impact / Minor exposure to unsafe work environment	<4 hours	Little or no image impact	Little or no impact	$0–$50,000

Table 9.3 BIA Financial Impact Worksheet

Financial Impact Worksheet	
Type of Impact	*Estimated Dollar Loss if Asset Were Unavailable Just beyond the Longest Tolerable Outage*
Loss of sales	
Regulatory fines	
Legal fines	
Cost of money (e.g., revenue collection delayed)	
Loss of competitive advantage	
Loss of investor confidence	
Loss of customer confidence	
Adverse public opinion	
Reporting delay (financial reports, etc.)	
Cost of disruption to business	
Replacement of employees	
Elimination of work backlog	
Use of alternate procedures	
Loss of productive time	
Replacement of lost information	
Equipment repair or replacement	
Decreased employee morale	
Operating delay	
Total estimated loss	

Table 9.4   BIA Worksheet

BIA Worksheet

If the Asset User Review Were Unavailable for:	Using the Provided BIA Impact Table, What Would Be the Impact to:				
	Health and Safety	Interruption of Production	Public Image	Environmental Release	Financial
<24 hours					
24–72 hours					
73 hours–5 days					
6–9 days					
10 days or more					

Table 9.5   BIA Worksheet Example 1 — Purchasing

BIA Worksheet

If the Asset User Review Were Unavailable for:	Using the Provided BIA Impact Table, What Would Be the Impact to:				
	Health and Safety	Interruption of Production	Public Image	Environmental Release	Financial
<24 hours	N/A			N/A	
24–72 hours					
73 hours–5 days		3	4		4
6–9 days					
10 days or more					

Table 9.6 BIA Worksheet Example 2 — Accounts Payable

BIA Worksheet

If the Asset User Review Were Unavailable for:	Using the Provided BIA Impact Table, What Would Be the Impact to:					
	Health and Safety	*Interruption of Production*	*Public Image*	*Environmental Release*	*Financial*	
<24 hours	N/A					
24–72 hours		2	4	3	3	
73 hours–5 days						
6–9 days						
10 days or more						

Chapter 10

Conclusion

The uses of qualitative risk analysis are limited only by what you can think of to do with it. The prescreening process can provide the information security or audit group with some important image enhancements when the business units see how important it is to smooth out the business cycle. The goal of an effective risk management process is to implement controls only where necessary.

Risk assessment is not done to fulfill audit requirements. It is not done because information security mandated it. It is not done to be in compliance with laws and regulations. Risk assessment is done because it makes sound business sense and provides management with the documentation to prove that it has performed its due diligence.

Being able to identify the assets of the organization and determine what threats are out there and what safeguards are available ensure that the limited resources of any organization are put where they will do the most good. Risk assessment supports the business objectives or mission of the enterprise and is conducted because it will improve the bottom line.

Risk assessment is an essential component in the successful management of any organization. It is a process that must start from the inception of the project and continue until the application or system is completed and its expected benefits have been realized. Risk assessment must be focused on the areas of highest risk within the scope of the review, with continual monitoring of other areas of the project to identify any new or escalating risks.

The success of a risk assessment strategy is dependent on:

- The commitment of senior management
- The skills and experience of the risk management team in the identification of threats and the development of effective risk controls
- The risk management team and the business unit working closely together to identify and manage information asset threats
- The risk assessment process being ongoing
- The use of a consistent risk assessment process
- Regular reporting of the performance of safeguards meeting the needs of the organization

Appendix A

Sample Risk Assessment Management Summary Report

Customer Information Held and Processed at GLBA Bank: October 21, 2004

Contents

Attendees 300

Assessment Team: 300

Risk Assessment Scope Summary: 300

Assessment Methodology Used: 301

Assessment Findings and Action Plan: 301

Full Findings Documentation: 303

Conclusion: 303

Attendees

Assessment Team:

Gilbert Godfried	Nicole Kidmann
Katherine Turner	Lloyd Nolan
Bill Aikman	Liane Bronco
Leonard Elmore	Gerry Lee
Myra Osmond	Melvinia Nattia
Mike Illich	Ryan Harris
Wayne Fontes	MaryJane Ashman
Linda Wright	

Facilitator:	Thomas R. Peltier	Peltier and Associates
Scribes:	Lisa Bryson	Peltier and Associates
	Julie Peltier	Peltier and Associates

Risk Assessment Scope Summary

On October 23, 2004 the GLBA Bank (GLBA) risk assessment team and Peltier and Associates met to review the scope of a risk assessment to be conducted on Nonpublic Personal Customer Information held and/or processed at GLBA. The team discussed the most recent Office of the Comptroller of the Currency (OCC) examination of GLBA. The team also reviewed the December 21, 2003 Visioneering, Inc. (VI) information system audit; the Gross Technology Partners (GTP) November 18, 2003 Penetration Test and Network Vulnerability Assessment report; and the GLBA Internal Audit report of November 30, 2003. The findings of these reviews, assessments and audits were used to develop a risk assessment scope statement.

On October 24, 2004, GLBA Bank (GLBA) staff at the 45 North Main Avenue, Buzzover, UT, conducted the risk assessment. The intent of this process was to identify threats that could signify risk to the integrity, confidentiality, and availability of Nonpublic Personal Customer Information being held and/or processed by GLBA.

Fifteen (15) GLBA employees participated in the process. These employees represented a variety of users with a broad range of expertise and knowledge of GLBA operations and business processes. The various Bank areas represented helped support a multidisciplinary and knowledge based approach to the risk assessment process. These employees were asked to participate within a candid, reflective atmosphere so that a thorough and clear representation of GLBA's potential business risks to customer information could be developed.

Assessment Methodology Used

The Facilitated Risk Analysis and Assessment Process (FRAAP) was created by Peltier and Associates in 1993. The FRAAP was received within the information security industry through its inclusion as a course in the 1995 Computer Security Institute's calendar of classes. The FRAAP was further promoted in the industry upon publication of the book *Information Security Risk Analysis* by Auerbach Publication CRCPress. The General Accounting Office (GAO) reviewed the FRAAP in 1998 and issued Government Accounting Office May 1998 Executive Guide for Information Security Management (GAO/AIMD 98-68). This executive guide supplemented the Office of Management and Budget revision of Circular A-130, Appendix III recommending qualitative risk analysis for government agencies.

The FRAAP process is consistent with the National Institute of Standards and Technology October 2001 Special Publication Risk Management Guide of Information Technology Systems and the FFIEC December 2002 Information Security Risk Assessment.

A senior facilitator led the process, assisted by GLBA Information Security personnel. Participants were asked to identify risks to the availability, confidentiality, and integrity of Customer Information held and/or processed by GLBA Bank.

All risks were reviewed and consolidated to eliminate redundancy. All risks were then examined to determine if an existing control or safeguard was in place at GLBA. Typically, the examination of existing controls is conducted after the risk level has been established. Due to time constraints, these steps were transposed to affect a more streamlined, accelerated risk assessment process.

Participants were asked to rate each risk in terms of probability of occurrence (high, medium, and low) and then business impact (high, medium, low). The GLBA risk assessment team, with assistance from Peltier and Associates, examined the controls identified to determine whether existing controls were adequate. Low criticality items are not included in final counts summarized in the assessment findings below, as they are normally deferred to a "Monitor" status in final recommendations

Assessment Findings and Action Plan

The risk assessment process identified one hundred and thirteen (113) potential risks in the areas of confidentiality, integrity, and availability. Approximately sixty percent of the risks identified were classified by the team as moderate to low level of risk. Of the remaining risks, six (6) were categorized as Priority A (requiring immediate correction), and fifty-four (54) Priority B (corrective action should be taken). The open number of priority risks has been significantly reduced through diligent efforts undertaken by the GLBA team.

The threat scenario categories with the highest rated risk levels are as follows:

Risk Level	Number of Similar Threats	Description of threat scenario
A	4	Physical intrusion
A	2	Power failure
B	10	Information handling and classification
B	4	Password weakness or sharing
B	4	People masquerading as customers
B	3	Firewall concerns
B	2	Computer viruses
B	2	Workstations left unattended
B	2	Employee training
B	27	Individual threats identified

The risk assessment identified five key areas of concern:

1. Restricted physical access areas should be considered throughout GLBA.
   Action Plan: A physical security risk assessment will be conducted to determine if there is a need to create restricted access areas and/or increase physical access controls.
2. Power failure could cause corruption of information or prevent access to the system.
   Action Plan: Network UPS may not be adequate for a power outage out of regular business hours. Install a backup domain controller at Ualena Street and connect it to the Ualena Street UPS.
3. Information classification scheme is incomplete.
   Action Plan: GLBA has created a draft Information Classification Policy that addresses five categories: Public, Internal Use, Restricted, Confidential and Classified. The new policy requirements are to be disseminated to the GLBA staff and will become part of the new employee orientation and the annual employee awareness program.

4. Concern that the weakness of passwords for some information systems user accounts could allow compromise of the password and permit unauthorized access to GLBA systems and information. *Action Plan:* The GLBA Passwords Policy is to be modified to require strong passwords. GLBA ISD will investigate software solutions to enforce a strong password requirement.
5. Someone could impersonate a customer to corrupt or access bank records or accounts
    Action Plan: Concern to be addressed in GLBA employee awareness program and new employee orientation.

Full Findings Documentation

The completed risk assessment worksheets have been turned over to the GLBA Information Security Officer and are available through his office.

Conclusion

The results of this risk assessment exercise proved to be fairly comprehensive in the breadth of the threat scenarios considered. The breadth of consideration can be directly attributed to the collaborative approach to the risk assessment process embraced by the GLBA participants. The results of this assessment should provide a solid foundation upon which to build and enhance future risk assessment efforts as GLBA moves forward to ensure that assessments are completed whenever changes to any relevant factors, such as new products, business processes, or new technologies, occur.

FACILITATED RISK ANALYSIS PROCESS — ACTION PLAN

Application: U Rent It System (URIS)   **FRAP Date: 1/8/01**

THREAT #	THREAT	ELEMENT	RISK LEVEL	POSSIBLE CONTROLS	OWNER SELECTED ACTION	RESPONSIBLE GROUP	DUE DATE
1	Information accessed by personnel not intended to have access	Integrity	B	3,5,6,11,12,16	ACF2 has been implemented and the Access control list will be reviewed to identify authorized users.	Owner& IP	7/15/04
2	Unclear or non-existent versioning of the information	Integrity	B	9,13, 26	Change management procedures already in place	Operations	complete
3	Database could be corrupted by hardware failure, incorrect, bad software	Integrity	D				
4	Data could be corrupted by an incomplete transaction	Integrity	C				

#	Description						
5	Ability to change data in transit and then changing it back in order to cover the activity	Integrity	C				
6	A failure to report integrity issues	Integrity	A	7,11,12,13,20,21	Employee training sessions scheduled	HR	8/15/04
7	Incompletely run process or failure to run a process that could corrupt the data	Integrity	B	1,2,12,13,14,15, 18,20,21,25	Backup SLA to be reviewed with Operations.	Owner & Operations	7/31/04
8	Lack of internal processes to create and control, manage data across functions	Integrity	A	7,13,17,20,23,25	SLA with service provider to be implemented.	Owner	8/20/04
9	No notification of integrity problems	Integrity	A	7,13,26	SLA with service provider to be implemented.	Owner	8/20/04
10	Information being used in the wrong context	Integrity	B	11,12,19	Train users on proper use of data	Owner/ InfoSec	9/28/04

THREAT #	THREAT	ELEMENT	RISK LEVEL	POSSIBLE CONTROLS	OWNER SELECTED ACTION	RESPONSIBLE GROUP	DUE DATE
11	Third party information may have integrity issues	Integrity	B	7,13,26	Implement edit checking controls to ensure data delivered is in correct format	Applications	10/31/04
12	Third party access to information	Integrity	A	3,4,5	Monitor access control lists bi-monthly		
13	Data updated internally but not being made externally	Integrity	B	11,12,13,19			
14	Verification of authentication of originator of request	Integrity	B	6			
15	Denied access to information that you are authorized to access	Integrity	C				
16	Impact to business by using information that is incorrect	Integrity	B	9,11,12,13,16,26			

17	Security and authorization procedures are so beaurocratic as to hamper the business process	Integrity	A	3,6,19,23,25			
18	Control process so 'B' that they are ignored	Integrity	B	3,6			
19	Personnel making changes are not adequately trained	Integrity	B	11,12,13,19			
20	Information could be published without proper authorization	Integrity	B	11,12,13,19,24			
21	Corporate embarrassment due to unauthorized changing of information	Integrity	B	3,4,5,6,11,12,13, 16,19,22,24			
22	Corporate information damaged due to information leakage	Integrity	B	4			

THREAT #	THREAT	ELEMENT	RISK LEVEL	POSSIBLE CONTROLS	OWNER SELECTED ACTION	RESPONSIBLE GROUP	DUE DATE
23	Not responding to requests in a timely manner	Integrity	A	7,9,15			
24	Internal personnel deliberately modifying data for personal/group gain/reason	Integrity	B	1,2,3,4,11,12,13, 16			
25	eBusiness integrity policies conflict with existing corporate policies	Integrity	A	9,11,12			
26	unwarranted trust in a third party business partner	Integrity	B				
27	Un-recorded changes to system/application software and/or data	Integrity	B	1,2,7,25,26			

28	eBusiness corporate policies cannot be implemented in other countries	Integrity	A	20			
29	Wrong document or data is published	Integrity	A	7,8,9,26			
30	Information from partners or suppliers has integrity problems	Integrity	B	7,12,13,17,22			
31	Audit and/or data integrity legislation causes integrity loss (trans-border)	Integrity	B	13			
32	Legal implications to the business due to misuse of Trademarks and registration	Integrity	B	3			
33	Use of an out-of-date copy of the data	Integrity	C				
34	Synchronization issues using recovery media	Integrity	C				

THREAT #	THREAT	ELEMENT	RISK LEVEL	POSSIBLE CONTROLS	OWNER SELECTED ACTION	RESPONSIBLE GROUP	DUE DATE
35	Incorrect use of the modification process in the application development process (change code without testing)	Integrity	B	7,8,9,16,25			
36	Old data or documents are not removed	Integrity	C				
37	Modification of data due to virus introductions	Integrity	B	2,10,11,12,13			
38	eBusiness product is not designed to meet user expectations	Integrity	B	8,13,23,25			
39	Timely reporting in status of users, customers, suppliers, developers, etc.	Integrity	A	3,5,11,12,13,20			

40	Unclear strategy from the business to support the use of eBusiness transactions	Integrity	B	8,13,23,25
41	Incomplete or non-existent of clear documentation defining or qualifying the information	Integrity	B	11,12,13,23
1	Information/data is incorrectly labeled	Confidentiality	B	7,11,12,13,23,
2	Shoulder surfing of information	Confidentiality	C	
3	Information/data is incorrectly classified	Confidentiality	B	11,12,13
4	Information/data is shared before it is released through proper channels	Confidentiality	B	11,12
5	Access to customer, employee, or partner supplier lists are made available unknowingly	Confidentiality	C	

THREAT #	THREAT	ELEMENT	RISK LEVEL	POSSIBLE CONTROLS	OWNER SELECTED ACTION	RESPONSIBLE GROUP	DUE DATE
6	Ex-developers still have access to secure data	Confidentiality	A	4,7,13,16,20			
7	Use of insecure systems to transmit sensitive information/data	Confidentiality	A	7,10			
8	Disclosure of information and violation of the privacy laws	Confidentiality	B	11,12,23			
9	Information on laptops is unprotected	Confidentiality	A	4,6,22,24			
10	'B' and complex processes for enabling secure e-mail capability	Confidentiality	B	6,11,12,13,25			
11	Government legislation prevents proper protection of sensitive information	Confidentiality	B				

12	Clear definition of confidentiality rules	Confidentiality	B	11,12,13				
13	Inability of the company to access confidential information between two parties at a later time	Confidentiality	B					
14	Improper protection of password lists	Confidentiality	C					
15	Uncontrolled access to printed confidential information	Confidentiality	A					
16	Introduction of 'back doors' into software, data and applications	Confidentiality	B					
17	Sensitive and non-sensitive information are mixed	Confidentiality	B	7,8,11,12,25				
18	Disgruntled admin staff with high security privileges	Confidentiality	A					

THREAT #	THREAT	ELEMENT	RISK LEVEL	POSSIBLE CONTROLS	OWNER SELECTED ACTION	RESPONSIBLE GROUP	DUE DATE
19	Downstream effects are not thoroughly analyzed before a change is applied	Confidentiality	B				
20	Allocation of security privileges not known to the organization	Confidentiality	A	3,11,12,13			
21	Removal of access to the developers after the project is complete	Confidentiality	A	3,11,12,13			
22	Trade secrets are sold without detection	Confidentiality	A	3,11,12,13			
23	Distribution lists have personnel who are not authorized	Confidentiality	B	3,11,12,13			
24	Wrong use of the security administration procedures in applications with sensitive information	Confidentiality	B	7,11,12,13,15, 19,23			

25	Authentication for access to sensitive information is inadequate	Confidentiality	A	3,4,5,6,13,16				
26	Collection of information in one place can cause confidentiality issues	Confidentiality	C					
27	Ability to assume another's identify	Confidentiality	A	3,5,6,7,13,16				
28	Unknowingly/knowi ngly releasing information to activist organization (deliberately or accidentally)	Confidentiality	B	3,4,13,16				
29	Assumption that developers require access to sensitive information	Confidentiality	C					
30	Access to sensitive information through the test environment	Confidentiality	B	3,5,13,16				

THREAT #	THREAT	ELEMENT	RISK LEVEL	POSSIBLE CONTROLS	OWNER SELECTED ACTION	RESPONSIBLE GROUP	DUE DATE
31	Individuals are unaware how to publish or store information on the web	Confidentiality	C				
32	Confusion over where to store sensitive information	Confidentiality	B	11,12,13,19			
33	Unclear/unknown process for classifying data	Confidentiality	B	11,12,13,19,20			
34	Granting access to individuals who don't have a business need for access	Confidentiality	C				
35	Information about internal systems is inadvertently released for potential later attacks	Confidentiality	B	7,13,15			

36	Sharing user Ids	Confidentiality	B	12					
37	Access to backups is not properly controlled	Confidentiality	B	14,20,22					
38	Broad Security access is granted for simplified in sake	Confidentiality	B	3,7,13					
39	Confidentiality contracts are un-enforceable	Confidentiality	B	23					
40	Personal information for staff might be posted on the internet without authorization	Confidentiality	A	9,12,13,15,26					
41	False sense of security due to firewall mentality	Confidentiality	A	12,13,23					
42	Third party breaks of confidentiality agreements	Confidentiality	B	13,23					
43	Unclear definition of what sensitive information in joint venture activities	Confidentiality	A	13,15,23					

THREAT #	THREAT	ELEMENT	RISK LEVEL	POSSIBLE CONTROLS	OWNER SELECTED ACTION	RESPONSIBLE GROUP	DUE DATE
44	New Technologies leading to breaches of confidentiality	Confidentiality	A	7,9,13,26			
45	Effort and planning involved in changing a security access model	Confidentiality	B	23			
46	How to explain confidentiality to non-employees	Confidentiality	B	12			
47	Loss of sales and increased costs due to release of competitive advantage information without company knowledge	Confidentiality	B	3,4,5,6,7,9			
48	Packet sniffing outside the Internet site by unauthorized personnel	Confidentiality	B	5,13			

49	Penalties for confidentiality agreement violations not sufficient to deter inappropriate activities	Confidentiality	C					
50	Electronic eavesdropping of company sites	Confidentiality	B	3,5,6,7,9				
1	Hackers could bring site down	Avaliability	B	1,2,3,5,6,10,21, 22,				
2	Intruders gaining physical access to computer facilities	Avaliability	B	22				
3	Hardware failure of the Internet server	Avaliability	C					
4	Communication provider service outage	Avaliability	C					
5	Hosting site lacks physical protection of information	Avaliability	B	20,22				

THREAT #	THREAT	ELEMENT	RISK LEVEL	POSSIBLE CONTROLS	OWNER SELECTED ACTION	RESPONSIBLE GROUP	DUE DATE
6	Manual process fails when eCommerce site is unavailable	Avaliability	B	8,12,17			
7	Links to back office systems fail	Avaliability	C				
8	Overly complex system design	Avaliability	B	25			
9	Incorrectly made hardware or software changes	Avaliability	B	8,9			
10	Unanticipated volumes/usage projections	Avaliability	B	20,25			
11	Contingency planning procedures not tested	Avaliability	B	1,2,8,14,20,21			
12	No guarantee of server availability by service provider	Avaliability	D				
13	Industrial action/strike at service provider	Avaliability	D				

14	Normal planned maintenance will cause system unavailability	Avaliability	B	18,20,21				
15	Topology design precludes effective/acceptable global service availability	Avaliability	C					
16	Inadequate funding for backup capability	Avaliability	C					
17	Planned attack by protesters	Avaliability	A	3,5,10,16,22				
18	Business partner unavailability	Avaliability	C					
19	Hardware configuration is inadequate for high availability	Avaliability	B	13,18,20				
20	Technical resources lack proper training	Avaliability	B	12,15				
21	Congestion on the Internet causes user dissatisfaction	Avaliability	B	13,20				

THREAT #	THREAT	ELEMENT	RISK LEVEL	POSSIBLE CONTROLS	OWNER SELECTED ACTION	RESPONSIBLE GROUP	DUE DATE
22	Applications design flaws may cause resource thrashing or internal resource contention	Avaliability	C				
23	Critical application may not be critical to service provider	Avaliability	B	12,13,20			
24	eCommerce application is designed to work with only a limited set of clients	Avaliability	C				
25	Introduction of virus may cause system/information unavailability	Avaliability	A	1,2,10			
26	Insufficient monitoring of web site may fail to report unavailability	Avaliability	B	13,20			

27	Router or firewall failure may cause inaccessibility to services	Avaliability	B	13,18,20,22
28	Backups are insufficient	Avaliability	C	
29	Loss of customers due to site unavailability	Avaliability	A	13,18,20,21
1	There were no deferred issues	Deferred Issue		
2		Deferred Issue		
3		Deferred Issue		
4		Deferred Issue		
5		Deferred Issue		

FRAP ATTENDEES

	NAME	PHONE
IS Security Center of Excellence (SCoE) Manager	Alex Rodriguez	
IS Information Management Center of Excellence (IMCoE) Manager	Alec Futon	
IS Technology Center of Excellence (TCoE) Manager	Alistair Cooke	
IS Manager Latin America Region (LAR)	Mitsuro Kincade	
Commercial Center of Excellence Lead for Latin America (LA)	Jorge George	
Information Security Area Manger for the Americas	Todd Buffington	
Information Security Specialist	Mary Jane Ashman	
Senior Project Consultant	Pam Salaway	
SAP/R3 Team Leader	Sherry Giordano	
Facilitator	Lisa Bryson	
Scribe	Julie Lanavich	

Appendix B

Terms and Definitions

Risk Assessment Terms

Acceptable risk — The level of residual risk that has been determined to be a reasonable level of potential loss/disruption for a specific IT system.

Annual loss expectancy (ALE) — A single loss expectancy (x) annualized frequency of occurrence.

Availability — Protection from unauthorized attempts to withhold information or computer resources.

Due diligence — The process of taking every reasonable precaution in the circumstances for the protection of the asset under review or in question.

Fiduciary responsibility — When one person has a legal responsibility to act in another's best interest, he has a fiduciary responsibility. For example, officers of a company have a fiduciary responsibility to the shareholders; i.e., they have to act in the shareholders' best interests, not in their own best interests.

Fiduciary responsibility, aspects of — In judging whether someone has fulfilled his fiduciary responsibility, two aspects tend to be considered:

Residual risk — The potential for the occurrence of an adverse event after adjusting for the impact of all in-place safeguards.

Risk — The probability that a particular critical infrastructure's vulnerability is being exploited by a particular threat weighted by the impact of that exploitation.

Risk alleviation — Senior management approves the implementation of the controls recommended by the risk management team that will lower the risk to an acceptable level.

Risk analysis — A technique to identify and assess factors that may jeopardize the success of a project or achievement of a goal. This technique also helps define preventive measures to reduce the probability of these factors from occurring and identify countermeasures to successfully deal with these constraints when they develop.

Risk assessment — The computation of risk. Risk is a threat that exploits some vulnerability that could cause harm to an asset. The risk algorithm computes the risk as a function of the assets, threats, and vulnerabilities. One instance of a risk within a system is represented by the formula (asset * threat * vulnerability). Total risk for a network equates to the sum of all the risk instances.

Risk assumption — After examining the threats and determining the risk level, the team's findings lead management to determine that it is the best business decision to accept the potential risk and continue operating. This is an acceptable outcome of the risk assessment process. If, after completing the risk assessment process, management decides to accept the risk, then it has performed its due diligence.

Risk avoidance — Where, after performing the risk assessment, management chooses to avoid the risks by eliminating the process that causes the risks, for example, foregoing certain functions or enhancements to systems or applications because the risk assessment results lead management to conclude that to proceed, the organization would be placed at too great of an exposure.

Risk limitation — The process to limit the risk by implementing controls that minimize the adverse impact of a threat. This is the standard process that is worked when a risk assessment is completed. By identifying threats, establishing the risk level, and selecting reasonable and prudent controls, management is limiting risk exposure.

Risk management — The total process to identify, control, and minimize the impact of uncertain events. The objective of the risk management program is to reduce risk to an acceptable level and obtain and maintain senior management approval.

Risk planning — A process where it is decided to manage risk by developing an architecture that prioritizes, implements, and maintains controls.

Risk transference — Management transfers the risk by using other options to compensate for a loss, such as purchasing an insurance policy.

Safeguard — A risk-reducing measure that acts to detect, prevent, or minimize loss associated with the occurrence of a specified threat or category of threats.

Standard of due care — The minimum and customary practice of responsible protection of assets that reflects a community or societal norm. Failure to achieve minimum standards would be considered negligent and could lead to litigation, higher insurance rates, and loss of assets. Sufficient care of assets should be maintained such that recognized experts in the field would agree that negligence of care is not apparent.

Threat — Any circumstance or event that could harm a critical asset through unauthorized access, compromise of data integrity, denial or disruption of service, or physical destruction or impairment.

- Natural threats — Floods, earthquakes, tornadoes, landslides, avalanches, electrical storms, and other such events.
- Human threats — Events that are either enabled by or caused by human beings, such as unintentional acts (inadvertent information entry) or deliberate actions (network-based attacks, malicious software, unauthorized access to confidential information).
- Environmental threats — Long-term power failure, pollution, chemicals, liquid leakage.

Threat impact — A measure of the magnitude of loss or harm on the value of an asset.

Threat probability — The chance that an event will occur or that a specific loss value may be attained should the event occur.

Vulnerability — A flaw in security procedures.

Vulnerability assessment — The systematic examination of a critical infrastructure.

Law Definitions

Federal Guidelines for Sentencing for Criminal Convictions

The federal sentencing guidelines define executive responsibility for fraud, theft, and antitrust violations, and establish a mandatory point system for federal judges to determine appropriate punishment. Because much fraud and falsifying corporate data involves access to computer-held data, liability established under the guidelines extends to computer-related crime as well. What has caused many executives concern is that the mandatory punishment could apply even when intruders enter a computer system and perpetrate a crime.

While the guidelines have a mandatory scoring system for punishment, they also have an incentive for proactive crime prevention. The requirement here is for management to show *due diligence* in establishing an effective compliance program. There are seven elements that capture the basic functions inherent in most compliance programs:

1. Establish policies, standards, and procedures to guide the workforce.
2. Appoint a high-level manager to oversee compliance with the policy, standards, and procedures.
3. Exercise due care when granting discretionary authority to employees.
4. Ensure that compliance policies are carried out.
5. Communicate the standards and procedures to all employees and others.
6. Enforce the policies, standards, and procedures consistently through appropriate disciplinary measures.
7. Implement procedures for corrections and modifications in case of violations.

These guidelines reward those organizations that make a good faith-effort to prevent unethical activity; this is done by lowering potential fines if, despite the organization's best efforts, unethical or illegal activities are still committed by the organization or its employees. To be judged effective, a compliance program need not prevent all misconduct; however, it must show due diligence in seeking to prevent and detect inappropriate behavior.

The Economic Espionage Act of 1996

For the first time, the Economic Espionage Act (EEA) of 1996 made trade secret theft a federal crime, subject to penalties including fines, forfeiture, and imprisonment. The act reinforces the rules governing trade secrets in that businesses must show that they have taken reasonable measures to protect their proprietary trade secrets to seek relief under the EEA.

In *Counterintelligence and Law Enforcement: The Economic Espionage Act of 1996 versus Competitive Intelligence*, author Peter F. Kalitka believes that given the penalties companies face under the EEA, businesses hiring outside consultants to gather competitive intelligence should establish a policy on this activity. Included in the contract language with the outside consultant should be definitions on:

- What is hard-to-get information?
- How will the information be obtained?
- Does the consultant adhere to the Society of Competitive Intelligence Professionals Code of Ethics?
- Does the consultant have accounts with clients that may be questioned?

The Foreign Corrupt Practices Act (FCPA)

For 20 years, the Foreign Corrupt Practices Act (FCPA) was largely ignored by regulators. This was due in part to an initial amnesty program under which nearly 500 companies admitted violations. Now the federal government has dramatically increased its attention on business activities and is looking to enforce the act with vigor. To avoid liability under the FCPA, companies must implement a due diligence program that includes a set of internal controls and enforcement. A set of policies and procedures that are implemented and audited for compliance is required to meet the test of due diligence.

Sarbanes–Oxley (SOX)

Sarbanes–Oxley (SOX) was signed into law on July 30, 2002, and the provisions of the act have a meaningful impact on both public companies and auditors. Two important sections of the act are:

- Section 302 ("Disclosure Controls and Procedures," or DC&P), which requires quarterly certification of financial statements by the CEO and CFO. The CEO and CFO must certify completeness and accuracy of the filings and attest to the effectiveness of internal control.
- Section 404 ("Internal Control Attest"), which requires annual affirmation of management's responsibility for internal controls over financial reporting. Management must attest to effectiveness based on an evaluation, and the auditor must attest and report on management's evaluation.

Health Insurance Portability and Accountability Act (HIPAA)

The Health Insurance Portability and Accountability Act (HIPAA), also known as Kassebaum–Kennedy, after the two senators who spearheaded the bill, passed in 1996 to help people buy and keep health insurance (portability), even when they have serious health conditions. The law sets basic requirements that health plans must meet. Because states can and have modified and expanded upon these provisions, consumers' protections vary from state to state. The law expanded to include strict rules for privacy and security of health information, giving individuals more control over how their health information is used. The privacy and security rules within HIPAA govern the use, disclosure, and handling of any identifiable patient information by covered healthcare providers. The law covers the information in whatever form it is seen or heard and applies to the information in whatever manner it is to be used.

Gramm–Leach–Bliley Act (GLBA)

The Gramm–Leach–Bliley Act (GLBA) was signed into law in 1999. Its primary purpose is to provide privacy of customer information by financial service organizations, and comprehensive data protection measures are required. Depending on the financial institutions' supervisory authority, GLBA compliance audits are conducted by either the Office of the Comptroller of the Currency (OCC), the Federal Reserve Systems (Fed), the Federal Deposit Insurance Corporation (FDIC), or the Office of Thrift Supervision (OTS). All financial service organizations must comply with GLBA data protection requirements. These requirements do not pertain only to providers receiving federal funds.

GLBA requires financial institutions to:

■ Ensure the security and confidentiality of customer records and information
■ Protect against any anticipated threats or hazards to the security or integrity of such records
■ Protect against unauthorized access

Appendix C

Bibliography

Anonymous. *Maximum Security: A Hacker's Guide to Protecting Your Internet Site and Network*, 2nd ed. Indianapolis: Sams Publishing, 1998.

Atkinson, R. Security Architecture for the Internet Protocol. *RFC 1825*, Naval Research Laboratory, August 1995.

Bryson, Lisa C. Protect Your Boss and Your Job: Due Care in Information Security. *Computer Security Alert* 146, San Francisco, May 1995.

Carroll, John M. *Computer Security*, 3rd ed. Woburn, MA: Butterworth-Heinemann Publishers, Ltd., 1996.

D'Agenais, Jean, and John Carruthers. *Creating Effective Manuals*. Cincinnati, OH: South-Western Publishing Co., 1985.

Depuis, Clement. CISSP Study Booklet on Operations Security. Posted at http://www.cccure.org, April 5, 1999.

Devlin, Ed, and Cole Emerson. *Business Resumption Planning*, 1999 ed. New York: Auerbach Publications, 1999.

Economic Espionage Act of 1996. U.S. Congressional Record of 1996. Available at http://cybercrime.gov/EEAleghist.htm.

Ermann, M. David, Mary B. Williams, and Michele S. Shauf. *Computers, Ethics and Society*, 2nd ed. New York: Oxford University Press, 1997.

Ford, Warwick, and Michael S. Baum. *Secure Electronic Commerce*. Englewood Cliffs, NJ: Prentice Hall, 1997.

Glass, Robert L. *Building Quality Software*. Englewood Cliffs, NJ: Prentice Hall, 1992.

Guttman, E., L. Leong, and G. Malkin. Users' Security Handbook. *RFC 2504*, Sun Microsystems, February 1999.

Hare, Chris. CISSP Certified CBK Study Guide: Business Continuity Planning Domain. Posted at http://www.cccure.org, March 1999.

Housley, R., W. Ford, W. Polk, and D. Solo. Internet X.509 Public Key Infrastructure Certificate and CRL Profile. *RFC 2459*, SPYRUS, January 1999.

Hutt, Arthur E., Seymour Bosworth, and Douglas B. Hoyt. *Computer Security Handbook*, 3rd ed. New York: John Wiley & Sons, 1995.

Icove, David, Karl Seger, and William VonStorch. *Computer Crime: A Crimefighter's Handbook*. Sebastopol, CA:: O'Reilly & Associates, 1995.

Imparl, Steven D., JD. *Internet Law: The Complete Guide*. Specialty Technical Publishers, 2000.

International Information Security Foundation. Generally Accepted Systems Security Principles (GASSP), Version 2.0. Gaithersburg, MD: International Information Security Foundation, June 1999.

International Standards Organization. Common Criteria for Information Technology Security Evaluation, Version 2.1. Geneva, Switzerland: International Standards Organization, August 1999.

International Standards Organization. Information Technology: Code of Practice for Information Security Management, ISO/IEC 17799:2000(E). Geneva, Switzerland: International Standards Organization, 2000.

Jackson, K.M., and J. Hruska. *Computer Security Reference Book*. Boca Raton, FL: CRC Press, 1992.

Kabay, Michel E. *The NCSA Guide to Enterprise Security*. New York: McGraw-Hill Computer Communications Series, 1999.

King, Christopher M., Curtis E. Dalton, and T. Ertem Osmanoglu. *Security Architecture: Design, Deployment and Operations*. Emeryville, CA: Osborn/McGraw-Hill, 2001.

Krawczyk, H., M. Bellare, and R. Canetti. HMAC: Keyed-Hashing for Message Authentication. *RFC 2104*, IBM, February 1997.

National Institute of Standards and Technology. Generally Accepted Principles and Practices for Securing Information Technology Systems, Special Publication 800-14. Washington, D.C.: U.S. Government Printing Office, September 1996.

National Institute of Standards and Technology. Contingency Planning Guide for Securing Information Technology Systems, Special Publication 800-34. Washington, D.C.: U.S. Government Printing Office, June 2002.

National Institute of Standards and Technology. An Introduction to Computer Security: The NIST Handbook, Special Publication 800-12. Washington, D.C.: U.S. Government Printing Office, October 1995.

National Institute of Standards and Technology. NIST Generally Accepted Principles and Practices for Securing Information Technology Systems, Special Publication 800-14. Washington, D.C.: U.S. Government Printing Office, September 1996.

National Institute of Standards and Technology. Risk Management Guide for Information Technology Systems, Special Publication 800-30. Washington, D.C.: U.S. Government Printing Office, January 2002.

National Research Council. *Computers a Risk: Safe Computing in the Information Age*. Washington, D.C.: National Academy Press, 1991.

National Security Agency. Online Course: Overview and Risk Management Terminology. Posted at www.ncisse.org/Courseware/NSAcourse/lesson1/lesson.PPT, 1997.

Parker, Donn. Risk Reduction Out, Enablement and Due Care In. *Computer Security Institute Journal*, Volume XVI, Number 4, Winter 2000.

Peltier, Thomas R. *Information Security Policies, Standards, Procedures and Guidelines*. Boca Raton, FL: CRC Press, 2001.

Peltier, Thomas R. *Information Security Risk Analysis*. New York: Auerbach Publications, 2001.

Peltier, Tom. How to Build a Comprehensive Security Awareness Program. *Computer Security Institute Journal*, Volume XVI, Number 2, Spring 2000.

Pfleeger, Charles P. *Security in Computing*, 2nd ed. Upper Saddle River, NJ: Prentice Hall, 1996.

Piper, D. The Internet IP Security Domain of Interpretation for ISAKMP. *RFC 2407*, Network Alchemy, November 1998.

Postel, Jon, and Joyce Reynolds. File Transfer Protocol. *RFC 959*, ISI, October 1985.

Russell, Deborah, and G.T. Gangemi Sr. *Computer Security Basics*. Sebastopol, CA: O'Reilly & Associates, 1991.

Scambray, Joel, Stuart McClure, and George Kurtz. *Hacking Exposed: Network Security Secrets and Solutions*, 2nd ed. New York: Osborne/McGraw-Hill, 2001.

Schneier, Bruce. *Applied Cryptography*. New York: John Wiley & Sons, 1996.

Stephenson, Peter. *Investigating Computer-Related Crime*. New York: CRC Press, 2000.

Summers, Rita C. *Secure Computing: Threats and Safeguards*. New York: McGraw-Hill, 1997.

Tipton, Harold F., and Micki Krause, Eds. *Information Security Management Handbook, 1996–97*, yearbook edition. New York: Auerbach Publications, 1997.

Tipton, Harold F., and Micki Krause, Eds. *Information Security Management Handbook*, 4th ed. New York: Auerbach Publications, 2000.

Tudor, Jan Killmeyer. *Information Security Architecture*. New York: Auerbach Publications, 2001.

U.S. Department of Defense. *Technical Rationale behind CSC-STD-003-85*. Washington, D.C.: U.S. Government Printing Office, 1985.

U.S. Department of Defense. *Trusted Computer System Evaluation Criteria*. Washington, D.C.: U.S. Government Printing Office, 1985.

U.S. Department of Defense. *Trusted Network Interpretation of the Trusted Computer System Evaluation Criteria*. Washington, D.C.: U.S. Government Printing Office, 1987.

Vallabhaneni, Rao S. *CISSP Examination Textbooks*, Vol. 1. Schaumburg, IL: SRV Professional Publications, 2000.

Index

A

Acceptance testing, 178, 200, 233
Access control, 179, 180, 199, 235, 239, 240, 243, 250, 255
Accidental acts, 109
Accidental threats, 89, 126
Action plan, 304–323
Air pollution, 85
ALE, *see* Annual loss exposure
Annual loss exposure (ALE), 48, 49
Annual rate of occurrence (ARO), 19
Antivirus, 176, 200, 231
Application(s)
    control, 178, 200, 233
    development, control requirements, 229
    FRAAP, 212
    security review, 230
    threat table, 214–215, 216–217
ARO, *see* Annual rate of occurrence
Assessment team attendance, 192
Asset(s)
    accounting of, 242, 252
    classification, 10, 179, 234, 242, 248
    control costs and, 26
    criticality, 51
    definition, 16
    headings, 44–45
    identification, 100
    information as, 42
    logical, 45
    measure of harm to, 25
    mission, 51
    physical, 45
    review schedule, 107
    standards for protecting, 57
    threats to, 16
    valuation, 101, 104
Assurance controls, 55, 93, 94
Audit
    controls, 150
    findings, 213
    logs, 228
    mission statement, 13
    staff, 83, 145
    trails, 228, 286
Authentication, 228, 230
Availability, loss of, 44
Avoidance controls, 55, 93, 94

B

Backup, 232
Bank information processing environment, audit of, 213
Basel Accords, 174, 227
BCP, *see* Business continuity planning
BDLC, *see* Business development life cycle
BIA, *see* Business impact analysis
Blizzard, 85, 117
Bomb threat, 88, 127
Brainstorming sessions, 125
BS7799-1, 27
Business associate contracts, 150
Business continuity
    management, 241, 244, 257
    planning (BCP), 82, 225, 230
Business development life cycle (BDLC), 8
Business disruption, 291

Business impact analysis (BIA), 51, 80, 101,
141–142, 158, 177, 289–295
creation, 290–295
definitions, 291
financial impact worksheet, 293
impacts, 292
overview, 289–290
worksheet, 294, 295
Business process
IT organizations supporting, 176–181
risk management as part of, 8

C

Catastrophic fire, 127
Change management, 177, 181, 200, 203,
232, 235
CIO, *see* Corporate information officer
CISO, *see* Corporate Information Security
Officer
CobiT (Controls Objectives for Information
and Related Technology), 250
CobiT Security Baseline, 174, 227
Communication protection, 228
Communications plans, 230
Competitive disadvantage, 291
Compliance, 244, 247
Computer Security Institute (CSI), 1
Alert, 108
Buyer's Guide, 77
Information Protection Assessment Kit,
121
Information Security Program of the Year
Award, 78
Computer viruses, 195, 302
Confidentiality, 44, 220
Configuration management, 228
Contingency planning, 285
Continuity planning, 228
Control(s), *see also* Mapping controls
assurance, 55, 93, 94
avoidance, 55, 93, 94
basis for establishing, 57
business-friendly, 42
categories, 55, 56, 94
cost–benefit analysis, 78
detection, 56, 93, 94
effectiveness of, 52
establishment of, 174
identification of, 93
nontechnical, 54, 112

recommendations, 107
recovery, 56, 93, 94
reliability, 53
requirements, 226
return on investment, 54
selection of, 223
standards, 57
technical, 54, 112
threat-based, 111
vulnerability, 218, 228
Controls list mapping, 28, 224, 226
information security layer, 228
information technology organization, 229
ISO 17799, 32–37, 229, 237–241
ISO 17799 and CobiT, 250
ISO 17799 and FSGCA, 245
ISO 17799 and GLBA, 236
ISO 17799, GLBA, and SOX, 245
ISO 17799 and HIPAA, 236, 242–244
ISO 17799, HIPAA, GLBA, SOX, and
FSGCA, 249
IT organization, 28–31, 231–236
security architecture layer, 230
security categories, 228
using NIST SP 800-26, 262–284
Copyright compliance, 225
Corporate communications, 82, 146
Corporate embarrassment, 103
Corporate information officer (CIO), 121
Corporate Information Security Officer
(CISO), 11, 12
Corrective strategies, 178, 203, 233
Cost–benefit analysis, 13, 15, 27, 96, 98
Cracker, 47
Crime prevention, incentive for proactive,
247
Crisis management planning, 230
Criticality impact level, 155
Cross-reference report, 194
Cross-reference sheet example, 197–198,
199–203
Cryptography, 241, 244
CSI, *see* Computer Security Institute
Customer confidence, loss of, 293

D

Dam/reservoir failure, 117
Data
availability, 109
backup, 149, 150

integrity, 109, 285
sensitivity, 109, 158
Database administration, 172, 229
Data stream, intercepted, 219, 220
Deliberate acts, 109
Deliberate threats, 127
Desktop computing, control requirements, 229
Detection controls, 56, 93, 94
Disaster recovery plan, 149, 230
Disclosure
accidental, 126
deliberate, 127
impact levels, 155
Due diligence, 247
documentation of, 52
management obligation to perform, 135
Duty of care, 135
Duty of loyalty, 134

E

Earthquake, 85, 117, 126
Electrical disturbance, 86, 126
Electrical interruption, 87, 126
Electrical storm, 117
Emanation, 87, 126
Emergency mode operations plan, 149
Employee(s)
acceptance of new control by, 133
emergency training, 49
morale, 291, 293
poorly trained, 47
replacement of, 293
responsibilities, 10, 11, 135, 225
sabotage, 88, 128
training, 195, 302
typical roles for, 12
union-represented, 146
workstations unattended by, 164
Encryption, 54, 180, 230
Enterprise assets, functional owner of, 7
Environmental controls, 54, 228
Environmental failure, 127
Environmental terrorist, 47
Environmental threats, 18, 86–87
Epidemic, 117
Equipment security, 242
Errors, prevention of, 223
Evacuation plans, 119

F

Facilitated Risk Analysis and Assessment Process (FRAAP), 3, 79, 128, 129–204, *see also* FRAAP facilitation skills; FRAAP variations
action plan, 189, 191
brainstorming definition, 169, 170, 171
deliverables, 183
development of, 132
impact definitions, 173
introduction of FRAAP to organization, 132–204
awareness program overview, 133–134
facilitation skills, 136–142
FRAAP session, 166–186
FRAAP team, 144–147
introduction of FRAAP, 134–136
post–FRAAP, 186–204
pre-FRAAP meeting, 159–165
prescreening, 147–159
session agreements, 143–144
management summary report, 190, 193
overview, 129–131
probability definitions, 173
project budget, 153
reason for creation of, 131–132
risk level matrix, 174
session agenda, 167
session agreements, 168
session summary, 183
team members, 145
threat identification, 168
threat table, infrastructure, 208–209, 210–211
tools kit, 142
worksheet, 172, 175, 182, 184–185, 187–188
Faulty programming, 219, 220
FBI, threats and, 48
FDIC, *see* Federal Deposit Insurance Corporation
Federal Deposit Insurance Corporation (FDIC), 236
Federal Emergency Management Administration (FEMA), 116
Federal Information Processing Standards Publications, 2, 174, 227
Federal Reserve System, 236

Federal Sentencing Guidelines for Criminal Activity (FSGCA), 121, 245
FEMA, *see* Federal Emergency Management Administration
FFEIC examination guidelines, 175
Financial losses, 101
Fire, 87, 127
Firewall concerns, 195, 302
Flooding, 50, 117, 126
FRAAP, *see* Facilitated Risk Analysis and Assessment Process
FRAAP facilitation skills
    authority, 140–141
    breaks, 141
    center, 138
    change behavior, 139
    confrontation, 137–138
    crisis intervention, 138
    expecting hostility, 140
    goal of facilitator, 141
    leadership, 137
    listening, 136–137
    neutrality, 140
    objective, 140
    observation, 139–140
    participation encouragement, 139
    problem solving, 139
    punctuality, 141
    reflection, 137
    stopping, 141–142
    summarizing, 137
    support, 138
    team involvement, 140
FRAAP variations, 205–222
    infrastructure FRAAP, 205–221
        application FRAAP, 212
        other variations, 213–221
        summary, 207–212
    overview, 205
Fraud, 88, 109, 128, 223, 291
Frequently asked questions, 2–5
    how success of risk analysis is measured, 5
    time to complete risk analysis, 4
    what results of risk management can tell, 5
    what risk analysis can analyze, 4–5
    when risk analysis should be conducted, 3
    who should conduct risk analysis, 3–4

who should review results of risk analysis, 5
who within organization should conduct risk analysis, 4
why risk assessment should be conducted, 2–3
FSGCA, *see* Federal Sentencing Guidelines for Criminal Activity
Full findings documentation, 190

G

GAO, *see* Government Accounting Office
General Motors Systems Corporate Activity (GMISCA) group, 1
GLBA, *see* Gramm–Leach–Bliley Act
GMISCA group, *see* General Motors Systems Corporate Activity group
Government Accounting Office (GAO), 78
Gramm–Leach–Bliley Act (GLBA), 57, 69–73, 174, 227, 236

H

Hacker, 47
Hardware
    failure, 87, 127
    maintenance, 228
Hazard impact analysis (HIA), 116
    impact categories, 117
    paralysis by analysis, 119
    process, 116
    threat list, 117
    worksheet, 118, 119, 120
Healthcare clearinghouse functions, 148
Health Insurance Portability and Accountability Act (HIPAA), 147, 227, 236
    baseline set of controls using, 148–151
    controls list, 57–65
    controls mapping, 69–73, 242
    mapping of to ISO 17799 standards, 66–68
HIA, *see* Hazard impact analysis
High winds, 117
HIPAA, *see* Health Insurance Portability and Accountability Act
Hostility, 140
Housekeeping 254
Human threats, 18
Hurricane, 85, 117, 126

I

Ice storm, 85, 117
IDS, *see* Intrusion detection system
Incident response, 228
    capability, 286
    procedures, 230
Information
    awareness program, 230
    classification, 246
        levels, 154
        policy, 10, 11, 225
    handling, 195
    labeling, 242
    losses, causes of, 114
    process for classifying, 43
    protection (IP) program, 121
    resource, value of, 43
    sensitivity, 51
Information Protection Assessment Kit
        (IPAK), 121
Information security (IS), 7, 41, 146
    baseline principles, 224–225
    compliance program, 225
    function of, 109
    layer, controls list by, 228
    life cycle, 11, 14
    mission statement, 13
    model, control categories, 94
    policy, 224
    professional, roles for, 12
    program, 43, 230
    risk analysis (ISRA), 108
        matrix, 109
        process, 109
        threat identification, 111
    steering committee, 225
    triad, 42
Information Security Administrator, 11
Information systems security officer (ISSO),
        1, 220
Information technology (IT), 81
Infrastructure FRAAP threat table, 208–209,
        210–211
Instrumentation, Systems, and Automation
        Society, 261
Insurance company, threats and, 48
Integrity, loss of, 44
Intellectual property, 26
Interface dependencies, 202, 231
Internal attacks, 114
Interruption prevention, 230

Intrusion detection, 230
    software, 54
    system (IDS), 82
Investigation tools, 230
IPAK, *see* Information Protection Assessment
        Kit
IP program, *see* Information protection
        program
IS, *see* Information security
ISO (International Standards Organization)
        17799, 27, 57, 224
    CobiT and, controls list mapping, 250,
        287
    controls list mapping, 69–73, 242–22
    controls list using, 32–37, 229, 237–241
    FSGCA and, controls list mapping, 250
    GLBA and, controls list mapping,
        246–247
    GLBA, SOX, and, controls list mapping,
        248
    HIPAA and, controls list mapping,
        242–244
    HIPAA, GLBA, SOX, FSGCA, and,
        controls list mapping, 249,
        251–257
    standards, mapping of HIPAA to, 66–68
ISRA, *see* Information security risk analysis
ISSO, *see* Information systems security
        officer
IT, *see* Information technology
IT organization, control list by, 28–31, 229,
        231–236

K

Kassebaum–Kennedy, *see* Health Insurance
        Portability and Accountability
        Act

L

LAN, *see* Local area network
Landslide, 117, 126
Law enforcement agencies, threats and, 48
Legal fines, 293
Legal liability, 291
Legal requirements, compliance with, 241,
        244, 257
Legal staff, 146
Legislation, new controls and, 227
Lightning, 85, 126
Liquid leakage, 127

Local area network (LAN), 51, 81, 109, 200
Logical access control, 228
Logical assets, 45

M

Maintenance, 202, 231, 232
Malicious software, 243
Management
    decisions, wrong, 291
    information security, 242
    summary report, 194, 196
    summary risk levels, 195
    support, 179, 203, 234
Mapping controls, 223–287
    control list examples, 227–286
        information security layer,
            228–229
        information technology organization,
            229, 231–236
        ISO 17799, 229–230, 237–241
        ISO 17799 and CobiT, 250–261,
            287
        ISO 17799 and Federal Sentencing
            Guidelines, 245–249
        ISO 17799 and GLBA, 236–245
        ISO 17799, GLBA, and
            Sarbanes–Oxley, 245
        ISO 17799 and HIPAA, 236
        ISO 17799, HIPAA, GLBA, SOX, and
            FSGCA, 249, 251–257
        NIST control list, 249, 258–261,
            262–284, 284–286
        other sources, 261–286
        security categories, 227–228
    creation of controls list, 224–227
        cautionary note, 226–227
        control requirements considerations,
            226
        information security baseline
            controls, 224–226
    overview, 223
Matrix table, 25
Media
    handling, 243, 254
    protection, 228
    reuse, 150
Mission statements, sample, 13
Mudslide, 117

N

National Institute of Standards and
        Technology (NIST), 2, 9, 174,
        227, 249
    controls list subset, 284–286
    800 series of special publications,
        258–261
National Weather Center, natural threats and,
        48
Natural threats, 18, 48, 85–86, 117, 126
Network
    access control, 240, 243
    administrator, baiting of, 140
    management, 229, 254
Network Vulnerability Assessment (NVA), 13
NIST, *see* National Institute of Standards and
        Technology
Nontechnical controls, 54, 112
NVA, *see* Network Vulnerability Assessment

O

OCC, *see* Office of the Comptroller of the
        Currency
Office of the Comptroller of the Currency
        (OCC), 236
Office of Thrift Supervision (OTS), 236–245
Organization
    definition of objectives, 81
    due diligence, documentation of, 52
    information classification policy, 100
    intellectual property, 26
    management, mission statement, 13
    reputation, damage to, 52
    security, 238, 246, 248, 250, 251
    system development life cycle, 9
OTS, *see* Office of Thrift Supervision
Out-of-control processes, 113

P

Passwords, 164, 195, 196
Penetration testing, 230
Personnel security, 54, 228, 242, 246, 250,
        253
Physical assets, 45
Physical controls, 228
Physical intrusion, 195, 196
Physical security, 145, 181, 203, 236
Post-FRAAP, 131, 186
Power failure, 195, 196, 302

Pre-FRAAP meeting, 131, 144
  checklist, 162–163
  definitions, 161
  deliverables, 165
  example, 155
  meeting mechanics, 160
  scope statement, 159
  summary, 165
Prescreening, FRAAP, 147, 152, 157
Privacy Act of 1974, 174, 227
Privacy loss, 291
Privacy officer, 148
Probability–impact matrix table, 24, 25, 26
Probability of occurrence, 91
Processing authorization, 228
Production control, control requirements,
  229
Project scope statement, 80, 82, 100, 101, 113
Public key infrastructure, 230

Q

QRA team, *see* Qualitative Risk Assessment
  team
Qualitative risk analysis, trade-off, 90
Qualitative risk assessment, 115–128
  attributes, 77, 78
  hazard impact analysis, 116–120
    paralysis by analysis, 119–120
    process, 116–119
  pros and cons, 79, 80
  questionnaires, 120–124
  single time loss algorithm, 124–128
Qualitative Risk Assessment (QRA) team, 81
Quantitative versus qualitative risk
    assessment, 77–114
  attributes, 77, 78
  pros and cons, 79, 89
  qualitative risk assessment basics, 79–99
    cost–benefit analysis, 96
    quality team, 81–84
    ranking of safeguards, 96–97
    risk assessment report, 97–99
    risk factor determination, 92–93
    safeguards and controls
      identified,93–95
    scope statement, 81
    threat impact, 90–92
    threats identified, 84
    threats prioritized, 84–80

qualitative risk assessment using tables,
    99–108
  asset valuation, 101–102
  risk evaluation, 102–106
  risk management, 107
30-minute risk assessment, 108–114
  documentation, 112–113
  ISRA matrix, 109
  ISRA process, 109–111
  objectives, 108–109
  out-of-control process, 113
  overview, 108
  threat-based controls, 111–112
Questionnaires, 120, 122–124

R

Records management policy, 225
Recovery
  controls, 56, 93, 94
  plan, 176, 177, 199, 231, 232
Regulatory affairs, 13, 82
Regulatory requirements, new controls and,
    227
Remote access, 256
Remote intrusion monitoring, 230
Resource owner(s)
  roles for, 12
  threats identified by, 132
Risk
  alleviation, 38
  assumption, 38
  avoidance, 38
  definition of, 41
  evaluation, 102
  factor determination, 92, 93, 98
  level matrix table, 54
  limitation, 39
  planning, 39
  transference, 39
Risk analysis, 231, 232
  opportunity statement, 124
  process, 15, 304–323
  success, 5
Risk assessment, 228
  advantages and disadvantages in
    conducting, 77
  deliverables, 221–222
  elements, standard, 206
  focus of, 297
  matrix, 110, 111, 112

questionnaire process, 121
reason for doing, 297
report, 74, 97
team members, 83
30-minute, 108
understanding, 133
values, qualitative, 103
Risk assessment management summary
    report, sample, 299–324
    assessment findings and action plan,
        301–303
    assessment methodology used, 301
    attendees, 300
    full findings documentation, 303
    risk assessment scope summary, 300
Risk assessment process, 41–75
    information as asset, 42–44
    level of receptiveness to, 133
    most important element in, 107
    most important step in, 96
    risk assessment methodology, 44–74
        controls and safeguards, 52–73
        cost–benefit analysis, 74
        documentation, 74
        elements of threats, 46–48
        risk level determination, 50–52
        threat occurrence rates, 48–50
Risk Factor Determination Worksheet, 84, 89
Risk management, 7–39
    business process, 8–10
    cost–benefit analysis, 27–38
    definition of, 7
    employee roles and responsibilities,
        10–11
    information security life cycle, 11–15
    overview, 7–8
    purpose of, 39
    results, 5
    risk analysis process, 15–16
    risk assessment, 16–27
        asset definition, 16–18
        controls recommended, 25–27
        documentation, 27
        impact of threat, 24–25
        probability of occurrence, 19
        threat identification, 18–19
    risk mitigation, 38–39
    SDLC vs., 10
    terms, 8

S

Safeguard(s)
    identification, 93, 98
    performance of, 298
    ranking of, 96
    recommendations, 98, 107
    threat worksheet with, 95
    vulnerability of, 218, 220
Safety risk, 291
Sanction policy, HIPAA, 148
Sandstorm, 86, 117, 126
Sarbanes–Oxley Act (SOX), 69–73, 175, 121,
        227, 245
Scope statement, 81, 97, 100, 124, 159
    management summary, 193
    review, 167
SDLC, *see* System development life cycle
Seasonal flooding, 117
Secure application architecture, 230
Security
    awareness, 180, 228, 234
    categories, controls by, 227, 228
    incidence, response to, 225
    planning, 228
    policy, 238
    program, level of receptiveness to,
        133
Segregation of duties, 223
Senior management, 12, 83
Service level agreements (SLAs), 146, 202,
        232
Session agreements, FRAAP, 143
Shoulder surfing, password, 164
Single time loss algorithm (STLA), 124,
        126–128
SLA, *see* Service level agreements
SMEs, *see* Subject matter experts
Snowstorm, 117
Software
    alteration, 89, 127
    error, 87
    maintenance, 228
    malicious, 243
Spam hits the fan, 3
Standards
    mapping to, 57
    testing, 230
STLA, *see* Single time loss algorithm
Strike, 88, 128
Subject matter experts (SMEs), 132, 140
Surge, 86

System(s)
  acquisition procedures, 228
  administrator, 146
  development, 240, 241, 256
  integrity, 228
  logs, monitoring of, 181, 235
  mission criticality, 153
  programming, 146, 229
  protection, 228
  security architecture, 230
System development life cycle (SDLC), 8, 9
  concepts, 9
  risk management vs., 10

T

Tables, risk assessment using, 99, 102
Team
  assembly, 100
  members, FRAAP, 145
Technical controls, 54, 112
Telecommunications
  control requirements, 229
  interruption, 87
Telecommuting, 256
Terms and definitions, 325–330
  law definitions, 327–330
    Economic Espionage Act, 328–329
    Federal Guidelines for Sentencing for
      Criminal Convictions, 327–328
    Foreign Corrupt Practices Act, 329
    Graham–Leach–Bliley Act, 330
    Health Insurance Portability and
      Accountability Act, 329–330
    Sarbanes–Oxley, 329
  risk assessment terms, 325–327
Terrorist, 47
Theft, 88
Third-party access, security of, 251
Third-party license agreements, 179
Threat(s)
  accidental, 89, 126
  agent, 46
  -based controls, 111
  bomb, 127
  definitions, 45, 84, 85–89
  deliberate, 127
  enterprise facility and, 47
  environmental, 18, 86–87
  evaluation matrix, 105
  human, 18

identification, 18, 45, 84, 98
impact, 24, 49, 90
  level definitions, 53
  probabilities, 91, 92
  table, 207
  value assignments, 92
individual, 195
motive, 46
natural, 18, 48, 85–86, 117, 126
occurrence rates, 48
prioritization of, 130
probability
  assignments, 91
  factor definitions, 90
  priorities, 89
rates of occurrence, 50
results, 46
risk level
  determination, 50
  establishment of, 171
scenario, description of, 302
sources, 45, 47
table, 20–23, 214–215, 216–217
worksheet with safeguards, 95
Tidal flooding, 117
Tornado, 86, 117, 126
Training, 178, 179, 201, 202, 233, 234
Transmission security, 150
Tropical storm, 117
Tsunami, 117, 126
Typhoon, 117

U

Unauthorized access, 164
Union-represented employees, 146
User
  access management, 243, 255
  responsibility, 243, 250
  training, 242

V

Vandalism, 88, 128
Viruses, 119, 195, 302
Volcanic activity, 117, 126
Vulnerability, 14
  assessment, 218, 230
    example, 220
    matrix, 221
  business areas for, 290
  probability vs., 219

Vulnerability Analysis Worksheet, 106

W

WAN, *see* Wide area network
Warning system, 119
Web administration, control requirements, 229
Web-based applications, 146

Wide area network (WAN), 81
Workstation(s)
  security, 149, 253
  unattended, 164, 195, 302

Y

Yellow snow, 86